... shows how to road test ideas and opportunities before writing a business plan and improve the chances of winning both customers and capital.

Business Monthly, July 2003

... provide[s] a reality check for anyone poised to jump into a new venture without thinking. Readers will enjoy discovering the nuggets of wisdom embedded in the case studies.

Financial Times, July 2003

I added this book on spec to a hefty order of business planning books I was buying. This book alone was worth the price of the total order!

My first impression upon seeing his seven domain model was that it's just another 'name-a-number steps to success' book consisting of made-up-to-sound-good rubbish. ABSOLUTELY NOT SO. The substantial nature of John Mullins' ideas is obvious in reading and seems so sensible in retrospect. Looking at his background and at the research that's behind his approach only goes to reafirm this impression.

It may be a long while before I next get a business idea that I actually attempt to put into action. In the meantime, at least I can derive some satisfaction in letting my newfound knowledge stop me before I throw money I haven't got at yet more businesses that are doomed to fail from the start!

I may one day make an entrepreneur but, even if not, I'm living with a renewed respect for those who do succeed.

absolutelyprobable from London

Superb. Stop reading the reviews – just buy it now! This book is immensely helpful, I can't recommend it too highly.

There probably isn't a single business person on the planet who wouldn't benefit from knowing the seven domain model – this alone is worth the price of admission, as it were.

A Reader, Surrey, UK

I read the book before going into my first venture and it made me look at my business plan in a whole different way. I was not only able to identify the loopholes but also the ways I could improve my business plans. Even today while I am looking at a new venture, I find myself always going back and referring to this book. Once read, it will make a place in your entrepreneurial life. This is a must-read book for entrepreneurs as well as venture capital aspirants.

Chintan Thumar, Mumbai, India

Having launched several major ventures over the past decades, I have learned that careful advance planning and analysis cannot be over-emphasized. Through the years, I have struggled to develop a robust framework to analyze opportunities before investing time and money.

Mullins has beaten me to the task. Full of frameworks and anecdotes, theory and practice. Thorough, logical, insightful, and easy to follow. An excellent roadmap for the novice and expert alike. My three copies are already dog-eared.

Kevin Conrad, New York

As an aspiring entrepreneur you are so convinced that your great idea will work that you want to go straight to the business plan. This book gives you the framework and discipline to force yourself to cut your emotional ties with your idea and pick it apart. If your idea still stands after having gone through the rigorous scrutiny described in the book then you have a very strong foundation for taking it to the next stage. An excellent book that I strongly recommend to anybody who has a great idea for a new business, product or service regardless of whether you are an entrepreneur or business executive.

Mikael Aberg, Brussels

As a successful entrepreneur in the satellite communication industry for the past 18 years, we were developing a new business idea for commercial launch and happened to talk with John Mullins. His book provided an overall check for our business plan and we were able to patch many holes. An excellent book providing an all round framework for new and established entrepreneurs.

Sanjay Singhal, President/CEO, Sintel Satellite Services, Inc., New York

If you are like me, when you have a good business idea all you want to do is to get going. Luckily I was persuaded to 'road test' my idea first, and I am very glad that I did. Going through John Mullins' framework has helped me to critically examine many business issues, some of which I hadn't previously thought about. As a result I have modified my plans, and I now feel that I have a better chance of securing funding and ultimately launching a successful venture.

K. McEnery, UK

The New Business Road Test is a great read: thought-provoking, and not 'business-lite' like so much entrepreneurial advice. It's also digestible for a manager in the thick of things, something many books overlook. The questions John Mullins asks are relevant to new ventures and existing businesses looking to move forward, and this book will help you do just that.

Max Aitken, Chief Executive, Ratio One

Whilst reading your book I found myself jotting ideas down and organising my thoughts. You have provided me with half a dozen sheets of paper full of scribbles and diagrams which between them feel like a very 'rounded' view of my business. We have been running for 18 months now, and it seems time to write a tentative business plan. Your book has provided a very welcome helping hand towards that plan.

Tim Craine, Managing Director, London Development Research

I first bought and read your book in early 2003 when I began to plan and research starting up my own business. I wanted to write to you then, when I read it for the first time, to say how much I enjoyed it and more importantly how clear and understandable it was for me ... somebody who had no business or commerce experience. Last Thursday was my last day in salaried employment and I am now up and running as a full-time enterprise, providing high-quality horticultural services to the B2B market. I am now updating my business plan, which is how I came to be reading your great book again.

Martin Costelloe, Rowan Landscapes

I am a Canadian entrepreneur who is having the profitable experience of reading your *New Business Road Test* book. Thanks for writing a terrific (and very sobering) book.

Christian Thwaites, President (Corporate Development), FORPAC BioSciences,
Vancouver, BC

At the moment I'm sitting in the classroom listening to Dr Al Davis, my co-teacher in the capstone strategy class, lecture on strategy in start-ups. Sitting next to me is a book he has been raving about over the last week, *The New Business Road Test*. Perhaps you have heard of it. Dr Davis is a successful entrepreneur and angel.

Eric M. Olson, PhD, Professor of Marketing and Strategic Management,
University of Colorado at Colorado Springs

I have added your book to my own entrepreneurship curriculum and I regularly give it to entrepreneurs we advise and in which we invest. I would like to thank you for penning such an important tome.

Vic Sarjoo, Chairman and CEO, Radical Funds, New York

I use your book regularly to assess the opportunities that come across my desk and it has been very useful in qualifying out of things that I might have wasted time on previously.

Jeremy Renwick, Kubernetes Ltd, Oxfordshire, UK

I picked up the current *HBR* and read the case about 'Good Money after Bad'. But most of all I picked up the trail to your book, *The New Business Road Test*. What a 'Eureka' moment I had. Your comments and seven domains just sharpened up our thinking several very large notches.

Dave Sutherland, Retrievall Inc., Ontario, Canada

FT Prentice Hall
FINANCIAL TIMES

In an increasingly competitive world, we believe it's quality of thinking that will give you the edge – an idea that opens new doors, a technique that solves a problem, or an insight that simply makes sense of it all. The more you know, the smarter and faster you go.

That's why we work with the best minds in business and finance to bring cutting-edge thinking and best learning practice to a global market.

Under a range of leading imprints, including Financial Times Prentice Hall, we create world-class print publications and electronic products bringing our readers knowledge, skills and understanding which can be applied whether studying or at work.

To find out more about our business publications, or tell us about the books you'd like to find, you can visit us at www.pearsoned.co.uk

The New Business Road Test

What entrepreneurs and executives should do
before writing a business plan

third edition

John Mullins

**Financial Times
Prentice Hall
is an imprint of**

Harlow, England • London • New York • Boston • San Francisco • Toronto • Sydney • Singapore • Hong Kong
Tokyo • Seoul • Taipei • New Delhi • Cape Town • Madrid • Mexico City • Amsterdam • Munich • Paris • Milan

PEARSON EDUCATION LIMITED

Edinburgh Gate
Harlow CM20 2JE
Tel: +44 (0)1279 623623
Fax: +44 (0)1279 431059
Website: www.pearsoned.co.uk

First published in Great Britain in 2003
Second edition published 2006
Third edition published 2010

© John Mullins 2003, 2006, 2010

Pearson Education is not responsible for the content of third party internet sites.

ISBN: 978-0-273-73279-2

British Library Cataloguing-in-Publication Data
A catalogue record for this book is available from the British Library.

Library of Congress Cataloging-in-Publication Data
Mullins, John W. (John Walker)
    The new business road test : what entrepreneurs and executives should do before writing a
    business plan / John W. Mullins. -- 3rd ed.
        p. cm.
    Includes bibliographical references and index.
    ISBN 978-0-273-73279-2 (pbk.)
    1. New business enterprises--Planning. 2. Marketing research. I. Title.
    HD62.5.M85 2010
    658.02'2--dc22
                            2010014286

10 9 8 7 6 5 4 3
14 13 12 11 10

Typeset in 9pt ITC Stone Serif by 30
Printed and bound by Ashford Colour Press Ltd, Gosport

Contents

Why read this book?

Right now there are 2 million entrepreneurs in the UK actively engaged in starting a new business. Many of their ventures will never get off the ground. Of those that do, the majority will fail. There are more than 15 million entrepreneurs in the USA doing the same thing. Most of their ventures will fail, too. Of those who submit business plans to business angels or venture capitalists less than 1 per cent will be successful in raising the money.

This picture of entrepreneurship is not a pretty one. The odds are daunting, the road long and difficult. Why, then, are a stunning one of every 19 adults in the UK – and one in ten in the USA – actively pursuing entrepreneurial dreams? In a word – opportunity! Opportunity to develop an idea that seems, at least to its originator, a sure-fire success. Opportunity to be one's own master – no more office politics, no more downsizing, no more working for others. Opportunity for the thrill, excitement, challenge and just plain fun inherent in the pursuit of entrepreneurial ventures. I know, because I've been there, too.

❝ most opportunities are not what they appear to be, as the business failure statistics demonstrate ❞

But there's a problem. Most opportunities are not what they appear to be, as the business failure statistics demonstrate. Most of them have at least one fatal flaw that renders them vulnerable to all sorts of difficulties that can send a precarious, cash-starved new venture to the scrapheap in a heartbeat. An abundance of research makes it clear that the vast majority of new ventures fail for opportunity-related reasons:

- market reasons – perhaps the target market simply won't buy;

- industry reasons – it's too easy for competition to steal your emerging market;

- entrepreneurial team reasons – the team may lack what it takes to cope with the wide array of forces that conspire to bring fledgling entrepreneurial ventures to their knees.

How can a mere book help you meet this challenge?

The research underlying this book (see the Appendix) suggests that the serious entrepreneur who wants to beat the long odds – who wants to work harder and smarter to beat their competition – should pause in their haste to write that great business plan. Yes, I'm referring to *you*. Before putting pen to paper, you should step back and give your opportunity a road test. Examine the seven crucial domains of attractive opportunities that this book illuminates. Find, if you can, the fatal flaw lurking in what looks like an attractive opportunity. Your prospective investors will be looking for it, so you'd better have looked first.

Why bother?

But why shouldn't a would-be entrepreneur simply skip the seven domains road test this book advocates and proceed directly to preparing a business plan? There are three key reasons.

- First, this book enables entrepreneurs to avoid impending disaster. For most entrepreneurs, that's the likely outcome – sad to say – according to the business failure data. Preparing a customer-driven feasibility study based on the seven domains – a concise memo addressed to oneself, really – affords the entrepreneur a chance to opt out early in the process, before investing the time and energy in preparing a complete business plan. Identifying the critical flaw early can save weeks or months of time that might be wasted on a fundamentally flawed opportunity.

- Second, for opportunities that do look promising, the feasibility study jump-starts the business planning process and provides a clear, customer-focused vision of why the proposed venture makes sense – from market, industry and team perspectives, viewed independently and collectively.

- Third, most business plans are not worth the paper on which they are printed. In my view, far too much time is spent crafting business plans in excruciating detail and far too little time is spent getting *real* data from *real* customers about *real* (or prototype) products. A customer-driven feasibility study together with a credible and focused plan for answering unanswered questions may be of far more value in many situations than a lovingly crafted – but hopelessly naïve and unfounded – business plan. But more about this subject in Chapters 5 and 14.

the feasibility study jump-starts the business planning process

Thus, by ensuring that all aspects of the opportunity are examined, the new business road test reduces the entrepreneur's risk of entering a venture that simply has no chance. What entrepreneur wants to be the next contributor to the sorry statistics of business failures? Surely not you. And it enhances the chances of starting a successful business that attracts both customers and capital.

Further, from a societal perspective, doing the seven domains homework – before writing and pitching business plans – can reduce the waste of precious entrepreneurial resources now devoted to crafting business plans for fundamentally flawed opportunities. Entrepreneurs are the drivers of the global economy. Their firms create the new jobs and offer role models for others to follow. Let's be certain that today's entrepreneurs are working on ventures that have at least a fighting chance of success!

Who should read this book?

Principally, this book is for serious, opportunity-focused entrepreneurs and those who support them.

- People who are dying to get out of the big, stifling, inflexible businesses where they work today to strike out on their own. People who have identified one or more opportunities that might just be the ticket out, but who need a way to test them. People who want to run their own business and benefit from the significant upside potential that could bring them economic freedom.

- Entrepreneurs already running a start-up who are finding the challenges more daunting than they had imagined. Perhaps they are wondering whether their chosen path is a good one.

- Engineers and inventors with ideas or technologies that can spawn something more than just a new product.

- The growing legion of advisers, consultants and others, all working to create more entrepreneurial ecosystems where they live and work.

There are three other groups, too, that can benefit from *The New Business Road Test* and its seven domains.

- General managers, new product managers and business development professionals in businesses now mired in stagnant performance or – worse – in an unforgiving economy. They know their companies must find attractive new markets and develop successful new products in order to grow. Business as usual won't cut it. But how, they wonder, can their company be made more entrepreneurial?

■ Investors – whether family or friends or business angels or even newcomers to venture capital – who want to sharpen their skills and bring more than their money to the entrepreneurial table. Independent, clear-sighted advice from investors is more valuable to entrepreneurs than the money they bring.

■ University faculty teaching students how to assess opportunities or write their first business plan. For such faculty, there's even a website to provide wide-ranging support: www.newbusinessroadtest.com.

What are these people – perhaps you are one of them – doing today? Some are spending every waking moment looking for an opportunity to join the ranks of today's growing entrepreneurial culture. Others are already engaged in conceiving or starting a new venture. Still others have recently done so, but the path to success remains unclear. Whichever of these types of entrepreneur or would-be entrepreneur you are, if you are serious about succeeding in your new venture – not simply starting one – this book is for you. It will help you avoid the disaster that's waiting to happen to the majority of new ventures. Yes, even to yours.

> ❝ if you are serious about succeeding in your new venture – not simply starting one – this book is for you ❞

What will be the result of reading this book?

Entrepreneurs or managers having an opportunity in mind – whether it's still in the planning stages or already navigating the turbulent waters that early-stage ventures must sail – will reach one of three conclusions after finishing this book and putting their opportunity through the new business road test.

■ Perhaps the most common outcome will be that the fatal flaw(s) will be uncovered. 'Whew! I'm glad I didn't write a business plan for *that* idea' is the likely sigh of relief. The disaster that would have ensued is now avoided, and all the time and energy that would have been invested in crafting the business plan can be invested more productively in a better idea. Those already in a new venture who reach this conclusion can plot a way to change the direction of the business – or sell it – before disaster strikes.

■ Another common outcome will be that flaws that are identified can be fixed. Opportunities are malleable, and the entrepreneur is often able to reshape an opportunity to improve its attractiveness by:

- targeting a different market;
- offering a different product or service than the one originally planned;
- playing at a different level in the value chain – as a distributor rather than a manufacturer, for example;
- adding skills to the entrepreneurial team that were missing in the original conception.

Opportunities can evolve, and the thought process outlined in this book hastens and strengthens that evolution.

■ A third possible outcome – the happiest, but most rare – will be that the seven domains test finds no fatal flaw. No matter how hard you look. Better yet:

- your homework identifies a real problem that someone – your prospective customer – has, and you offer a solution that's better, faster or cheaper than current solutions;
- your proposition stands a chance to establish sustainable competitive advantage with a business model that works;
- the market is large enough to make the effort worthwhile;
- the industry is sufficiently attractive;
- your entrepreneurial team has what it takes to succeed.

The best news about this kind of outcome is that, in jump-starting the start-up process, the seven domains homework provides the evidence-based research foundation for a persuasive and compelling pitch.

Why John Mullins? What does a business school professor know about starting an entrepreneurial business?

This book brings together, from a single author, the hands-on, done-it-before experience of a three-time entrepreneur with the research expertise found among faculties at only a handful of the world's leading business schools. Put simply, I've practised what I preach and I have the entrepreneurial badges and scars to prove it. I've learned the way most entrepreneurs learn, from both failure and success.

I served as vice president in the early high-growth days at a then young company with great clothing stores called Gap; I founded Pasta Via International and took it public before market and technological changes took our company down; and I pioneered chimney-type charcoal starters for American barbecue enthusiasts. From all these experiences and from the extensive research effort that underlies this book, I have drawn insights that deliver powerful lessons from which every entrepreneur – and many investors, for that matter – can learn.

As a professor at London Business School, where my entrepreneurship colleagues and I – most of us successful entrepreneurs in our own right – develop world-class entrepreneurs and train and provide talent for the venture capital industry, I am well positioned to have written what I hope you will find is an accessible and eye-opening book. Once you have read it, I believe you'll agree with me that ignoring even *one* of the seven domains can be a road map to entrepreneurial disaster. Entrepreneurs who start writing a business plan without putting their idea to the new business road test do so at their peril!

> **ignoring even *one* of the seven domains can be a road map to entrepreneurial disaster**

Why a third edition?

The first and second editions of *The New Business Road Test* were rousing successes, not only in the English-speaking markets where the book was first introduced, but also in translations into several other languages. 'But are the case histories still current?' we wondered, as the book neared six years in print.

This new and fully updated editions brings each and every case history up to date, adding an important and timely 'What happened' to each of the stories. More important, though, is the addition of a new chapter, 14: Determining the viability of your business model. In this new chapter, you'll find a field-tested process to help you transform your initial idea – plan A, we'll call it – into a more vibrant and viable plan B. As many investors hasten to say, 'I've made far more money on plan B than I ever made on plan A.' This new chapter draws on my most recent work with dozens of start-ups and my latest research to provide the tools to get you to plan B largely unscathed. Though I know you've barely begun reading *The New Business Road Test*, if you'd like to add another great book to your bedside pile, you'll find a more complete exposition of the ideas in this book's Chapter 14 in my newest book, coauthored by noted venture capital investor Randy Komisar, *Getting to Plan B: Breaking Through to a Better Business Model*.

To clarify the structure of the book, it's made sense to present this edition in two parts. Part 1 is all you'll need to know to road test your new business idea while Part 2 provides you with the practical toolkit to carry out your road test.

In 20 seconds or less

This book helps serious entrepreneurs and business professionals avoid impending disaster. It shows them what to do *before* they write a great business plan, to enhance their chance of winning both customers and capital and actually achieving their entrepreneurial dreams. And it reveals the seven key issues that astute investors examine *before* they invest. Intrigued? Read on.

JWM
January 2010

Author's acknowledgements

For the ideas that have coalesced into this book, there are more people who deserve thanks than there are stars in the Milky Way splashed across the midnight sky in Colorado, where most of this book's first edition was written in the summer of 2002. But two people stand out. First is John Bates, my friend and colleague at the London Business School, whose clear thinking and entrepreneurial insights and instincts inform many of its pages. John's access to the venture capital community in the UK was instrumental in the research that underlies the book. Without it, the book simply would not exist. Thank you John, and Wendy too. Second, Suzanne Stoller uncovered and researched the companies whose case histories – successful and otherwise – would bring to life the lessons of the seven domains. Her opening vignettes in each chapter make the book more engaging and readable, and her humour and intellect made the work more fun and engaging. Many thanks Suzanne. But the case histories have moved on, and thanks go to Laura Hemrika for doing the research in the autumn of 2009 to bring each of them up to date.

At the heart of the book, informing the research that led to the seven domains model, are some two dozen venture capitalists and entrepreneurs in the UK and USA who shared their time and candid insights with me. If the ideas in this book make a difference in how the current generation of aspiring entrepreneurs fares, it is these thoughtful men and women who deserve the thanks. Most of the good ideas are probably theirs. Any errors in fact or interpretation are, of course, mine. Thanks, too, to Grant McCracken's *The Long Interview* for teaching me how to interview them. Thanks go to Ginny Potter, who performed the content analysis that identified in the set of interview transcripts the recurring themes and relationships. Michael Denny, thank you for your encouragement at an early stage of the writing. And to Nicole Callahan and a dozen or so entrepreneurs who helped me see how this work might best contribute to entrepreneurial practice, thanks to you too.

To my students who, over the years, helped these ideas grow, many thanks for challenging them as they took shape in our class discussions. Just like opportunities, ideas can be shaped. The very best thing about being a teacher is how much one learns. To my teachers of a lifetime – my parents Jack and Alice Mullins, the late Larry Cummings, and many, many more – who taught me to always ask questions and helped me learn how to think clearly in search of answers, this book is but one manifestation of my thanks to you all.

My readers and I owe thanks to everyone at Pearson, especially my editors Stephen Partridge, Linda Dhondy and Liz Gooster, whose gentle candour and careful reading made this a more readable book, and Rachel Kay, whose market savvy helped the first edition of this book find its way into readers' hands. Thanks, too, to Stephanie Lewis, whose suggestions in an early round of editing lent punch and a clearer rationale to the way the book and its chapters are structured, and to Peter Kelly, whose careful look at the first nearly-final manuscript sharpened its logic and filled in some blanks. To those who commented on the seven domains framework as its form emerged over several iterations and to those who kindly read portions of the manuscript, thanks too. There are fewer factual errors and fewer erroneous insights thanks to you.

I would be remiss if I did not thank my family – Donna, Kristina and Heather – for embracing both our temporary move from our home in Colorado to the PhD programme at Minnesota more than 20 years ago and my flitting to and fro between Colorado and London these past several years. I'm one of those fortunate people who loves his work, but I couldn't do it without you.

Conducting research like that which forms the basis of this book takes both time and money. Thanks to the University of Denver's Daniels College of Business for financial support and for the sabbatical that took me to London to begin the research and to the London Business School for providing a livelihood that permits me to write. Thanks too to the Marketing Science Institute, whose research grant was crucial. Likewise to my friends and incomparable colleagues at the London Business School, who from the beginning supported, believed in and helped with this project. It remains a genuine pleasure working with all of you.

Finally, to tomorrow's entrepreneurs, whose passion and dreams will make this a better and more humane world for all of us, thanks in advance for your entrepreneurial inspiration, vision and efforts and for the jobs and economic development you provide. If this book helps you in any way, please tell me about it. If it doesn't, please tell me that too. I'd love to hear from you.

John Mullins
London and Colorado, January 2010
jmullins@london.edu
http://faculty.london.edu/jmullins

Publisher's acknowledgements

We are grateful to the following for permission to reproduce copyright material:

Epigraph on page 3 from William P. Egan II in 'Venture capital has gone from one unreality to another', Knowledge at Wharton, http://knowledge. wharton.upenn.edu/, with permission from William P. Egan II; Epigraph on page 27 – this extract was published in *The Effective Executive* (*Classic Drucker Collection*), Drucker, P., p. 53, Butterworth-Heinemann Ltd., 2nd revised ed., Copyright Elsevier, 2007; Epigraph on page 79 from Warren Buffett, quoted in Herb Greenberg, 'How to avoid the value trap', *Fortune*, 10 June 2002, p.194. The material is copyrighted and used with permission of the author, Warren Buffett; Epigraph on page 105 from 'Best beats first', *Inc*, August, pp. 48-51 (Collins, J. 2000), with permission from Jim Collins; Epigraph on page 209 from Margaret Mead, with permission from Sevanne Kassarjian. The slogan 'Never doubt that a small group of thoughtful, committed citizens can change the world®' is a registered mark under United States Trademark Law; Extract on pages 245-253 adapted from the work of Robert McGowan and Paul Olk of the University of Denver, with permission from Paul Olk and Robert McGowan; Extract on pages 255-262 adapted from *Getting to Plan B: Breaking Through to a Better Business Model*, Harvard Business School Press (Mullins, J. W. and Komisar, R. 2009) Boston, MA 2009, reprinted by permission of Harvard Business School Press. Copyright © 2009 by the Harvard Business School Publishing Corporation; all rights reserved; Chapters 15 and 16 adapted from *Marketing Management: A Strategic Decision Making Approach*, 4th ed., McGraw-Hill Companies (Mullins, J., Walker, O. C. and Boyd Jr., H. W. 2001) Chapter 7 © 2001, reproduced with permission of The McGraw-Hill Companies, Inc.

In some instances we have been unable to trace the owners of copyright material, and we would appreciate any information that would enable us to do so.

Part 1

Road test your new business idea

1

My opportunity: why will or won't this work?

> You may have capital and a talented management team, but if you are fundamentally in a lousy business, you won't get the kind of results you would in a good business. All businesses aren't created equal.
>
> **Long-time venture capitalist William P. Egan II**[1]

Passion! Conviction! Tenacity! Without these traits, few entrepreneurs could endure the challenges, the setbacks, the twists in the road that lie between their often path-breaking ideas – opportunities, as they call them – and the fulfilment of their entrepreneurial dreams. The very best entrepreneurs, however, possess something even more valuable – a willingness to wake up every morning and ask a simple question about their nascent opportunity: 'Why will this new business work when most will fail?' Or, to put it more realistically, 'What's wrong with my idea, and how can I fix it?'

They ask this simple question for a very simple reason. They understand the odds. They know most business plans never raise money. They know most new ventures fail. Most of all, they don't want to end up starting and running what Bill Egan would call a 'lousy business', one that consumes years of their energy and effort, only to go nowhere in the end. Despite asking this crucial question every day, their passion remains undaunted. So committed are they to showing a reluctant world that their vision is an accurate one that they want to know before bad things can happen why they might be wrong.

If they can find the fatal flaw *before* they write their business plan or *before* it engulfs their new business, they can deal with it in many ways. They can modify their idea – shaping the opportunity to better fit the hotly competitive world in which it seeks to bear fruit. If the flaw they find appears to be a fatal one, they can even abandon the idea before it's too late – before launch, in some cases, or soon enough thereafter to avoid wasting months or years in pursuit of a dream that simply won't fly.

Better yet, if, after asking their daily question and probing, testing and especially experimenting for answers, the signs remain positive, they embrace their opportunity with renewed passion and conviction, armed with a new-found confidence that the *evidence* – not just their intuition – confirms their prescience. Their idea really is an opportunity worth pursuing. Business plan, here we come!

Tools to answer the question 'why will or won't this work?'

Just as most car buyers take a road test before committing to the purchase of a new vehicle, so serious entrepreneurs run road tests of the opportunities they consider. Each road test resolves a few more questions and eliminates a few more uncertainties lurking in the path of every opportunity.

❝ serious entrepreneurs run road tests of the opportunities they consider ❞

This book provides a road test toolkit that any serious entrepreneur can use to resolve these questions and eliminate these uncertainties *before* writing a business plan. It addresses the seven domains that characterize attractive, compelling opportunities. It recounts the vivid case histories of path-breaking entrepreneurs who understood these domains, to their enduring advantage. Perhaps more importantly, the book brings to life the less happy stories of other entrepreneurs whose opportunities ran foul of one or more of the seven domains and who, as a result, failed to achieve their goals. Learning from failure is something most successful entrepreneurs do quite well. As many entrepreneurs put it, in talking about their battle scars, 'If I can make each mistake only once, I'll be in good shape.' The common as well as some not so common mistakes are here in this book for all to see.

What this book is and what it is not

This book is not about how to write a business plan. It's about what to do *before* you write your business plan to ensure that your plan has a better chance to compete for the time and attention – and hopefully the money

– of the financiers and other resource providers you will approach, be they the three Fs (family, friends and fools, as the saying goes), angel investors, bankers, venture capitalists or prospective partners or employees.

This book doesn't just tell the story of one entrepreneur's route to glory – there are already plenty of books in that category – for it's grounded in solid research into what characterizes attractive opportunities across a wide variety of market and industry settings (see Appendix). This research brings together new insights gleaned from leading venture capital investors and successful serial entrepreneurs. Their insights apply equally to high-potential ventures and to lifestyle businesses that can enable you to be your own boss and get out of the corporate rat race.

It's also not a book about the personalities and traits of successful entrepreneurs, for an abundance of research has made clear that successful entrepreneurs come from all walks of life, from all strata of society.[2] The sources of their opportunities, however, do show some patterns, which we examine later in this chapter.

❝ **this book is not about how to get rich quickly** ❞ Finally, this book is not about how to get rich quickly. It's about how serious entrepreneurs – whether embarking on a new start-up or building something new within the confines of an existing organization – can prepare a solid foundation for the development of an enduring business that creates and delivers value for its customers and owners alike. There's nothing more fun in business than doing this, and the results are well worth the effort, as any successful entrepreneur will attest.

So what *is* this book? It's a map for the opportunity-assessing, opportunity-shaping process. It provides a useful framework – the seven domains – to lay a solid foundation on which to build a business plan or to create a successful entrepreneurial venture.

The seven domains of attractive opportunities

At its heart, successful entrepreneurship is comprised of three crucial elements: markets, industries and the one or more key people who make up the entrepreneurial team. The seven domains model (Figure 1.1) that drives this book brings these elements together to offer a new and clearer way to answer the crucial question that every aspiring entrepreneur must ask themselves every single morning: 'Why will or won't this work?' The model offers a better toolkit for assessing and shaping market opportunities[3] and a

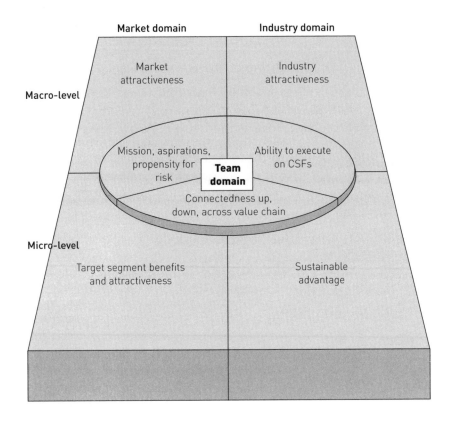

figure 1.1   The seven domains of attractive opportunities

better way for entrepreneurs or entrepreneurial teams to assess the adequacy of what they themselves bring to the table as individuals and as a group. The model also provides the basis for what I call a customer-driven feasibility study that entrepreneurs may use to guide their assessments – *before* they invest the time and effort in writing a business plan.

At first glance, the seven domains model appears simply to summarize what everybody already knows about assessing opportunities. So it does. Upon more careful scrutiny, however, the model goes further to bring to light three subtle but crucial distinctions and observations that most entrepreneurs – not to mention many investors – overlook:

■   markets and industries are not the same things;

■   both macro- and micro-level considerations are necessary: markets and industries must be examined at both levels;

■ the keys to assessing entrepreneurs and entrepreneurial teams aren't simply found on their resumés or in assessments of their entrepreneurial character.

Moreover, the model's seven domains are not equally important. Nor are they additive. A simple scoring sheet won't do. Worse still, the wrong combinations of them can kill your venture. On the other hand, sufficient strength on some factors can mitigate weaknesses on others. Good opportunities *can* be found in not-so-attractive markets and industries.

❝ good opportunities *can* be found in not-so-attractive markets and industries ❞

As the model shows, it is comprised of four *market* and *industry* domains, including both *macro-* and *micro-*levels, and three additional domains related to the entrepreneurial *team*. These seven domains that emerged from my research address the central elements in the assessment of any market opportunity.

■ Are the market and the industry attractive?

■ Does the opportunity offer compelling customer benefits as well as a sustainable advantage over other solutions to the customer's needs?

■ Can the team deliver the results they seek and promise to others?

Before examining these questions, let's address the first of the three crucial distinctions, that between markets and industries.

Markets and industries: what's the difference?

A market consists of a group of current and/or potential customers having the willingness and ability to buy products – goods or services – to satisfy a particular class of wants or needs. Thus, markets consist of buyers – people or organizations and their needs – not products. One such market, for example, consists of businesspeople who get hungry between meals during their workday. We'll call this the market for workplace snacks.

❝ markets consist of buyers, not products ❞

An industry consists of sellers – typically organizations – that offer products or classes of products that are similar and close substitutes for one another. What industries serve the market for workplace snacks? At the producer level, there is the salty snack industry, the confectionery industry and the fresh produce industry, to name but three. There are also industries providing the distribution of these products to workplaces, including the supermarket industry, the restaurant industry, the coin-operated vending machine industry, the coffee bar industry and so on. Clearly, these industries offer varying bundles of benefits to hungry workers. Some of these industries are more attractive than others to would-be entrants seeking to serve the workplace snack market.

Why is the market–industry distinction important? Because judgements about the attractiveness of the *market* one proposes to serve may be very different from judgements about the *industry* in which one would compete. This should not be – but often is – surprising, for the questions asked to assess market attractiveness are different from those for industry attractiveness, a point easily obscured when words like 'sector' and 'space' are used indiscriminately or carelessly in the opportunity assessment process. (Does the user of these terms mean 'market' or 'industry'? See Case Study 1.1.) So, if market and industry attractiveness are both important, how should each be assessed?

> ❝ **an industry consists of sellers** ❞

---

case study 1.1

A lesson learned from the dot.com crash

In the late 1990s entrepreneurs stumbled over one another in a mad race for first-mover advantage in the dot.com space. But what did they mean by 'space'?

Did they mean the *market* of individuals and organizations who would use the Internet for shopping, information, communication and other purposes? In hindsight, we now know that this market was and is extremely attractive: it was growing fast and would soon include most segments of the population, as the so-called digital divide shrank rapidly.

Or did they mean *industries*: Internet service providers, e-tailers, e-publishers and so on. In hindsight, we now know that some industries on the Web were and still are unattractive, because numerous new competitors can enter easily, differentiation is difficult to establish and competitive advantage is hard to sustain with competitors only a mouse-click away.

As entrepreneurial efforts, business plans and venture capital followed like lemmings from business-to-consumer to business-to-business to

▶

peer-to-peer models in the late 1990s, it soon became clear that, while many of these models served potentially attractive *markets*, they were in not very attractive *industries* in which to compete. Unfortunately for the many dot.com entrepreneurs whose ventures failed, the recognition of this crucial distinction came too late.

As time has healed some of the Internet wounds, significant numbers of attractive Internet opportunities have emerged. They share in common many of the attributes – attractive markets and industry settings, clear customer benefits and sustainable competitive advantages, all delivered by capable management teams – that characterize many of the pre-dot.com case histories in this book. As we now know, the Internet, while perhaps not the change-the-world phenomenon in as many ways as was predicted at the turn of the millennium, is alive and well!

Is the market attractive? Macro- and micro-considerations

All else being equal, most entrepreneurs and investors would prefer to serve attractive rather than unattractive markets, of course. How might such market assessments be made? My research showed that assessments must be made at both macro- (broad, market-wide) and micro- (particular to a specific segment, one customer at a time) levels. The macro/micro distinction is important, for the assessment questions differ.

Macro-level

It is actually quite straightforward to conduct a macro-level market assessment. One first assesses – usually by gathering secondary data from trade publications, the business press and so on – how large the market is. Market size can be measured in many ways – the more the better. Measures include:

■ number of *customers* in the market, say for workplace snacks;

■ the aggregate *money spent* by these customers on the relevant class of goods or services, in this case workplace snacks;

■ the number of *units* of relevant products or usage occasions, such as workplace snacks, bought annually.

One also collects recent historical data, to ascertain how fast the market has been growing, together with any available forecasts about how fast it is likely to grow in the future.

The venture capitalists and entrepreneurs we interviewed in researching this book concurred with this view:

We want to know the size and growth rate of the market, so that if the product catches on, we should have a substantial upside.[4]

HH, UK

We want to know that the overall market opportunity is big, and we have to be able to demonstrate that the market size of this particular offering is robust.

TP, USA

One then assesses broad macro-environmental (macro for short) trends – demographic, sociocultural, economic, technological, regulatory and natural – to determine whether things are likely to get better or worse in the future.[5] Do the trends favour the opportunity, or will the entrepreneur be swimming against a powerful tide?

I think that being able to assess, spot, and maybe even create trends is very big – a key to decision making. There are many problems that don't have solutions yet. Just look at the cell phone . . . As you know, in many countries today, the penetration of mobile telephony now surpasses the penetration of desktop or wireline phones.

CM, USA

The broad, macro-level market assessment is important to the entrepreneur, for he or she risks investing years committed to an idea that, in the end, may not be large enough to be worth all the time and effort. It's important for the entrepreneur to know whether the opportunity is a substantial one, serving a large and attractive market, or a niche opportunity with limited potential. Either may be acceptable. It depends on the entrepreneur's aspirations. It is also important to know which way the tides are flowing. Thus, reaching a clear conclusion about market attractiveness is critical. But this macro-level assessment – done at the 30,000-foot level, so to speak – is only half the market domain story. It is essential aerial reconnaissance and a good look at the road ahead, but for the full picture you need observers on the ground.

Micro-level

❝ aspiring entrepreneurs who say 'We have no competition' are simply naïve ❞

No matter how large and fast-growing a market may be, entering it in the face of other competition is likely to be difficult, since customers are probably already satisfying their needs – though perhaps not optimally – in some way. In this sense, there's no such thing as a new market in customer terms. Aspiring entrepreneurs who say 'We have no competition' are simply naïve. Thus, most successful entrepreneurs, rather than targeting the entire market, identify a much smaller segment of customers *within* the overall market. The micro-level market assessment involves asking four key questions relevant to such a segment.

- Is there a target market segment where we might enter the market in which we offer the customer clear and compelling benefits, or – better yet – resolve their pain at a price he or she is willing to pay?

- Are these benefits, *in the customers' minds*, different from and superior in some way – better, faster, cheaper or whatever – to what's currently offered by other solutions? Differentiation is crucial. With the possible exception of niche markets in which small entrants can safely fly 'below the radar' of competitors, the vast majority of me-too products fail.

- How large is this segment, and how fast is it growing?

- Is it likely that our entry into this segment will provide us entry into other segments that we may wish to target in the future?

This new service concept is turning the existing business model in the market on its head, making it a cost-effective alternative in a market that hasn't been properly serviced in the past. Customers are lining up for it.

JS, UK

How can these questions be answered? Most commonly, a combination of first-hand primary data (gleaned from talking to or surveying prospective customers) and secondary data (data collected previously and available on the Internet or in libraries or from other sources, to determine segment size and growth rate) can deliver the understanding that the entrepreneur needs.

66 many aspiring entrepreneurs make the mistake of examining only the macro-level 99

As we shall see later in this chapter, many aspiring entrepreneurs make the mistake of examining only the macro-level. This behaviour appears to be especially common in technologically driven firms. Through failing to identify the first customers who will buy – almost by name – and why they would benefit,[6] and in ignoring how entry into this segment might create one or more options for growth into other market segments,[7] they risk pursuing a dead-end path on two counts:

- without differentiated benefits, most customers won't buy;

- without a pathway to growth, most investors won't invest.

Most market segments are simply too small to sustain a high-growth business for very long, although such segments may be quite attractive to entrepreneurs seeking to establish niche-market or lifestyle businesses that fly 'below the radar' of larger competitors and grow more slowly. The story of Nike's entry and subsequent growth in the athletic footwear market demonstrates the importance of the micro-level assessment of market attractiveness (see Case Study 1.2).

---

case study 1.2

Nike wins at the micro-level

The story of Nike's origins is now a familiar one. Phil Knight, a distance runner, and his track coach Bill Bowerman used Bowerman's wife's waffle iron and some latex to develop a running shoe for distance runners that was lighter (benefit: faster race times), had better cushioning (benefit: fewer shin splints and stress fractures from miles and miles of training) and had superior lateral stability (benefit: reduced chance of ankle sprains caused by running on uneven terrain).

At the macro-level, the market for athletic footwear was stagnant at the time. Most people had only one or two pairs of trainers and saw no need for another. From a micro-perspective, however, distance runners loved Knight's and Bowerman's new shoes, and the new company's success in the distance running segment led to later successes in tennis, basketball and other sports that have made Nike one of the world's leading brands.

In opportunity terms, what Knight and Bowerman saw initially was a chance to offer a demonstrably superior product that customers – distance runners – would prefer and pay for, one that could then lead to similar success in other sharply targeted footwear niches. Their sport-by-sport advance across the formerly stagnant athletic footwear market, accompanied by astute marketing that made high-priced athletic shoes a fashion item, led to that market's stunning growth (how many pairs of different athletic shoes are in *your* wardrobe today?) and to Nike's leading position in today's athletic footwear industry.

Is the industry attractive? Macro- and micro-considerations

Just as serious entrepreneurs prefer to serve attractive markets, so they also prefer to compete in industries in which most participants are successful and profitable, rather than in industries where many firms struggle to survive. Serious entrepreneurs also prefer to compete on the basis of some sustainable advantage that their competitors do not enjoy. How might these crucial judgements be made?

Macro-level

Michael Porter, in the late 1970s, identified the forces that determine industry attractiveness.[8] These forces – five of them – are powerful determinants of the overall profitability of any industry, not a bad thing for an aspiring entrepreneur to know:

■ threat of entry;

■ buyer power;

■ supplier power;

■ threat of substitutes;

■ competitive rivalry.

Assessing these forces and any ongoing or likely future changes therein lies at the heart of a macro-level assessment of industry attractiveness.

So, how should a five forces analysis be done? What should be its outcome? The aspiring entrepreneur first identifies what industry his or her new business will be in – retailing, food manufacturing, software, or whatever. Doing this is not a trivial exercise. Industries can be defined broadly or narrowly, as we shall see in Chapter 4.

The entrepreneur then asks a series of questions (discussed in detail in Chapter 4) about each of the five forces to determine whether that force is favourable or unfavourable on balance. The more forces that are favourable, the more attractive the industry, and vice versa. As it turns out, most industries are not very attractive. Would-be entrepreneurs should note that severe problems on just one force can be enough to tip the balance, so the weighing must be done in a thoughtful manner. Identifying such problems in advance enables the entrepreneur to craft plans to deal with them, or to abandon the opportunity altogether, if the problems are too severe.

Once all five forces have been assessed, the key outcome is to reach a clear conclusion about the attractiveness of one's industry. This step is crucial to the overall assessment of your opportunity, and it is one issue that professional investors always examine. If necessary, admit that your industry just isn't very attractive. Note, however, that all is not necessarily lost if the verdict is unfavourable. Other factors elsewhere in the seven domains analysis may compensate for these concerns.

❝ most industries are not very attractive ❞

As in the case for the macro-level assessment of market attractiveness, gathering secondary data is necessary here, but such data tell only part of the story. Additional, first-hand industry knowledge or primary data are usually required to develop a clear understanding of how the industry works and how it is changing.

We research where the industry is heading and what factors are affecting it. We want to know that the industry is here to stay and that it's not about to be replaced by technology.

JS, UK

One might imagine that a macro-level assessment of industry attractiveness would be sufficient, provided the micro-level market assessment has indicated that customers want to buy what the new entrant offers. For entrepreneurs who seek to build small but stable firms serving narrow market niches, this may sometimes be true. For more growth-oriented entrepreneurs, however, there's another important piece of the puzzle: the micro-level.

Micro-level

Even if customers like what the prospective new entrant offers and most firms in its industry are successful due to favourable industry structure, a new venture is not likely to grow over the long term if the initial advantage it brings to its customers cannot be sustained in the face of subsequent competitors' entry or if its business model lacks economic viability. Thus, identifying and assessing the sustainability of the proposed new firm's competitive advantage is necessary to fill in the micro-level industry piece of the opportunity assessment puzzle.

How might these micro-level industry judgements be made? Assessing the sustainability of the proposed venture's competitive advantage requires examining, in relationship to its competitors, the proposed venture itself – whether a new firm or a venture within an existing firm. The goal is to determine whether certain factors are present that would enhance the ability of the venture to sustain any advantage that it might have at the outset. These factors are the following.

▓ The presence of proprietary elements – patents, trade secrets and so on – that other firms are unable to duplicate or imitate.

▓ The likely presence of superior organizational processes, capabilities or resources that others would have difficulty duplicating or imitating.[9]

▓ The presence of an economically viable business model – one that won't quickly run out of cash! This factor, in turn, involves a careful look at some more detailed issues:

  – revenue, in relation to the capital investment required and margins obtainable;
  – customer acquisition and retention costs, and the time it will take to obtain customers;
  – contribution margins and their adequacy to cover the necessary fixed cost structure to operate the business;
  – operating cash cycle characteristics, i.e. how much cash must be tied up in working capital such as inventory, how quickly will customers pay, and how slowly may suppliers and employees be paid, in relation to the margins the business generates.[10]

  Information on the economic structure of most industries can be found from published sources such as the Risk Management Association's *Annual Statement Studies*, available in most business libraries and on the Internet, e.g. the Risk Management Association's website, www.rmahq.org

Aspiring entrepreneurs who plan to compete based on price should note that building a business by giving away your products for less than they cost to acquire or produce is not a sustainable strategy in the long run, as numerous dot.com entrepreneurs learned in the turn-of-the-millennium dot.com bust. Another economic viability issue often overlooked by entrepreneurs is this:

Too often entrepreneurs fail to understand how long it will take (and thus how much capital) to actually close a sale, no matter how good the opportunity looks.

RJ, UK

It's worth noting here that first-hand experience in the industry makes all the difference in addressing these issues. Entrepreneurs who know the territory will have the necessary answers. Those who don't must find people who do. Adequate answers for most of these issues are not likely to be found on the Internet. If the entrepreneur doesn't have such experience, then they must obtain it from others. Picking up the phone and calling those who they know can help, and it helps build your network, too, a topic we address further later on.

> **first-hand experience in the industry makes all the difference**

The point addressed by the micro-level assessment on both the market and industry sides is that even in generally attractive markets and industries – such as financial services and pharmaceuticals – not all new ventures succeed. Favourable industry conditions at the macro-level are not a panacea. Positive results from your investigations into these micro-level conditions are typically far more important.

Can the team deliver?

When pressed to name the single most important factor in their investment decisions, many of the venture capitalists we interviewed said, simply, 'Management, management and management.' But we learned that assessing 'management' involves more than judging character and reading CVs. Our research identified three domains relating to the entrepreneur or entrepreneurial team itself, and we include any investors therein. Examining these domains is necessary in order to complete the opportunity assessment task.

- Does the opportunity fit the team's business mission, personal aspirations and risk propensity?

- Does the team have what it takes, in a human sense – in experience and industry know-how – to deliver superior performance for this particular opportunity, *given its critical success factors*, i.e. those factors that, done right, almost guarantee superior performance, even if other things aren't done so well; or done wrong, will have severely negative effects on performance regardless of doing other things right?

- Is the team well connected up, down and across the value chain so it will be quick to notice any opportunity or need to change its approach if conditions warrant?

Let's take a look at each of these final three domains.

The team's business mission, personal aspirations and risk propensity

For a variety of reasons, individual entrepreneurs and investors come to the opportunity assessment task with certain preconceived preferences, often defined in terms of:

- markets they wish to serve (Nike's founder, Phil Knight, an athlete himself, wanted to market to athletes);

- industries in which they are willing to compete (for Knight, athletic footwear);

- their own aspirations (how big a venture, how soon, if at all, do we wish to exit, are we committed to this opportunity, or are we buying an option to see whether it pans out?);

- risks they are willing to undertake (with how much money, how certain must we be of a successful venture, must we have control, or are we willing to share it?).

Opportunities that do not match these preferences will be seen as unattractive, even though other observers having different sets of preferences and dreams might view them more favourably.

We've turned down opportunities because they didn't meet our criteria for investing, and sometimes they go on to do well with another firm. But when you change your threshold, you let in a lot more false positives. Your level of scrutiny should be exactly proportional to how much risk you are willing to take on in bringing in deals that may actually turn out to be bad. False positives are what you worry about, not false negatives.

TP, USA

The team's ability to execute on the critical success factors

The backgrounds and prior experiences brought to the venture by particular entrepreneurs and investors make them better prepared to execute on some sets of critical success factors than on others. Understanding the critical success factors relevant to a particular opportunity and the industry within which it will compete and matching them against the team's ability to perform on them is among the most compelling questions most investors ask in assessing opportunities. Entrepreneurs should do the same.

66 understanding the critical success factors is among the most compelling questions 99

We really dig into the management team. We want to be totally confident that this team can deliver on the promises they have made. We do that by looking at their experience, by assessing how well they understand their industry and their customers. We want to know about their leadership in terms of the CEO and the heads of engineering, R&D and marketing. Probably those were the most important functions for this opportunity.

OD, USA

I don't mess with products or markets I don't know how to read.

PB, UK

Entrepreneurs who fail to assess accurately whether they and their team have what it takes to execute on the critical success factors they will face take a huge personal risk – beyond the business risk they already take – if they seek external capital. It is all too common for venture capital investors who like an opportunity to tire of the team they first back and bring in a new one at the first sign of trouble. Losing their companies is not something most entrepreneurs are keen to do.

The team's connectedness up, down and across the value chain

A favourite saying among venture capital investors is: 'I've made more money on plan B than I ever made on plan A.' In other words, the ability to combine tenacity with a willingness to change course – sometimes due to changes in the marketplace, fortuitous or otherwise – can make all the difference. Thus, good luck can help a new venture, but those best prepared to take advantage of good luck are those whose leading-edge information connections enable them to respond to market changes quickly and adroitly. Entrepreneurial teams should ask how connected they are, both up and down the value chain – with suppliers and customers – and across their industry to address this concern. How can they get connected if they are not? One partial answer: network, network, network.

❝ I've made more money on plan B than I ever made on plan A ❞

We had three products when we entered the business, and we thought we knew their order of importance in the marketplace. We lost the market for what we thought would be our biggest product, and things looked really bad. But we had an outstanding board that brought to the team a lot of experience and partnerships and connections. One of our salespeople told a story about a customer's interest in our third product, a network interface card. The board seized upon the story and talked to some people that knew. It turned out that the board had spotted an early trend, and this is where we made all of our money. Without a doubt, the thing that carried us through was the quality of the team and all of its connections.

HH, UK

By assessing themselves in the three *team* domains as part of their broader opportunity assessment efforts, entrepreneurs and entrepreneurial teams gain in three ways.

■ If the team needs to be strengthened to better suit an otherwise promising opportunity, the best time to do so is *before* writing a business plan. Doing this early enables the business planning effort to benefit from the talents, insights and perspectives of the team's new members.

■ Viewing investors as part of the team also builds trust and can reduce the risk investors perceive in the venture, since many investors like to help build the team. Entrepreneurs who are willing to admit they don't have all the skills required often rate highly with the investor community.

■ If external funding is to be sought, then pitching an inadequate team is not only likely to be unsuccessful but also undermines the credibility and reputation of the team members, thereby hampering their ability to raise capital in the future. Get the team right first, then pitch. You'll need to make a convincing case that the team will be able to deliver the results it seeks and those it promises to investors and other stakeholders.

These benefits are important, even for entrepreneurs in emerging industries who may not appreciate the need for well-developed connections. (For more on this topic, see Case Study 1.3.)

---

case study 1.3

What about entrepreneurs bearing new paradigms?

A visionary entrepreneur can change the world, or at least some part of it. They may be tempted to say, 'Our new paradigm [e.g. the Internet] changes everything. The old rules no longer apply.' But is this true? The not very pretty record of dot.com ventures at the turn of the millennium suggests that entrepreneurs pitching new paradigms must understand clearly the realities of the old ones. Otherwise, they risk being blindsided by market or industry forces they fail to foresee or facing critical success factors they are ill prepared to address.

Including both old- and new-paradigm people and perspectives on the entrepreneurial team is one way to ensure that this does not happen.

Putting the seven domains model into action

Using the seven domains model requires a considerable amount of data. Mere opinions that an opportunity is attractive will not suffice and will destroy the credibility of the aspiring entrepreneur in the eyes of others. How, then, should the entrepreneur obtain and interpret the necessary data?

In Chapter 10, we address this question in considerable detail. For now, however, let us note that some of the data the model calls for can be obtained quickly from secondary sources: trade and other business publications in the library or on the Internet, government reports and so on. Typically, though, an abundance of primary data – from interviews, observation, surveys of prospective customers and/or industry participants, or market experiments – are necessary for the two micro-level assessments comprising the lower row in the model and for understanding the industry's critical success factors. So, build a simple mockup or prototype, pick up the phone and get some feedback! Make the connections up, down and across the value chain that your team will need to assess fully your opportunity and to run a successful venture.

As for interpretation (and as was noted earlier in this chapter), using the model is not a simple matter of constructing a score sheet that adds scores for the seven domains. The domains are not additive and their relative importance can vary. Thus, a simple checklist will not suffice. The wrong combination of factors can kill your new venture, and enough strength on some factors can mitigate weaknesses on others. We address these situations in Chapter 9. For now, however, if a checklist is not sufficient, then how should the entrepreneur who completes a seven domains analysis draw conclusions about what it means?

Why *won't* this work?

Along the seven domains path, concerns inevitably crop up that may be potentially fatal flaws that can render one's opportunity a non-starter. The key task in answering the crucial question 'Why won't this work?' is to find that major flaw that cannot be resolved, the opportunity's Achilles' heel. Thus, the crucial things to look for on the downside are elements of the market, industry or team that simply cannot be fixed by shaping the opportunity in a different way.

> **find that major flaw that cannot be resolved, the opportunity's Achilles' heel**

If flaws that cannot be fixed are found, then the best thing to do is to abandon the opportunity at this early stage and move on to something more attractive. Persisting with a fundamentally flawed opportunity is likely to have one of two outcomes, both of which are unpleasant.

■ *Best case:* The best and most likely outcome is that experienced investors or other resource providers – suppliers, partners and so on – will identify the flaws that you have ignored and refuse to give you the resources you need, even if you have gone to great lengths to craft a business plan that papers over these flaws. Fortunately for you, their refusal will save you the agony of investing additional months or years of your life in actually running a lousy business, though your efforts in preparing and pitching your business plan will have been wasted. The harsh reality is that this is the case with the vast majority of business plans, for the opportunities they seek to pursue are fatally flawed. Most business plans should have been abandoned before they were written.

■ *Worst case:* The second, though less likely, outcome of pursuing a fundamentally flawed opportunity through the business planning stage is that, in spite of the flaws, you are able to secure the resources you need and actually start the business. At some point, the flaws will rear their ugly heads, and you'll need to scramble to recast the business before it goes under. Some readers of this book may find themselves in this unhappy predicament today. It's not a pretty place to be.

Why *will* this work? Can the opportunity be shaped?

The good news in all this is that opportunities are not static. They can be shaped and developed in many ways. Potentially fatal flaws are there to be fixed. You can choose a different target market, one more receptive to the proposed offering. The product offering can be adapted to make it better fit what the market needs. Decisions can be made to pursue the opportunity at a

❝ potentially fatal flaws are there to be fixed ❞

different level in the value chain – as a distributor, rather than as a retailer or a manufacturer, for example – if a different industry setting would be more hospitable. Finding additional individuals who can help the team deliver on the critical

success factors or who bring appropriate connections up, down or across the value chain can strengthen the entrepreneurial team.

Mapping a route to your entrepreneurial dreams

Completing the seven domains road test provides the light to see through the fog of uncertainty that surrounds every opportunity. It enables the entrepreneur to make the necessary mid-course corrections to reshape the opportunity so that it becomes worth pursuing – *before* writing a business plan. Most likely, your initial conception of your opportunity isn't quite optimal. It can probably be improved. This book provides the tools for doing so.

In this chapter, I've provided an overview of the seven domains framework and shown how it can protect entrepreneurs against pursuing ill-advised ventures that are fatally flawed, and how it can help entrepreneurs to achieve their dreams. In the next seven chapters, taking each of the seven domains in turn, the book relates the case histories of successful entrepreneurial heroes from around the world whose businesses exemplify 'getting it right' in seven domains terms. Each chapter also examines one or more case histories of entrepreneurs who violated the precepts of that domain – and paid the price. To complete each of these chapters, I draw on the research that underlies this book to outline what investors look for in each of the seven domains. And I summarize the powerful lessons the case histories offer to aspiring entrepreneurs who hope to avoid the mistakes of others who have ventured down the entrepreneurial path before them.

Finally, Chapters 9 and 10 bring it all together. Chapter 9 shows how the seven domains can work together to spring traps that wary entrepreneurs should look out for in their own opportunities and shows how and where attractive opportunities can be found in stagnant or otherwise unattractive markets and industries. It also points out the kinds of opportunities that are particularly well suited to niche-market entrepreneurs – those who hope to build a fly-below-the-radar business that they can operate for many years or pass on to their children.

Chapter 10 examines where the best opportunities usually come from and addresses the practicalities of conducting the necessary market research and preparing the evidence-based forecasts that are so crucial in the development of an effective business plan. This chapter then outlines the steps that aspiring entrepreneurs should take in researching and writing a customer-driven feasibility study for their own opportunity. Such a study – a short memo to oneself, really – documents and clarifies the conclusions of the seven domains road test. It provides a clear, customer-focused vision about why the proposed venture makes sense – from market, industry and team perspectives. Best of all, it takes the entrepreneur halfway home in preparing a compelling business plan, thereby jump-starting the business planning process and ensuring it rests upon a firm foundation. So, read on and enjoy the ride!

2

Will the fish bite?

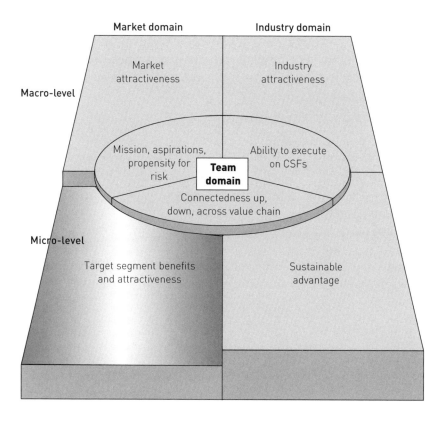

It's a crisp July morning in Lewistown, Montana, where you are on holiday. You wake up at 5:30 a.m. to overcast skies (perfect for fly-fishing) and nothing on your calendar but a date with the brown trout on the Upper Missouri River. Within an hour, you find your way to one of the most pristine fishing spots in the western USA. Wearing your waders, and sporting a vest full of home-tied flies, you trudge along the banks until you reach the perfect spot. About ten yards away is a pod of what must be 30 or 40 trout, feeding contentedly on the morning's hatch. And these are not small fish. By the looks of their mouths, they must be a good 20 inches long.

Having spent enough time on the river, you know these fish are smart. They won't bite at just anything. So, you take a few minutes, checking the air and the surface of the water to figure out what they are eating. Instead of hastily casting your line with the Royal Coachman fly from your last fishing trip, you sit down on a rock and carefully attach a mid-sized Caddis fly. After casting five or six times, you feel a tug at the end of your line and proceed to fight a strong and able brownie for three exhausting minutes. With your forearm throbbing, you finally pull this 21-inch beauty out of the water. Its colours are magnificent. You unhook the fly and place the fish back in the water, proud of your first catch of the day.

When fly-fishing, patience is a virtue. When the fish are feeding like mad, it is all too tempting to start casting as soon as is humanly possible. But experienced anglers know it's far wiser to take a few moments to assess what the fish are eating than to start fishing impulsively with the wrong fly. The same is true for entrepreneurs. When a target market seems ripe for a new venture, it is appealing to launch a business hastily. While it's tempting to go quickly to market to attain first-mover advantage, the rewards of haste are by no means guaranteed. More often, it's better to take some time to identify and understand the target market, figuring out what the customers really need, rather than to dive in prematurely.

Do customers matter?

The customer . . . is the ultimate reason for whatever the organization produces.

Peter Drucker[1]

As Peter Drucker says, it's all about customers. Without customers, there can be no business. Without satisfying what the customers want or need, or – better yet – resolving their pain, there will be no customers. It's simple, really. So, why do most aspiring entrepreneurs, when asked about the businesses they hope to start, begin with words like these:

■ 'We provide . . .'

■ 'Our new product is . . .'

■ 'With our new technology . . .'?

It's not about *you*. It's not about your revolutionary products or services. Successful entrepreneurial ventures are about serving customers and their needs and resolving their pain. Not just any customers. Target customers. It's about providing differentiated benefits that are so compelling that customers abandon their allegiance to former providers and give their business to you.

> **❝ it's not about *you*. It's not about your revolutionary products or services ❞**

But you've already got an idea for a new business, and you know it's a good one, or you probably wouldn't be reading this book. 'Of course customers will buy it!' you argue. 'It's much faster (or better, cheaper, or whatever) than what they're using now.' While you may be right, the chances actually are, based on the accumulated learning of generations of entrepreneurs who have gone before you, that you are either *not quite* right, or perhaps even dead wrong! And as most venture capital investors will tell you, more money gets made on plan B (or C or D or Z) than ever gets made on plan A.

So, before you get too far into the book, turn to Chapter 11, where you'll learn about a powerful interviewing technique that will show you how to find out what you don't know you don't know about your new venture idea. Or more to the point, how to learn what you don't know you don't know about what customers *really* could use in the small bit of their lives that you propose to target. Yes, you've read these sentences correctly – you need to learn what you *don't know* you don't know.

When you return here from Chapter 11, you'll be all set to dig into the lower left quadrant in the seven domains model. Why begin here, as opposed to one of the other quadrants? Because it's worth listening to Drucker. Because without target customers whose needs you satisfy, the rest of the model doesn't matter very much.

As you learned in Chapter 1, there are four crucial questions you need to ask to understand your specific opportunity in micro-market terms. These questions are repeated in Box 2.1. The answers you are looking for, however, will vary depending on the kind of venture you hope to build.

If your dream is to build a high-growth venture that will put you in Richard Branson's or Michael Dell's league some day, you'll need to answer 'Yes' to the first two questions, 'Large, fast-growing' to the third and 'Very likely' to the fourth. If, on the other hand, your dream is to build a simple and satisfying lifestyle business that flies below the radar of major competitors, then a small target market with limited scope for expansion may be just fine. The local fly-fishing shop in Lewistown, Montana, is just such a business, and those who are stuck in the big-city rat race may well envy its proprietor.

---

box 2.1

Four crucial micro-level questions about target markets

1   Is there a target market segment where we might enter the market in which we offer the customer clear and compelling benefits, or – better yet – resolve their pain, at a price he or she is willing to pay?

2   Are these benefits, *in the customers' minds*, different from and superior in some way – better, faster, cheaper or whatever – to what's currently offered by other solutions?

3   How large is this segment, and how fast is it growing?

4   Is it likely that our entry into this segment will provide us entry into other segments that we may wish to target in the future?

In this chapter, we examine the case histories of three companies that have achieved some measure of success largely because of their ability to understand and capitalize on the needs of carefully defined target markets. First, we look at NTT DoCoMo, the Japanese company that found a whole new market for mobile phones with its iMode service.

Next, we go back in time to the USA more than 30 years ago, where, in a then-novel approach to beer marketing, Miller pitched its new, low-calorie beer to beefy, 20-something sports spectators. In doing so, Miller created an entirely new product class – light beer – that now wins a huge share of the American beer market.

Finally, we look at competitive advantage that two entrepreneur–athletes gained from their initial entry into the niche market of elite distance runners. Today, their company, Nike, serves almost every segment of the athletic shoe market, each with carefully targeted products and creative marketing that have made Nike one of the world's best-known brands.

We then examine the other side of the coin and turn to the troubles of OurBeginning.com, a company that thought it knew who its target market was but spent large amounts of cash for promotion in media not well suited to that target. The results, as it turned out, did not exactly ring wedding bells.

To wrap up the chapter, we consider the investor's perspective and we examine the lessons learned. We consider how entrepreneurs can use these lessons to determine whether their opportunity makes sense from the target customer's perspective. Will the fish bite? Without an affirmative answer to this crucial question, an entrepreneur has little to offer, either to customers or to investors.

iMode delivers what Japanese mobile phone users want

How many companies can boast of acquiring nearly 20 million customers in just two years?[2] Not many! The ones that are capable of such rapid market penetration must be doing something right. In the case of Japan's NTT DoCoMo's iMode, the company had conceived a product with carefully targeted appeal. Launched in February 1999, Japan's wireless phone service

> **❝ iMode's success in the wireless market is an example of how important it is to have a product offering clear and compelling benefits to a carefully targeted market ❞**

iMode had signed up nearly 20 per cent of the total Japanese population by the middle of 2001, or 25 per cent of the population between the ages of 15 and 64.[3] Even more impressive, in just two years the company became the most widely used mobile Internet service in the world.[4] iMode's success in the wireless market is an example of how important it is to have a product offering clear and compelling benefits to a carefully targeted market.

iMode's target markets

In 1999, the Japanese population numbered 126 million. Of this 126 million, only 12.2 per cent of the population had Internet access,[5] compared with 39 per cent of the US population, 21 per cent of the British population and 23 per cent of the Korean population. In a study conducted by AOL and Roper ASW, 69 per cent of Japan's online population said the Internet was essential to everyday life, but 29 per cent said that dial-up telephony costs were the biggest obstacle to Internet access.[6]

While seemingly behind the times with respect to Internet access, mobile phone use in Japan was more prevalent than in many other industrialized countries. At the end of 1999, 44.5 per cent of the Japanese population had mobile phones, compared with 40 per cent in the UK and 31 per cent in the USA. In a country where dial-up telephone access was expensive and consumers were obsessed with media – from information about stock quotes to comic strips and weather reports – Japan was ripe for an inexpensive wireless data service that targeted carefully defined segments of users with what they needed, any time, any place.

One target market that intrigued Takeshi Natsuno, Executive Director of NTT DoCoMo, included consumers interested in the financial markets and their own personal finances. To appeal to this group, iMode developed relationships with the banking industry: 'Of the more than 700 content partners we have, 320 are banks,' said Natsuno.[7]

Another target market comprised customers with an eye for comics. To serve this segment, iMode contracted the publishing firm Shueisha to provide weekly comic strips for a monthly fee of 300 yen (less than £2) for the transmission of a weekly comic strip. The toy company Bandai sold *charappa* or cartoon characters. For less than £1 a month, subscribers received a different cartoon image on their phone every day. By February 2000, Bandai had 400,000 iMode subscribers.[8]

As Natsuno said, 'The success of iMode is because we adjust our site to Internet users.'[9] Furthermore, unlike a dial-up Internet connection, iMode Web access was always on, allowing customers to use the Internet without dialling the phone. Even the phones were appealing to the Japanese market, with colour screens, lightweight handsets, multi-link navigation and better graphics capabilities. The only disadvantage of the product was its transmission speed of 9.6 kilobytes per second.

The price was right

With its slow transmission speed, iMode knew it was not in its best interest to charge customers based on the amount of time spent on the Web. Instead, iMode priced its services based on the amount of information downloaded, not the connection time. The pricing format was reasonable. Emails cost 1 yen (5p) per 20 Japanese characters (40 roman letters). Downloading still images cost 7 yen (4p), checking share prices cost 26 yen (14p), and transferring funds from bank accounts cost 60 yen (33p). While some of iMode's content providers charged a flat monthly fee, others were free of charge.[10] In 1999, iMode charged a basic monthly fee of 300 yen (£1.60) and a packet fee (based on the volume of data sent or received) of 0.3 yen (2p) per 128 bytes of information. iMode was also sure to price its phones reasonably, comparable to a normal mobile phone.[11]

Not only was the price low, but the billing method was also convenient for users. Instead of paying iMode for service fees and paying the content providers for subscription fees, iMode customers received one monthly bill with all of their mobile charges. 'The iMode system has made m-commerce [mobile commerce] a reality in Japan by introducing information billing systems that attach charges directly onto telephone bills,' said Natsuno.[12]

Suppliers have needs too

NTT DoCoMo's insight into the needs of its content providers was an important contributor to its early success. By taking care of the customer billing, iMode made business easy for content providers, who were hesitant to sell online because handling the billing was a large and expensive burden. By paying NTT DoCoMo to do the billing, the content providers were able to concentrate on what they did best – providing content –

and still generate earnings.[13] In return for this, iMode charged its content providers 9 per cent of revenue.

❝ iMode made business easy for content providers ❞

The company also kept a firm grip on its business, controlling all aspects of the iMode service. Unlike some European promoters of wireless application protocol (WAP), another mobile data technology, DoCoMo knew that developing content would be crucial. DoCoMo required its content providers to create wireless content from the ground up, specifically generating content to fit the mobile phone format. DoCoMo's success lay not in its technology, which actually was not state-of-the-art, but in its ability to bring together and control all these pieces and thereby deliver content that its target customers wanted.

Results

NTT DoCoMo created iMode at a time when the Japanese market for mobile phones was reaching maturity and users were in need of new services. Its foresight and customer understanding led to impressive results:

- 4.5 million subscribers in iMode's first year of operation;[14]
- 50,000 new customers each day over the next two years;[15]
- by May 2001, iMode had 22 million subscribers, approximately 20 per cent of Japan's population,[16] making DoCoMo's domestic customer base twice the size of its closest rivals.

In 2003, after four years of red-hot growth, iMode faced a two-pronged challenge: fighting off rivals that wanted a piece of iMode's market and sustaining the growth. With iMode maintaining its dominance in Japan, management decided to take its offering overseas through licensing agreements with local telecom operators.[17] Could iMode duplicate its success abroad, or was it strictly a Japanese cultural phenomenon? Its key target was Europe.

Although Europeans already enjoyed widespread domestic Internet access, consumer demand for mobile content was high. Sports and news updates, previously sent to phones in SMS text messages, along with ring tones, were especially popular.[18] With the support of the mobile networks, many of which were spending billions to update to the latest 3G mobile infrastructure, iMode was set to take off. Once again, the growth was promising.

By the middle of 2004, overseas iMode subscriber numbers had grown to 3 million, on top of more than 46 million subscribers in Japan.[19] But competition and cultural differences have made the going in Europe more difficult. Despite promising partnerships with some of Europe's leading mobile operators, such as KPN (Netherlands), O2 (UK and Ireland), Bouygues and Orange (France), and E-plus (Germany), iMode did not enjoy the growth it had experienced in Japan. By mid-2009, several of these operators had stopped supporting iMode.[20]

Though the newly updated 3G networks in Europe made iMode even easier to use, the iMode technology itself didn't. iMode required handsets and content specifically designed for iMode, unlike the conventional Internet browsers provided on the majority of handsets in Europe. In the UK, for instance, mobile operator O2 sold only 12 types of handset supporting iMode technology, compared to 240 types supporting conventional Internet browsers. In Europe, as the mobile industry matured, the customer simply had many more easily accessible options both in handsets and content. Translating success from one region to another – from Japan to Europe, in iMode's case – is often more difficult than it looks!

American beer drinkers see the Lite

To revolutionize an industry is a goal most companies can only dream of. For Miller Brewing Company, its decision to introduce light beer in 1975 had exactly this kind of impact. Barely on the radar in 1975, light beers made up only 1 per cent of beer consumption in the USA. By 1994, they accounted for 35 per cent of all domestic beer sold in the USA, some $16 billion in sales.[21] Miller Lite, the brand that built the light beer category, was credited for this monumental shift in consumer purchasing. How did Miller make this happen?

Miller's achievement can be attributed to two simple principles: segmented marketing and saturation advertising to reach the target market. Through consumer research, Miller realized there was a beer-drinking market segment of young men who were interested in a lower-calorie beer.[22] This appeal for lower-calorie beer stemmed from trends towards health and fitness in the 1970s. As we saw in Chapter 1, trends like these can have powerful effects on demand. The beer market was no exception. And, unlike what had been assumed previously, men were just as interested in light beer as women were. In this section, we examine how Miller identified a new target market for its beer, how it appealed to that new market and the results of its efforts.

❝ trends can have powerful effects on demand ❞

A new target market

There were a number of trends occurring in the mid-1970s. First, a nationwide health kick was in the works.

Led by maturing baby boomers and fitness fiends, Americans are breakfasting on less bacon and fewer eggs, forgoing the lunchtime Scotch, and seeing a lot more sparkling water and chicken breasts at dinnertime. The new abstinence has touched the lives of so many people that it is creating havoc in some very large industries. For marketers of products spurned, or favoured, by increasingly health conscious Americans, abstinence is either a problem of historic proportions or a magnificent opportunity.[23]

Second, in 1975, of the 76 million strong baby boomer population, nearly 20 million were in their mid- and late-twenties.[24] The result of these two trends was a large but changing beer-drinking demographic, one increasingly concerned with its health.

Realizing that its customer demographics were changing, Miller took action, conducting extensive consumer research to determine how best to appeal to its evolving target market. The research results were like music to Miller's ears, despite the fact that brewers overall were suffering (along with distillers of hard liquor) from declining per capita consumption as health and fitness trends took hold.

The beer-drinking generation was made up predominantly of men – no change there – in their mid-twenties, a segment quite different from the late-teens/early-twenties males who had traditionally attracted the lion's share of beer marketers' attention. The beauty of this demographic was that it was quite large (some 10 million in 1975) and it was growing. There were still 20 million male baby boomers yet to reach the legal drinking age. And all evidence suggested that the trend towards health and wellness would not be short-lived. If Miller could brew and market a beer that would appeal to this somewhat older, more health-conscious segment of the beer market, then the opportunity looked attractive. But would real men buy light beer?

Reaching its target market

Miller's goal from the onset was making light beer a mainstream, acceptable choice for young, macho, albeit health-conscious, men. To appeal to this target segment, Miller focused its advertising predominantly on sports. As

Miller's Alan Easton said, '. . . the sports fan and the beer consumer are essentially the same'.[25] Miller's research also showed that this group of once-in-shape athletes was growing up and out of sports participation. Increasingly, they were becoming spectators whose beer guts replaced rippling six-pack stomachs. As Easton commented, 'Once you're into the demographics of sports, you are also into the total demographics of beer drinking. You get them all, from the couch-potato spectator to the high-action, participating jocks – joggers, softball players, bowlers.'[26]

But how could a beer company promoting something as prissy as low-calorie beer attract this testosterone-fuelled group? Miller's answer is now legendary. When they introduced Miller Lite in 1975, they had the wit to hire famous ex-athletes to endorse it in hilariously funny television commercials. Beefy ex-jocks, like football player Bubba Smith, who tore the cover off a Lite can, demolished the idea that real men didn't drink light beer.[27] And, like Miller's target market, the athletes in the ads were all somewhat past their prime. 'We try to choose the sort of guys you'd love to have a beer with,' said Bob Lenz, the ad executive who conceived of the Lite campaign.[28] The idea was to show that low-calorie beer appeals to a man's kind of man.[29] The clear message was that this brew was not for sissies.

Sparkling results in a flat beer market

Throughout the 1950s and 1960s, two brewers, Anheuser-Busch and Joseph Schlitz, had dominated the American beer industry. In 1970, the fragmented industry comprised 10 major brewers accounting for 69 per cent of the country's beer production, and consumption was as flat as a day-old beer. Miller ranked seventh, with a 4 per cent share.[30] But then things changed.

■ By 1977, following its hugely successful introduction of Miller Lite, Miller had jumped from seventh to second place among US brewers and was threatening the long-time leader, Anheuser-Busch.[31]

■ By 1980, light beers accounted for 13 per cent of total US beer shipped, with Miller Lite the runaway leader.

■ One year later, Miller Lite became the third largest selling beer in the USA after Budweiser and Miller High Life. Selling 12.5 million barrels, Miller Lite had more than 50 per cent of the low-calorie beer market.

■ In 1985, Miller Lite, originally a brand extension, for the first time outsold its parent, Miller High Life, to become the company's flagship brand.[32]

Miller's insights ten years earlier about trends in the American beer market had borne fruit beyond its wildest dreams. The target market Miller had spotted – consumers concerned with health and fitness who didn't want to give up their beer – had proven far larger than Miller had imagined. 'Americans' taste appears to be turning lighter,' said Peter Reid, editor of *Modern Brewery Age*, an industry publication, in 1997. 'Five of the top 10 beers are light and those are the only ones showing any kind of growth.'[33] Light beer, once a niche product, now comprised 35 per cent of domestic beer consumption.

Nike: running away with the athletic market

Anyone's shortlist of the world's leading brands would surely include Nike, the global icon for the athletic set. Anyone under the age of 20 probably thinks Nike has been around since the beginning of time, but in reality the story of Nike is only 45 years old. While today's consumers know Nike as a broad-based athletic footwear, equipment and apparel company, Nike's beginning was rooted exclusively in shoes for elite distance runners.

“ how a company started on a mere $1000 investment became one of the world's best-known brands ”

As we saw briefly in Chapter 1, the story of Nike provides a compelling case study of how a company entered one target market, then used its success therein as a springboard to expand into other segments. Here, we look in greater depth at Nike's entrepreneurial roots, at how the capabilities Nike developed in running shoes enabled the company to expand into other market segments, and at how a company started on a mere $1000 investment became one of the world's best-known brands.

One waffle iron plus two entrepreneurs equals better shoes for distance runners[34]

It was 1964, and Phil Knight was still thinking about the business plan he had developed for a class assignment at Stanford's Graduate School of Business. Knight's plan had argued that there was an opportunity to build a business around American-designed, Japanese-made shoes for distance runners. Knight, a former distance runner at the University of Oregon with a 4:10 personal best in the mile, and Knight's former track coach at Oregon,

Bill Bowerman, thought the German-made shoes everyone wore at the time were too expensive. More crucially, in their view the German shoes weren't really designed with the unique needs of distance runners in mind.

Distance runners, especially elite distance runners like Knight and others who Bowerman had coached, had different needs in athletic footwear from other athletes, different even from sprinters who did most of their running on tracks. Distance runners ran several miles every day, often more than 100 miles a week. Most of these miles were run on dirt trails, whose uneven surfaces and the occasional rock led to sprained ankles, or on country roads, where the miles and miles of pounding could lead to shin splints or stress fractures of the bones in the feet, ankles and legs.

Bowerman, a lifelong tinkerer and innovator, believed distance runners could benefit from shoes that provided greater cushioning (against the repetitive impact from the miles and miles of training), that gave better lateral stability (to protect against ankle sprains), and that were more flexible and lighter than the shoes then on the market (to improve his runners' race times).

Knight's work at Stanford had shown him that athletic shoes could be sourced from factories in Asia at costs that were low enough to compete favourably with the dominant German competitors. The question, then, was how to design a shoe that would meet distance runners' needs. The now legendary answer was found in Bowerman's kitchen, where, with his wife's waffle iron and some latex, he created the waffle sole, which, together with a lightweight nylon upper, would revolutionize the running shoe.

" in 1964, Blue Ribbon Sports sold about 1300 pairs of running shoes, generating a mere $8000 in revenues "

Knight, now with a day job as an accountant, and Bowerman each chipped in $500 to form a new company, Blue Ribbon Sports, that would import Bowerman-designed shoes made by Onitsuka Tiger in Japan. There was no angel investor, no venture capital and no inkling of the potential that lay ahead. In 1964, Blue Ribbon Sports sold about 1300 pairs of running shoes, generating a mere $8000 in revenues. During their first five years in business, Knight's ageing station wagon could be found at track meets all over California and the Pacific Northwest, where Knight peddled his shoes to an increasingly accepting market. As runners wearing Tigers won more and more races, word spread. By 1969, with the business having grown to 20 employees and a handful of retail outlets, Knight quit his day job and began to devote all his energies to the growing business.

Creating a brand

At the US Olympic trials in 1972, Blue Ribbon Sports introduced its Nike brand after a dispute led to the break-up of the relationship with Onitsuka Tiger. In the 1972 Olympic marathon that soon followed, four of the top seven finishers wore Nike shoes. By 1974, after ten years of effort, the Nike shoe with the waffle sole had become America's best-selling training shoe. Nike was on the map at last, and in 1978 Blue Ribbon Sports changed its name to Nike.

One segment leads to another

By the mid-1970s, Nike had developed some capabilities that would serve it well. It had mastered low-cost outsourced production, using factories in Asia that could produce the innovative shoes created by Knight's designers. These designers had learned how to build relationships with elite athletes to identify their footwear needs and design shoes that would not only contribute to better performance but also protect them from injury. Knight and his team realized that these capabilities could now be applied in other athletic shoe segments to develop high-performance shoes tailored specifically to the needs of each sport.

In 1978, tennis great John McEnroe signed with Nike, and tennis became another growth business. That same year, the Boston Celtics and the Los Angeles Lakers began wearing Nike's new basketball shoes. By 1983, Nike had expanded its offerings to include apparel as well as shoes. In 1985, a promising rookie basketball player named Michael Jordan signed a deal with Nike for a new line of basketball shoes based on the air-cushioned technology developed by Nike for its running shoes. Air Jordan shoes became the envy of every American teenager, as Jordan became the best player ever in basketball.

Soaring results

By 1985, after 20 years in business, Knight's and Bowerman's little company reached the billion-dollar mark in worldwide sales, and Nike was acknowledged as the technological leader in the athletic footwear industry. Though it stumbled for a time in the late 1980s, as Reebok won the aerobics market with sleek, stylish shoes that consumers preferred to Nike's clunky, more functional designs, Nike regained its touch by renewing its focus on the customer and understanding both the psychological and functional benefits that its brand offered.[35] Its progress continued:

by 1985, Knight's and Bowerman's little company reached the billion-dollar mark in worldwide sales

■ in 1990, Knight said: 'Our goal is simple: to be the market share leader and the most profitable brand in all 39 footwear, apparel and accessory lines in which we compete';[36]

■ by 2000, with worldwide revenues having passed the $10 billion mark, with 22,000 employees doing business in 120 countries, and with more than a one-third share of the world's athletic footwear market, Nike was named the number one consumer goods and services company to work for in *Forbes* magazine's annual ranking.[37]

Nike's dominance in the athletic shoe and apparel market continued into the twenty-first century, with new inroads into golf and football (soccer, to the Americans in Nike's Oregon headquarters), the latter the most prominent sport in much of the world and one in which Nike had lagged. But Nike's next key challenge was women, a segment for which many of its products seemed to hold limited appeal. Though women were definitely interested in sports apparel, spending more than $15 billion on it in 2001, nearly $3 billion more than men's apparel, Nike was low on their shopping list.[38] It was time for Nike's marketers to discover why.

Nike's researchers soon learned that for most active women the key issue was fitness, rather than a specific sport. Clothes also needed to do double duty – handle an intense workout then look good worn on the street: 'We never appreciated the whole world of the active lifestyle', conceded Mark Parker, Co-president of the Nike brand.[39]

From these insights came new product lines, designed as coordinating fashionable collections, with the performance for which Nike gear was known. The new lines paid dividends. In 2005, Nike's combined women's business grew by almost 20 per cent, outpacing the company's overall growth, and performing strongly in every region and in apparel as well as footwear.[40]

Nike's women's business became one of seven key performance and lifestyle categories, along with action sports, basketball, football, men's training, running and sportswear, all of which Nike counted upon to lead the brand through the turbulent economic conditions that pervaded the globe in 2008 and 2009. This new categorization sought to connect better with consumers across seven key regional markets in Brazil, China, India, Japan, Russia, the UK and the USA. Despite the difficult economic environment, Nike proved its consumer and competitive mettle. Its fiscal 2009 revenues grew 3 per cent over the prior year, to $19.2 billion.[41]

OurBeginning.com's marketing bomb

Choose the correct answer to this question:

A company that shells out over $5 million on four television ads in one day:

(a) is large and very profitable

(b) has a consistent revenue stream

(c) has a marketing budget the size of Coca-Cola's

(d) has a significant amount of cash on hand

(e) has almost no other cash on hand?

If you chose (e), you would be correct, referencing OurBeginning.com's audacious marketing endeavour during Super Bowl XXXIV in early 2000. The story was not uncommon in the dot.com era, when many companies spent inordinate amounts of investors' money on poorly targeted marketing campaigns. The results of such campaigns were typically mediocre results and a waste of crucial cash.

Having seen in this chapter three examples of companies whose successes were based in large part on getting it right in micro-market terms – the stories of iMode, Miller Lite and Nike – we now examine the case of a company that got it wrong.

It's the story of a company that failed to focus its efforts on a clearly identified market segment. In this section, we consider OurBeginning.com's offering, we identify who its target market was, we examine its decision to advertise during the Super Bowl, which enjoys the single largest television audience each year in the USA, and we discuss its results.

The offering

Launched in early 1999 by Michael and Susan Budowski, OurBeginning.com took its first order in March 1999. Susan was a wedding planner. Michael had started several successful businesses of his own. Based on Susan's experience with wedding planning, the site was originally designed to meet couples' needs for wedding invitations: 'We launched the original OurBeginning.com site with a focus on weddings – providing the Internet's largest selection of invitations, as well as a focus on convenience and personalized service.'[42]

Once the customer decided on the style, design, paper and wording, he or she could place an order. OurBeginning sent the orders to outside printers, who printed and shipped to customers under the OurBeginning label. Boasting that its invitations were 10–30 per cent cheaper than those from retail stores, the company was, according to an early press release, the 'first Internet resource for selecting and purchasing high-quality wedding invitations online'.[43] OurBeginning.com also included a number of other services, providing suggestions about invitation wording, advising on invitation content and allowing friends and family to look at the invitations before placing an order.

Target market

By focusing on weddings, OurBeginning had a very specific target market. Customarily in the USA, women and their mothers plan the wedding, including choosing the wedding invitations. In order to use OurBeginning's site, customers needed access to the Internet. Thus, the company's target market was quite specific – women planning a wedding who had access to the Internet. In 1999, there were approximately 2.4 million weddings in the USA, a rate of 8.3 weddings per 1000 adults.[44] At the same time, approximately 55 per cent of the US population of marrying age had access to the Internet.[45] Thus, the size of OurBeginning's target market was approximately 1.3 million women in 1999.

The marketing plan

To increase brand awareness and generate sales, OurBeginning developed a marketing strategy. The key element would be three pre-game advertisements and a fourth one during the Super Bowl football game on 30 January, 2000. The total cost of this effort, including $1 million to create the ads and another $1 million to beef up the site to handle the planned increase in Web traffic, would be $5 million. In Michael Budowski's view, these ads would 'put a turbocharger in the company', and would create a database of some 5 million customers: 'It's the largest captive audience of the year,' said Budowski.[46]

This statement, of course, was true. In 2000, approximately 130 million people would tune in to watch Super Bowl XXXIV. But, how many of those 130 million viewers were interested in purchasing wedding invitations? Of those 130 million, 45 million were women.[47] What percentage of these 45 million was planning a wedding? If there are 8.3 weddings per 1000 adults (including both men and women, or 16.6 weddings per 1000 women), then of the 45 million women viewers (assuming conservatively that they are all adults, a significant overstatement), there were perhaps about 750,000 weddings in the works among this audience. With an interested audience of such a small size, how effective was this $5 million marketing decision?

Results

In January, the company reported 284,049 unique visitors to its site, an average of about 10,000 per day. What kind of response did its Super Bowl advertising generate?

- Traffic on the company's site jumped by 82 per cent on the Monday following the Super Bowl.[48]

- In February, after the ads aired, the site had 510,730 unique visitors, more than a 50 per cent increase to be sure, but far less than the 5 million-strong customer list Budowski had hoped to build.

- By March, however, the number of visitors plummeted to 92,292.[49] One of the reasons for this sharp drop-off was that there is no consistent relationship between advertising spending and lasting brand awareness for dot.com companies, according to a study by Greenfield Online, an Internet marketing research company.[50]

How much did the increased traffic spend with OurBeginning.com? In the first quarter of 2000, visitors to its site spent a total of $510,000.[51] While this was a 350 per cent increase in revenues from the previous quarter, the figure pales in comparison to the $5 million it took to generate the increased sales. If an average OurBeginning customer spent, say, 20 per cent less than the reported industry norm of $350 on invitations, i.e. $280,[52] then there were approximately 1800 customers in the first quarter of 2000. Thus, put another way, the company spent about $2800 to acquire each customer, or ten times what the customer spent, and probably 20 times the gross margin achieved on each sale. Suddenly, these results don't look as impressive. Perhaps the Super Bowl wasn't the most efficient way to reach OurBeginning's target market.

To be fair, its Super Bowl advertising netted OurBeginning additional press coverage, including 450 press mentions and more than 100 broadcast hits.[53] These side benefits enabled OurBeginning and its agencies to put a brave face on its results. But awareness and business results are two different things.

By June 2000, OurBeginning had a watchful eye on its dwindling six-month cash reserve and was reducing its marketing expenses.[54] By the beginning of 2001, the company was still not profitable and had revised its marketing strategy significantly. The marketing budget for 2001 would be $1 million, a small share of its budget the previous year. When asked about advertising in the 2001 Super Bowl, Budowski said he would 'merely be a spectator'.[55] By 2002, however, the Budowskis had become spectators not just of the Super Bowl but of the wedding invitation business *per se*, with their site having been quietly taken over by an already established, traditional printer of wedding invitations. Details of the transaction were not publicly disclosed.

Why did OurBeginning.com fail?

There were probably several reasons, including the fact that the business model Budowski conceived simply was not viable, a topic we address in Chapter 5. But the crucial flaw appears to have been a lack of understanding of who its target market really was and the unfocused marketing effort that ensued.

What investors want to know

Not every entrepreneur needs investors to get started. As we saw earlier in this chapter, Phil Knight and Bill Bowerman each contributed $500 to get their business rolling, and then nursed it for years until it reached a sustainable status. For many entrepreneurs, however, raising money is essential, whether from family and friends or from more established sources, such as banks, business angels or venture capital investors. Doing so typically requires the entrepreneur to prepare some kind of business plan, so the would-be investor can ascertain the likelihood of at least getting their money back and hopefully earning an attractive return on the investment. Such a business plan must, at its heart, be driven by the lessons of this chapter.

What do investors – arguably the most important readers of your business plan – want to know from a micro-market perspective?

■ First and foremost, they don't want to know about your ideas or products – they really couldn't care less about you and your idea. They want to know about the customer pain that your offering will resolve. No pain, no gain. If you can identify the customer pain, *then* their attention will be piqued.

■ They want to know who the target customer who has the pain is, and they want evidence that the target customer will buy what's to be offered at a price that works for you.

We ask, 'Who will be your first ten customers – names and addresses, please – and who will be your largest customer in five years?'

JT, London

The biggest shortcoming of the business plans we see is the complete absence of market research. Dreams of demand just won't do. Hard evidence is what attracts our money.

IC, London

❝ any entrepreneur who cannot answer these questions simply won't raise the money ❞ Any entrepreneur pursuing a business-to-business opportunity who cannot answer these questions – for consumer marketers' names and addresses are not relevant, although the same clarity of purpose is still needed – simply won't raise the money in today's demanding venture capital markets. The days when entrepreneurs could scrawl a dot.com business plan on the back of an envelope and raise millions from eager investors are long gone.

What sort of evidence do investors require? Marketing research is good. Blind faith doesn't count. Better, though, are actual sales or customer commitments based on some sort of market test – using a prototype, perhaps, or even a test on eBay. A little market experimentation can go a long way towards instilling investor confidence, not to mention, of course, your own!

The clear lesson here is that the entrepreneur must be painstakingly clear about who makes up the target market that he or she seeks to serve, and they must show tangible evidence that the customers in that market will buy. Why will they buy? To obtain benefits other solutions don't offer – faster, better, cheaper and so on. Without benefits – without pain relief – there will be no customers. Without customers, there will be no business.

Lessons learned

While world domination may be their ultimate goal, most successful entrepreneurs start with a single, sharply targeted market, often a niche that's really quite small. How are such markets defined? In simple terms, there are three ways to do so, as described in Box 2.2. Many new ventures succeed because their founders see a new way to segment and target an existing market, often in behavioural terms. Doing so enables the entrepreneurial venture to target a behaviourally defined segment with benefits suited uniquely to that segment, benefits not offered by existing solutions.

┌─ box 2.2 ───

Three ways to define market segments

1 By *who* the customers are, i.e. in demographic terms (age, gender, education, income, etc.). For business-to-business opportunities, demographics refer to the industry in which the customers do business, plus firm size and other firm characteristics.

2 By *where* the customers are, i.e. in geographical terms.

3 By *how* the customers behave, i.e. in behavioural or lifestyle terms. For business-to-business opportunities, behavioural segmentation specifies differences in how the products are used. For example, makers of pumps serve a broad variety of market segments, depending on what is to be pumped (liquid or gas, high or low viscosity, etc.) and the conditions under which the pumping occurs (e.g. the cold temperatures under which oil is pumped from wells in the Siberian tundra versus the hygienic conditions in a dairy facility).

Different market segments have different needs, thereby calling for different solutions. Entrepreneurs are renowned for finding new ways to segment markets that they serve, often behaviourally, thereby creating new segments that they can dominate.

└───

But it is not enough to know that there is a market for a product. In order to understand your opportunity in micro-market terms and to demonstrate that your customers will really buy, it is essential to become intimately familiar with the needs of the target segment or segments most likely to purchase your product. Ideally, you'll want evidence of purchase intentions or – better yet – purchase orders or letters of intent for your still-hypothetical product. You'll need this evidence *before* you write your business plan, since writing a business plan for a product for which there's no evidence that customers will buy is a waste of your time.

Knowing why they'll buy comes down to benefits, because customers buy benefits, not features, a distinction many entrepreneurs fail to understand. Benefits are the lead actor. Features are simply the supporting cast – a mere delivery system for the benefits customers seek. What do we mean by 'benefits'? Benefits are the often-measurable end-use consequences of using the product – the pain relief – as opposed to some physical attributes of the product itself. The waffle sole and nylon upper of Bill Bowerman's early running shoes were features – tangible product attributes – but that's not why runners bought his shoes. They bought them for protection from injury while training and because, when wearing them, they ran faster. These benefits differentiated the shoes from others and made the sale.

Lessons learned from iMode

As the iMode case history demonstrated, DoCoMo's new service was an instant hit because of its designers' intimate familiarity with the Japanese market on a segment-by-segment basis. Identifying clearly who its target markets were allowed the company to offer an Internet-access mobile phone service that appealed to a large number of customers. DoCoMo segmented its markets behaviourally and designed offerings of different downloadable information for each segment: those interested in financial markets, comic strips, cartoons and so on.

ɩɩ it's not so important whether recognition of the need comes first, or whether the technology comes first ɩɩ

The iMode story also provides an example that answers the often-asked question, 'Which must come first, the idea (or technology) or the customer need?' In iMode's case, Internet and communications technology created the possibility of delivering information to mobile customers, any time, anywhere. The application of those technologies to the particular set of consumer needs that iMode targeted then followed. Thus, it's not so important whether recognition of the need comes first, or whether the technology that makes new things possible comes first. Either route can be successful. What's crucial, though, is that, at the end of the day, there's a clear target market, a clear customer need, and that what the opportunity offers satisfies that target market's need in a way that's faster, better, cheaper or otherwise more beneficial – again, benefits, not features – than other solutions.

Lessons learned from Miller Lite

Entrepreneurial behaviour, as the Miller Lite story shows, can occur within established firms, as well as in nascent start-ups. In a brutally competitive industry serving a stagnant market, Miller Brewing Company needed to find a way to grow. The company used consumer research to determine whether and where there was an unfilled or under-served need. Miller identified a large and growing market segment, the 10 million, 20-something male baby boomers interested in low-calorie beer.

Thus, before introducing its light beer, Miller knew it had a sizeable target market with needs that were not served currently and effectively by other brewers. Unlike iMode, which segmented its market behaviourally, Miller identified a demographically defined market segment, although it used its customers' affinity for sports, a behavioural factor, in further targeting its marketing effort. Given the powerful demographic surge that lay ahead – with

20 million male baby boomers yet to reach drinking age – the segment had attractive potential for growth as well. As we shall see in more detail in the next chapter, demographic and other macro-trends can lead to the creation of new market segments waiting to be served by entrepreneurs whose customer insights uncover unserved or under-served needs that others have overlooked.

The Miller Lite story also shows that market niches sometimes turn out to be far larger than an entrepreneur might originally anticipate. From the 10 million males in its original target market, the light beer segment grew to encompass one-third of US beer consumption 20 years later – a $16 billion market. For entrepreneurs – especially those having resources more limited than Miller's – niche markets aren't bad places to begin.

Lessons learned from Nike

From Nike, we've seen how entry into one segment, if successful, can lead to success in additional segments. The additional value that such a successful entry offers can constitute an important part of the value that entrepreneurs bring to investors who back them. Understanding these options *before* writing a business plan and articulating them effectively can help entrepreneurs pitch the upside of what they propose to investors, thereby making their opportunity more compelling.

ff Nike's segment-by-segment success raises several questions that entrepreneurs should ask JJ

Unlike the Miller Lite story, where the entrepreneurial behaviour took root in an established firm, Nike's story began with two runners passionate about running. And unlike iMode, where the technology came first and made the concept possible, in Nike's case the venture was driven by customers' needs, needs that Knight and Bowerman, as runners themselves, knew intimately.

Nike learned its trade in one segment, elite distance runners, clearly a niche market then and now. There it built crucial capabilities:

- the art of understanding the needs of such athletes;
- the engineering of products that appealed to these athletes;
- the business of sourcing these products in low-cost offshore manufacturing locations;
- the marketing savvy to build on the performance of these runners to attract interest from the rest of the athletic pyramid.

Nike then used these capabilities when entering other segments. In almost every segment it entered, Nike won the match.

Nike's segment-by-segment success raises several questions that entrepreneurs should ask.

- What can I learn from this first market segment that will allow me to make waves in additional segments?
- What other segments exist that could benefit from a related offering?
- Can we develop capabilities that are transferable from one segment to another?

By answering these questions, entrepreneurs can identify additional value in the opportunity at hand – value that lies beyond the market targeted originally. As the Nike case history shows, that extra value can be more than small change!

Lessons learned from OurBeginning.com

It is one thing to identify a target market; it is another thing to market effectively to this segment. OurBeginning may have had a good sense for who its target market was, but the company made decisions about how to reach this segment that reflected a lack of understanding about target marketing. And when men placed a whopping 35 per cent of its early orders (do men buy most wedding invitations?), it might have given careful thought to the implications of this figure.[56] Was the marketing reaching the real target market? As the Monday morning quarterbacks noted and more savvy marketers would have foreseen, 'You're a stationery company, focusing on etiquette and customer service – not exactly the market that watches the Super Bowl.'[57]

Thus, understanding one's target market is a good start, but it requires effective execution, as we'll explore further in Chapter 7. Without clearly articulating one's target market up front, that execution is very likely to miss the mark. And, of more immediate concern to entrepreneurs about to

ΓΓ will the fish bite? ͻͻ

prepare a business plan, without a clear definition of the target market and compelling evidence to show why its customers will buy – Will the fish bite? – no investor will invest.

The new business road test: stage one – the micro-market test

■ What customer pain will your offering resolve? How strong an incentive do customers have to give you their money? Will the fish bite at a price that works?

■ Who, precisely, are the customers who have the pain? Do you have detailed, accurate and current information about who they are, where they live or do business, or what they do?

■ What differentiated benefits does your offering provide that other solutions don't?

■ What evidence do you have that customers will buy what you propose to offer?

■ What evidence can you provide to show that your target market has the potential to grow?

■ What other segments exist that could benefit from a related offering?

■ Can you develop capabilities that are transferable from one segment to another?

3

Is this a good market?

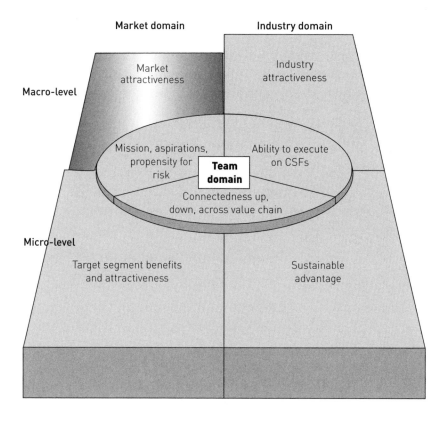

After years of searching for your dream car, a 1950s Austin Healey, you happen upon a mint-condition 1956 100 series BN2. With the exception of its price tag, it is perfect. Pillar-box red exterior. Leather seats. A dashboard more vintage than the car itself. With the money you saved over the past year, you hop on a plane to Las Vegas, ready to enjoy the desert sun and win yourself enough money to buy the car. Sure, you could have gone to a nearby casino on a riverboat or to an Indian reservation, but the jackpots are bigger in Las Vegas.

When you walk into the casino, you are entranced by the commotion. Readying (or steadying) yourself for a day of gambling, you sit down at the bar for a quick shot of vodka and a glass of freshly squeezed orange juice. At the bar, you notice a blank lottery ticket sitting in front of you. The payback in this game called Keno is enormous. For a small price of $7, all you need to do is pick seven numbers. If all seven numbers are included in the 20 selected during the lottery drawing, your winnings are $77,777. Not a bad return on an investment – if you hit the right numbers, of course. Your other gambling choice is a bit less rewarding. You sit at the bar and calculate how long it might take you to win $77,777 at the blackjack table. Your realization is that $77,000 is more than a day's work when playing blackjack under the very best of circumstances. Choosing games in Las Vegas is a bit like choosing markets, you reflect. Choose the right game – or the right market – and the payoff can be huge. But the size of the possible payoff isn't the only thing to consider.

Knowing that the odds of picking all seven numbers correctly in Keno are about 41,000 to 1, whereas you have about a 50 per cent chance of winning a hand in blackjack, which game do you choose?

Do markets matter?

There is a tide in the affairs of men, which, taken at the flood, leads on to fortune . . . We must take the current when it serves, or lose our ventures.

William Shakespeare[1]

Most entrepreneurs consider both risk and reward when starting a new business. As we have seen, the odds against hitting the jackpot as an entrepreneur can be nearly as daunting as those in Las Vegas or Monte Carlo. One way to mitigate the long odds, as we saw in Chapter 2, is to make sure you've identified an attractive market segment, one where the customers, according to evidence you've gathered, are almost certain to buy what you'll offer. But let's pause to ask some more questions.

- What if you are offering clear and compelling benefits to a carefully targeted market (as NTT DoCoMo did with iMode)?

- What if (like the 10 million young, diet-conscious, beer-drinking men that Miller identified) you have plenty of customers willing to buy your new product?

- What if the segment you'll target takes you naturally into other segments (as did Nike's distance runner segment)?

Is it time to write your business plan? No. Not even close.

As we'll see in this chapter, I've only scratched the surface in giving you the tools you need to assess your opportunity. One domain down, six to go. Having a target market whose customers are likely to buy is like table stakes. It gets you into the game, but it's by no means the end of the story. Thus, the next piece of the game we'll examine is the upper left quadrant of the seven domains model, the attractiveness of the market at the macro-level.

As Chapter 1 showed, one of the best ways to improve your odds for success – apart from serving an attractive target market – is to seek to do business in a market that's attractive overall. As we saw in Chapter 2, the assessment at the micro- or the target segment level involves looking very closely at your target market to make sure that you offer clear and differentiated benefits to a clearly defined group of customers. Here, as we deal with assessing markets at the macro-level, we view them from 30,000 feet.

❝ having a target market whose customers are likely to buy is like table stakes ❞

What you are looking for here is big enough to be seen from the air and you'll need some distance – a macro-perspective – to understand what you're looking at. What you want to find is evidence of market size and market growth, both today and tomorrow. Doing so involves asking the three key questions listed in Box 3.1. Chapter 12 provides a market analysis worksheet for digging into these questions in more detail. It also highlights the importance of reaching an overall conclusion about market attractiveness, at the macro-level, once you've gathered the evidence necessary to answer the questions.

In asking these questions as an aspiring entrepreneur, you must know what you want. If you take a long-run perspective and your aspirations include building a large and lasting venture that creates value over time, then you'll

---

box 3.1

Three crucial questions about markets

1   Is your market large enough today to allow different competitors the opportunity to serve different segments without getting in each other's way?

2   What are the predictions for your market's short-term growth rate? (In the absence of other information to the contrary, the recent rate of growth in your market may be the best available predictor of growth in the near future.)

3   What are the predictions for your market's long-term growth rate? (This is likely to be influenced heavily by macro-trends: economic, demographic, sociocultural, technological, regulatory and/or natural.)

be concerned with the answers to all three questions. If you plan to exit quickly, selling your business and perhaps moving on to another one, or you plan to build a small business in a protected market niche, then questions 2 and 3 might be less crucial for you.

In this chapter, we examine the case histories of three entrepreneurial success stories driven largely by the attractiveness of the market in macro-terms. First, we travel to India to examine the story of Hero Honda, a joint venture between a local bicycle manufacturer and a global leader in small-engine technology. This venture reaped the benefits of an enormous Indian population in need of affordable transportation, one having still modest but growing buying power.

We then see how the tide of growing demand for natural and organic foods propelled Whole Foods Market into the front-runner position in a rapidly growing segment of the American supermarket industry.

Finally, we discuss how EMC, a data storage company, succeeded in tracking and anticipating technological trends through 20 years, outperforming its competitors and just about every public company in the USA. We also look briefly at its efforts to reinvent itself after the dot.com bust and more recently amid a faltering economy.

On the other side of the coin, we examine the story of Thinking Machines, a supercomputer company whose failure can, to a large degree, be attributed to insufficient market size. Despite its founders' hopes, Thinking Machines simply couldn't find a large enough market to sustain its ambitions.

To conclude the chapter, we explore the investors' perspective on market attractiveness, we examine lessons learned, and we consider how you can use these lessons to determine whether your overall market is attractive in macro-terms. Will you find yourself swimming against the tide? Or, like a sailor with the wind at your back, will you benefit from a favourable breeze?

'Fill it, shut it, forget it':[2] Hero Honda's rise to the top in India

In 1983, Hero Cycles of India signed an agreement with Honda Motor Corporation, forming Hero Honda. This agreement, between an Indian firm that got its start making bicycle parts and the world's largest motorcycle manufacturer, marked Honda's entrance into the Indian market for motorized two-wheeled transportation. While the country was already crowded with competitors such as Suzuki, Yamaha, Bajaj and Kinetic,[3] Honda's executives and Hero's founder and CEO, Brijmohan Lall Munjal, saw significant potential in the Indian two-wheeled market.

Why was the market attractive?

At first glance, the Indian market was attractive because of its sheer size and significant growth. India boasted a population of approximately 725 million in 1983,[4] growing at a rate of 2.2 per cent per year.[5] At that rate of growth, the Indian population was expected to grow by 163 million people in the 1980s[6] and to surpass 1 billion people by 2000.[7] Not only was the total population of India enormous, but Munjal also knew that the adult age group most likely to purchase two-wheelers (15–65-year-olds) was expected to grow to over 500 million by 1990 and to an estimated 695 million by 2005.[8]

> **but why would one want to pursue a market where 35 per cent of the population was impoverished?**

But why would one want to pursue a market where 35 per cent of the population was impoverished?[9] Mitigating this fact was growth in the purchasing power of the Indian population, expected to grow per capita by 5.2 per cent between 1983 and 1993.[10] Furthermore, even in the early 1980s, the country was wealthy enough to support an infrastructure of 1.4 million kilometres of highway.[11] In total, Munjal saw that a large population coupled with a substandard economic situation was an ideal environment for inexpensive, motorized, two-wheeled scooters.

Honda also saw the potential. With air pollution from industry and vehicle emissions topping India's environmental concerns, emissions regulations had become increasingly stringent. These regulations made environmentally friendly vehicles more attractive, and two-wheelers with their fuel efficiency and low emissions fitted the bill. Honda also recognized that Asian countries such as India and China, with their huge populations and relatively low levels of economic development, were likely to embrace two-wheeled vehicles as a popular means of transport.[12]

In short, India offered a large and growing market for two-wheelers, supported by several favourable macro-trends that boded well for the future: growth in numbers in the demographic group most likely to buy two-wheelers, growing purchasing power across the Indian population and regulatory encouragement.

How did Honda enter the market?

Rather than enter the Indian two-wheeled market alone, Honda opted to join hands with the established bicycle manufacturer Hero Cycles, a company with proven manufacturing, distribution and management practices. Founded by Brijmohan Lall Munjal and his brothers in 1945, Hero Cycles was an ideal partner for Honda. In business for nearly 40 years, Hero had manufactured and distributed bicycle parts and bicycles in India for as long as Honda had produced motorcycles.[13] And, with strong distribution channels and well-honed supplier management, the Hero Cycles name was as reputable in India as was Honda's in Japan.

But Hero Cycles was no ordinary partner. The Munjal family's management practices had led to exceptional results, low employee turnover and never a day of strikes in 40 years.[14] The company used modern manufacturing concepts such as just-in-time supply chain management, multi-tasking assembly line workers and stringent quality assurance programmes. Most importantly, Hero's management brought an intimate familiarity with the Indian economy, government, business culture and people. 'What drew Honda to Hero was the philosophy and value of the group. It's good management and customer-oriented thinking,' said Honda's Kazumi Yanagida, one of two Honda directors on the Hero Honda board.[15]

Macro-trends steer India's two-wheeled market

In the company's early years, the geared scooter with a four-stroke engine was Hero Honda's most popular two-wheeled vehicle, providing inexpensive and reliable transportation to India's largely rural population and growing middle class. Hero Honda had seen something that all the motorcycle manufacturers had missed. The biggest chunk of demand was to come from villages, small towns and the middle-class office-goers in cities for whom the fuel economy of a four-stroke engine was a bigger draw than the looks and the power of two-stroke bikes. As Brijmohan Lall Munjal remarked, 'Looking into the rear-view mirror today, the choice of a four-stroke bike in the 1980s may sound providential, but we knew that buying a product is one thing and running it for a long time is quite another. That is why we wanted the running cost of our vehicle to be low.'[16]

The advantages of four-stroke engines were threefold. Not only did they produce less pollution than a two-stroke engine (commonly used in other motorcycles) but they were also more fuel-efficient and ran for longer than the more powerful two-stroke engine.[17] Fuel efficiency and product longevity translated directly into money saved. Saving money appealed strongly to India's middle-class consumer. Hero Honda had the first and for many years only four-stroke vehicle.[18] As its early ads said, 'Fill it, shut it, forget it.' Yet demand for these scooters would last less than a decade. The growing purchasing power of India's expanding middle class would soon change what they wanted in two-wheeled transportation.

In 1988, to understand its market better, Hero Honda conducted a massive customer survey, collecting some 25,000 responses. The survey told Hero Honda a surprising story. India's consumers had changed their minds. Scooters were no longer the vehicles of choice. Motorcycles were to become the two-wheel vehicles of the 1990s. Atul Sobti, Senior Vice-president of Marketing and Sales for Hero Honda said, 'It's thanks to that survey that today we sell over a million motorcycles in a year.'[19]

66 India's consumers had changed their minds 99

Sobti couldn't have been more accurate. In response to these surveys, Hero Honda set up a second plant in Gurgaon to allow for additional manufacturing capacity. Ravi Sud, Vice-president of Finance said, 'With additional capacity, we found it easier to cash in on the trend in favour of motorcycles.'[20] By 2000, motorcycles were the choice of 58 per cent of India's two-wheeled customers, up from 33 per cent in 1996.[21]

By making efforts to gauge and understand its market and the trends therein, Hero Honda cemented its reputation as a market-driven company, one that anticipated and acted upon these trends. As Brijmohan Lall Munjal said, 'The excellent results achieved by Hero Honda can be attributed to our continued focus on understanding and satisfying customer needs to the finest detail. We are committed to maximizing value to all our stakeholders, by delivering "value for money" products with the best in technology and service, to our customers, consistently, wherever they are.'[22]

In response to its customers' desires, Hero Honda introduced other customer-friendly innovations to the Indian two-wheeled market, extending motorcycle warranties from six months to two years, and developing a Passport Scheme that included accident insurance and reward points for purchases and service.

The results of great market understanding

Being market-driven has its benefits. The proof of that mantra is in the pudding.

■ Hero Honda won 5 million customers and achieved 40 per cent average annual growth in sales between 1996 and 2000.

■ In 2000, Hero Honda's Splendor, a model introduced in 1994, became the world's largest-selling motorcycle.[23]

■ In the first quarter of 2001, Hero Honda became the number-one-selling two-wheeled manufacturer in India, usurping arch-competitor Bajaj Auto Limited's 43-year reign. In the first four months of 2001, Hero Honda outsold Bajaj by 40,000 vehicles, grabbing nearly 50 per cent of India's motorcycle market.[24]

■ In its year ending 2001, Hero Honda sold 1 million motorcycles, becoming the largest two-wheel company in Honda's worldwide family.

Despite mounting pressure from domestic rivals and the entrance of Japanese and Korean motorcycle manufacturers into the fast-growing Indian motorcycle market, Hero Honda man-aged to continue its dominance. By 2003–04 Hero Honda had increased its unit sales to a record 2 million motorcycles, double its 2000–01 sales figures.[25] However, future growth seemed in peril when, in 2004, the non-competition clause was dropped from Hero's agreement with Honda.[26]

❝ being market-driven has its benefits ❞

With Honda, its technological partner, as a new entrant to the already competitive motorcycle market, Hero Honda decided to look to its original scooter market for growth. After years of stagnation, industry experts reported that the gearless scooter segment was taking off, with sales accelerating at a 20 per cent pace year on year, largely due to improved technology and styling.[27]

'The scooter market has revived. Our scooter will cater to niche demands that have been created by fast urbanization. We expect that more and more women will be buying scooters for commuting within cities,' claimed Pawan Munjal, CEO of Hero Honda.[28] But the gearless scooter market turned out to belong to new entrant Honda, which by 2008 achieved a market share of 55 per cent in the scooter segment.[29] Honda quickly became the number-four industry player, though Hero Honda remained the overall two-wheeler leader.[30]

Hero Honda maintained its market leadership by focusing its sales efforts on large but fragmented rural markets, where motorcycles still dominated and where it had superior distribution. The rural markets provided the added advantage that they were relatively more immune to the 2008–09 credit crunch, as consumers there relied less on financing than those in urban areas. But while the competing players initially focused on different segments, both were increasingly encroaching upon one another's areas of strength.[31] The chapter is far from closed on the Hero Honda/Honda competition. But whichever way the trends go in the Indian market for two-wheeled transportation, Pawan Munjal is certain about one thing. He isn't about to cede his company's market-leading position to anyone.

It would be myopic to attribute Hero Honda's successes simply to the size and growth of the Indian market. As the company's case history shows, Munjal and his team have done many things well. Among the most important of these, though, is keeping a watchful eye on market trends in order to stay in tune with changing customer needs, appropriately matching their offerings to what customers want. They understood the opportunity in 1983. Their ability to stay in touch with changes in the market has enabled them to continue to seize new opportunities as they have presented themselves.

Tofu and toothpaste: the rise of Whole Foods

In the USA in 1980, retail sales of organic products totalled just $178 million, and natural and organic products and foods appealed to just 2 per cent of the population.[32] The market for natural and organic foods was a small one, thought John Mackey, owner of Safer Way, a small health-food store in Austin, Texas.

But Mackey had noticed that his customers were asking more and more for natural foods and organically grown fruits and vegetables, so he figured the market would grow. Mackey joined hands with Craig Weller and Mark Siles of the Clarksville Natural Food Grocery to form what would become the first Whole Foods Market. The new store would serve a relatively tiny clientele: an eclectic group of vegetarians, macrobiotic dieters and others whose diets included a variety of supplements with near-unpronounceable names – ginkgo biloba, echinacea and others that collectively formed an entirely new lexicon for the three grocers. Like other 'mom-and-pop' organic shops elsewhere, the store was friendly, intensely concerned with its products' purity and very expensive.

Happily for the three entrepreneurs, consumers were more numerous and more responsive than Mackey and his partners would have predicted in their wildest dreams. In its first year, their small 10,500-square-foot store sold $4 million of natural products and organic foods.

Whole Foods' subsequent expansion from small-town natural foods grocer to a $4 billion grocery store chain is not just a fairy tale. It is a story of real-life market savvy. In a class of their own, Whole Foods' executives not only understood consumer demand for natural and organic products; they also knew what else drove Americans' supermarket purchasing patterns.

Understanding the trends

The decade that followed was the beginning of the nutrition movement in the USA and, soon thereafter, in the UK and elsewhere. 'The word "nutrition" was launched into the headlines more than in any previous decade,' according to Elaine McIntosh, a biologist and writer on nutrition.[33] Sparked by increasingly widespread interest in health, food companies began to introduce more products that claimed to have less fat, fewer calories and lower cholesterol, while at the same time providing more nutritional value such as fibre, vitamins and minerals. This trend augured well for Mackey and his partners, and for others who saw these developments.

When organic supermarkets started springing up in the 1980s, their proprietors figured that the aisles would be populated by a nation of granola eaters happy to pay a substantial premium for the halo of purity. They were wrong. Americans remained a nation of committed junk-food eaters even while welcoming organic foods to the table. Further, there were limits to the premiums consumers were willing to pay for organic foods, and they were unwilling to give up any of the conveniences of shopping in large stores that stocked everything from tofu to toothpaste.[34] So, what did Mackey and his team do to meet consumers' desires?

For starters, they built larger stores. With an average store size that soon reached 26,000 square feet, the stores offered chemical- and preservative-free foods, organic produce, hormone-free meats, cruelty-free cosmetics and ecologically friendly household products. Each store had at least one aisle of nutritional items for homeopathic and alternative healthcare. But, unlike the old niche stores, Whole Foods Markets were not ascetic: you could buy beer and wine as well as non-organic produce, foods with refined sugar, and even household cleaners – of the environmentally friendly kind, of course.

When the so-called home meal replacement market started growing in the 1990s, Whole Foods responded by selling quick entrées, side dishes, soups, rotisserie-grilled items, sushi and sandwiches, all of which were made fresh daily with natural ingredients from around the store.[35] They even added tables where customers could sit down and eat. A McKinsey & Company survey soon found that one of the dominant eating places for baby boomers aged 35–54 and mature middle-aged consumers aged 55–64 was the supermarket prepared-food section.[36] Prepared foods became one of the fastest growing and most lucrative elements of Whole Foods' business.[37]

Whole Foods also responded to its customers' growing interest in information by offering printed and Web-based information to help shoppers maintain a healthy lifestyle. The company also had an entire section of its website devoted to health issues and references.

Tasty results

As demand for natural and organic foods and products grew, so too did Whole Foods. The natural products market reached $25 billion in sales in 2000 and the organic industry was growing at a rate of 20–24 per cent per year,[38] with US organic sales topping the $10 billion mark in 2002.[39] Whole Foods enjoyed the ride.

- From one store in 1980 to ten stores in 1991, Whole Foods Market grew to 117 strong by 2001, with the help of several acquisitions financed by an initial public offering along the way.[40] It accomplished this feat in two ways. First, it kept pace with the growing interest in natural foods and products. Second, it drove demand for these products by offering consumers conveniently located, well-designed stores and an enjoyable shopping experience.

- In 2000, Whole Foods customers forked out an average of $826 per square foot, compared with the number-two natural-foods chain Wild Oats' $538, far outpacing average supermarket sales of $487 per square foot.[41]

- By 2004, even as they continued their aggressive expansion plan, Whole Foods Market's success had been nothing short of impressive. As Chairman John Mackey stated in the company's 2004 report, 'In a year that was challenging for most food retailers, we grew sales 23 per cent to just under $4 billion. Our 14.9 per cent comparable store sales increase set a new company record.'[42]

- The recession of 2008–09, however, provided a new set of challenges for the retailer sometimes referred to as 'Whole Paycheck'. Despite continuously growing sales figures reaching nearly $8 billion in its year ending September 2008, comparable-store sales fell in 2009. Mackey and his team were forced to reduce spending and lay off staff, as well as limit store expansion.[43] They set to work on shedding their luxury image through initiatives such as 'value tours' to highlight good deals and good value items in stores. By mid-2009, Whole Foods' sales were still soft, in keeping with a dismal US economy, but they came in ahead of analysts' expectations, so investor outlook – and Whole Foods' stock price – was looking up once again.

Catching the natural and organic foods wave and riding it early had served Whole Foods well. And Mackey and his shareholders are still enjoying the ride!

EMC: matching technology to customers' changing needs

There are no better markets than technology markets for examining what happens when wave after wave of high-tech disruption washes up on every beach. Michael Ruettgers, former CEO of EMC, a data storage company, uses an analogy of 'a surfer spotting, catching, and riding successive waves, each one representing an opportunity created by a disruptive technology, new market, or new business model'.[44]

❝ radical and continuous change is a simple fact of life in any technology-based business ❞

Radical and continuous change is a simple fact of life in any technology-based business. Why can some companies keep pace with such change, reinventing themselves and their technologies to keep customers happy and competitors at bay, while others come and go as one-hit wonders? And what lessons can such companies teach budding entrepreneurs about assessing opportunities based on the next high-tech breakthrough?

EMC is hardly a household name. The company, founded in 1979, managed brilliantly for more than two decades to keep pace with the changing needs of its customers brought about by the changing capabilities of the computer software and hardware solutions it employed. During the 1990s' bull market, EMC's 84,000 per cent stock price increase was the best in the US market, outperforming better-known companies such as Dell and Cisco. In 2001, however, another round of change hammered EMC's margins and market share. For the first time in more than a decade, EMC posted a loss for the year, losing $508 million on sales of $7.1 billion. Its once-hot stock plummeted to $7.20 in 2002, a loss of more than 90 per cent of its value since its peak in September 2000.[45]

Spotting a market – decentralized minicomputers

In August 1979, Roger Marino and Richard Egan opened shop. The two computer industry veterans were intimately familiar with the corporate computer landscape. They saw that companies were moving away from mainframe computers to minicomputers, resulting in an increasingly decentralized minicomputer marketplace.[46]

Business needs were driving the trend. Minicomputers and workstations enabled department managers and individual engineers to control their own projects and accomplish time-sensitive business tasks more effectively than centralized IT departments. With less centralized computing, data storage moved from the mainframe in the corporate data centre to decentralized servers and workstations. Egan and Marino realized that with such decentralization, there would be a growing need for additional memory for the rapidly proliferating number of minicomputers.[47]

In response, the two concentrated on selling add-on memory for mini-computers. Their first product, introduced in 1981, was a 64-kilobyte memory board, developed for Prime Corporation. Sales for this board reached $3 million in 1982 and $18.8 million by 1984. The company soon sold improved memory capacity for minicomputers to customers like IBM, Hewlett-Packard, Wang and Digital Equipment. By the time of EMC's initial public offering in 1986, the company reported net income of $18.6 million on $66.6 million in sales.[48] Not bad for a five-year-old start-up!

Market two – data storage

By the late 1980s, the memory business was becoming one of high volume and low margins, unappealing economics for a company like EMC accustomed to fat profit margins. To compound the problem, EMC was suffering from quality problems and was losing money. 'The quality of our products makes me puke,' said new Executive Vice-president for Operations Michael Ruettgers, having distributed airsickness bags to top executives to make his point graphically.

ʟʟ Ruettgers distributed airsickness bags to top executives to make his point graphically ʟʟ

So in 1989, with Ruettgers' promotion to President and Chief Operating Officer, the company changed its focus from memory and memory enhancement to data storage. As Richard Egan recalled, 'We realized that [EMC] could reach a big but underpublicized market: disk storage.'[49] The trend towards decentralized computing had generated huge amounts of new data, all of which had to be stored somewhere. EMC entered the IBM mainframe storage market with the introduction of a mainframe-compatible solid-state disk subsystem, the Orion.[50] Orion's compatibility with a variety of IBM and other mainframes, coupled with its speed, allowed EMC to steal some of IBM's storage market. EMC continued to grow.

Market three – open storage

Technology shifted again in the mid-1990s. By then, most large companies had a number of different computer systems, most of which couldn't communicate effectively with one another. Data were everywhere, except, as it often seemed, where they were needed. Now CEO, Ruettgers realized 'There was a desire to consolidate data storage, but it would require a reliable storage system able to communicate with the variety of computers that usually exist within an organization.'[51] Ruettgers spent over $1 billion developing software that would make its storage units compatible with many types of server.

With the introduction of its Symmetrix 5500 in 1994, EMC introduced the first platform-independent storage system, capable of simultaneously supporting virtually all major computer operating systems.[52] In 1995, EMC overtook its competitors, becoming the data storage leader, with a 41 per cent market share, up from just 5 per cent three years earlier.[53]

Market four – networked data storage

By the mid-1990s, distributed computing had become unmanageable, notwithstanding EMC's efforts to support centralized but open data storage architectures. Complicating matters was a growing tension between centralization and decentralization of computing power, data storage and IT systems management.[54]

EMC's answer was networked information storage, whereby far-flung data storage systems of various kinds could communicate with a company's typically far-flung network of servers.[55] EMC's enterprise storage networks wove together the hotchpotch of storage, switches, hubs and servers into a coordinated infrastructure that central IT departments could manage and scattered users running different operating systems on different platforms could use.[56] As new EMC President Joe Tucci asserted, the Symmetrix 8730 'is the industry's best-performing, most functional, most reliable, most scalable and by far most open enterprise information storage architecture'.[57] Of the 14 largest makers of servers worldwide, eight sold EMC units with their computers.[58]

Market five – along comes the Internet

Every time an Internet surfer purchases a book from Amazon, buys stock online or clicks on a banner ad, data are created that must be stored and tracked. For a data storage company like EMC, the advent of the Internet was a veritable gold mine.[59] But EMC almost

> **EMC almost missed the Internet party**

missed the Internet party. 'In our business, only a few large companies provided the majority of data storage, so we focused on companies with more than $500 million in revenue, 150 people in the IT department, and so forth. But suddenly there were companies with little or no revenue who were poised to immediately buy as much storage as some of our largest customers,' said Ruettgers. 'The Internet wave turned out to be much bigger and faster than we thought. It could have crashed over us.'[60]

Realizing the size of this emerging new market for data storage, EMC focused its efforts not just on its usual Fortune 500 companies but also on smaller Internet companies. EMC posted a record year in 2000, with sales of $8.9 billion and prospects for $12 billion in 2001.

What goes up must come down

In early 2001, the bottom dropped out of high-tech, and EMC was hit hard. The market for data storage fell off a cliff:

- EMC's sales in the third quarter of 2001 fell by 47 per cent;
- the company posted a $1 billion loss in 2001, including one-time charges;[61]
- by 2002 EMC's revenues had fallen 40 per cent in two years to just $5.4 billion, and its stock price had plummeted from $100 to $4.[62]

Tucci, having taken the CEO's baton from Ruettgers in January 2001 when everything looked rosy, was faced with reinventing the company once more. Once again, EMC was up to the challenge. Tucci slashed prices, cut costs and strengthened relationships with EMC's customers.[63] With a rising tide of data sloshing its way through most businesses, Tucci also saw that the storage game had changed. 'I want to solve your information needs, not your storage needs,' Tucci says. '[We want to be a company] you can't live without.'[64]

Embarking on an aggressive stream of acquisitions, Tucci transformed EMC into an end-to-end data management solutions company, a strategy that worked. By 2005, EMC was growing at twice the rate of the industry, with first quarter sales up 20 per cent year over year.[65] Once again, EMC was a growth machine, with revenues reaching $14.9 billion in 2008, up 12 per cent over 2007, and earnings up 7 per cent. But in the first quarter of 2009, amid a faltering economy, sales slipped, down nearly 10 per cent from 2008.[66]

Will Tucci be able to work his magic once more as the global economy begins to recover? Time will tell. But if any company can successfully ride wave after wave, history suggests it is EMC.

Thinking Machines: I thought I had a market . . .

There is no question that bright people founded Thinking Machines, a supercomputer maker in Cambridge, Massachusetts. The company's founder Danny Hillis was, at the time, a graduate student at the Massachusetts Institute of Technology's Artificial Intelligence Lab.[67] For his thesis, he conceived of what is known as a massively parallel processing (MPP) computer. His idea was simple but ingenious. Unlike a regular computer that has one processor working on one piece of data at a time, parallel machines have thousands of processors working on data simultaneously.[68] As Hillis said, 'Instead of trying to do one thing fast, a parallel processor does a lot of things at once.'[69]

❝ his idea was simple but ingenious ❞

Even folks like MIT's artificial intelligence guru Marvin Minsky supported the concept of starting a company that develops and sells MPPs.[70] How, then, is it possible that a company with such bright people, working on what seems to be such a clever idea, could last only 11 years before filing for bankruptcy?

A brief history of Thinking Machines

Started in 1983 with lofty ambitions but no clear business plan, Thinking Machines had two goals: to find a way to develop artificial intelligence software programs without worrying about university research funding, and to manufacture and sell supercomputers based on MPP technology. Market? Who cares?

The company was off to a running start when, in 1984, they won a $4.5 million Defense Advanced Research Projects Agency (DARPA) contract to build supercomputers for the US defense industry. With the money from DARPA, Thinking Machines developed its first MPP machine. The 5-foot-square box with flashing red lights called Connection Machine number one (CM-1) was completed in 1985 and had a $5 million price tag.[71] CM-1 had limited appeal. Its only real application was artificial intelligence, and its only buyer was DARPA. Fortunately for Thinking Machines, DARPA bought seven machines.

In 1986, Thinking Machines launched CM-2. Unlike CM-1, the newer model was able to run FORTRAN, the then-standard science computer language, and was therefore more appealing to a wider community of scientists. Capable of doing complex scientific modelling, CM-2 was an appealing purchase for anyone who:

- was interested in computational fluid dynamics, particle physics, global climate modelling, geophysics, astrophysics, linear and nonlinear optimization, magnetohydrodynamics, electromagnetism, computational chemistry, computational electromagnetics, computational structural mechanics, materials modelling, evolutionary modelling and neural modelling;

- had a budget that could support a multimillion-dollar computer expense.

While somewhat more practical than the CM-1, the CM-2 still needed special software, and users still needed to learn new programming techniques. With its wider appeal, Thinking Machines sold CM-2 machines to Los Alamos National Laboratory, American Express, NASA and others,[72] but by 1989 the company had still sold only 35 CMs, booking profits of $700,000 on $45 million in revenues.

In 1991, Thinking Machines announced its newest model, the CM-5. Like the earlier CMs, the CM-5 used anything from 32,000–64,000 processors. In techno-speak, it had teraflop capabilities, capable of performing a trillion calculations in a second. With a much more reasonable starting price of $750,000, the goal was for the CM-5 to have even broader appeal, attracting businesses as well as the scientific community. Though Hillis claimed it had the highest 'theoretical' performance of any supercomputer ever made, there was just one problem. The CM-5 was actually slower than its predecessor, the CM-2.[73]

Later in 1991, the *Wall Street Journal* uncovered a scandal between DARPA and a number of technology companies, Thinking Machines being one of them. Over the course of their seven-year relationship, DARPA had subsidized the sale of 24 CMs – sometimes offsetting the entire purchase price – translating into $55 million or 20 per cent of Thinking Machines' lifetime revenues.[74]

The party ended quickly. With the end of a cushy era of government subsidies, Thinking Machines found itself selling its CMs on a level playing field. No longer protected from its competition, the company went head to head with the likes of Intel, Kendall Square Research, MasPar Computer and nCube. By 1992, with products that just wouldn't sell, the company reported a loss of $17 million for the year. Not long later, Thinking Machines filed for bankruptcy protection under Chapter 11, the US equivalent of insolvency in the UK.

Why did Thinking Machines fail?

While Thinking Machines did last a decade, it was not because the company had a solid footing in the supercomputer market. Rather, the company stayed afloat almost entirely because of the fortuitous, albeit somewhat scandalous, relationship it had formed with DARPA. Without DARPA, the market for MPPs was not big enough to keep Thinking Machines in business.

The root of Thinking Machines' problems can be found in both micro- and macro-market domains. In micro-market terms, it neither identified nor understood its target market. Rather than examining its market, understanding the needs of its prospective customers and then building a machine, Thinking Machines built powerful computers and hoped they would appeal to someone. As one of the company's research directors Lew Tucker remarked later, 'Our charter wasn't to look at a machine and figure out the commercial profit. Our charter was to build an interesting machine.'[75]

In macro-market terms, the bottom line was that Thinking Machines' interesting machines were not interesting to a big enough market. For the academic community, the CMs were far too expensive and few academics needed such power. For most applications, PCs or workstations were more than sufficient.

For the corporate community, CMs were more technology than was needed. Even for the biggest corporations, the market for computers with the CM's power was very small. Buying a CM was like using a sledgehammer to kill a fly. According to Gartner Group Vice-president Howard Richmond, 'The key is industrial acceptance, and industry does not do grand challenge applications. It makes automobiles and engines and other mundane things.'[76]

“ there were few such grand challenges on the radar, and even fewer entities to fund them ”

The only real market for CMs consisted of that part of the scientific community involved in solving 'grand challenges' like decoding the human genome.[77] But there were few such grand challenges on the radar, and even fewer entities to fund them.

What went wrong? With no clear understanding of market size or market needs before launching the company – or afterwards, for that matter – Thinking Machines had little chance of success. Observers noted that CEO

Danny Hillis was so intent on building MPP computers that he neglected to notice that the market was voting with its feet to buy networked work-stations and clustered architectures.[78]

What investors want to know

As we saw in Chapter 2, not every entrepreneur wants or needs investors. Some investors – like the three Fs: family, friends and fools – don't really need returns on their investments, although they'll be happy if they get them. While they *hope* for returns, the real motivation for most of this group is to support someone they love. Aspiring entrepreneurs should not mistake such expressions of love for confidence in the venture, nor should they treat them as affirmation of their opportunity's merit!

> **❝ aspiring entrepreneurs should not mistake such expressions of love for confidence in the venture, nor should they treat them as affirmation of their opportunity's merit ❞**

Most other investors – business angels and venture capital investors – invest in order to achieve returns on their investments. Knowing that most new ventures fail, they expect spectacular returns in order to make it worth their while to bear the significant risks they know are involved. What sort of returns do such investors require?

A successful venture capital portfolio might, at the end of its life, have one or two in ten of its investments hit the jackpot, returning ten times their investment or more. Three or four more – the living dead, as they are called in the trade – may return their capital, but little more. The remaining deals – lemons – lose the firm's entire investment. It's not a pretty picture. On the other hand, if the one or two good deals are good enough, then the fund earns an overall 25 or 30 per cent annual return over the five- to ten-year life of the fund, enough to reward the partners handsomely and to make the pension funds and others who provide their capital happy indeed.

Given this picture, what sort of return do you suppose a venture capital firm seeks from each deal it invests in? A typical rule of thumb is ten times their investment over, say, five years, a figure that amounts to something like a 60 per cent *annual* return on their investment. Angel investors might invest in deals with returns projected at only half this level. But what does all this have to do with market attractiveness at the macro-level?

Do you know any (legal) business that returns that kind of money year after year? Invest ten pounds or ten dollars, return six, again and again? No, neither do I. The only way venture capital investors can get the kind of returns they require is for the business to grow so fast that it becomes worth far more tomorrow than it is worth today. They then sell the business, either to another company or to the public in an initial public offering. This kind of growth doesn't happen in niche markets, for there simply isn't the market potential to make it happen. Large markets are required. Nike did well in running shoes, but the overall athletic shoe market provided the scale that enabled Phil Knight and his team to grow the business substantially.

Thus, if you are a would-be entrepreneur seeking venture capital to start your company, market attractiveness – in macro-terms – is a big deal indeed.

We need to know whether the opportunity has the potential to be big – in other words, scale.

RJ, UK

A large and growing market is not the entire story, by any means, but an opportunity lacking such a market is unlikely to be funded by professional investors. Why? Large and growing markets offer two things that investors like. First and foremost, large and growing markets offer the opportunity to build a large company, one worth much more tomorrow than today. That's good for returns. Equally important, large markets offer the chance for multiple players to be successful, each serving a different segment perhaps in a different way. That's good for reducing risk, because it offers multiple pathways to success.

Lessons learned

We've seen why large and growing markets are important to investors and, in turn, to those who pursue high-potential opportunities through venture finance. On the other hand, if your purpose in becoming an entrepreneur is to build a business that you can control and run for a long time, without having to worry about bosses, boards of directors or others looking over your shoulder – except bankers, perhaps – then market attractiveness may work in reverse. Large, growing markets invite competitors – not exactly what you had in mind.

For you, a small and perhaps stable market or market niche – too small for the big guys to worry about – may be far more attractive. Unless you have intellectual property that can protect you from the competition that larger, faster-growing markets usually bring on – an issue to be addressed in Chapter 5 – then a smaller market where you can fly low, under the competitors' radar, may be more attractive.

So, what have we learned from the case histories we've studied in Chapter 3?

Lessons learned from Hero Honda

In 1983, could Honda Motor Company and Hero Cycles have predicted that the Indian market would buy 320,000 motorized two-wheelers each month in 2001?[79] Probably not. But Honda and Hero were confident of significant market potential for motorized two-wheel vehicles in India, given the sheer size of the Indian market and its emerging middle class. At the same time, they understood the limitations in the still-modest purchasing power of their target customers, so they offered products whose reliability and overall economy were unmatched by their competitors. Hero Honda's ability to identify an under-served market – one that was large and would grow – and match its offering to that market's needs were the twin factors that separated them from larger competitors who had targeted more upscale urban customers having quite different needs. These are simple ideas – marketing basics, really – but they comprise the foundation for many successful entrepreneurial ventures.

Lessons learned from Whole Foods Market

The story of Whole Foods Market provides dramatic evidence of the power of macro-trends to create opportunities that savvy entrepreneurs can capitalize on. Such trends – in this case, sociocultural ones – create groups of customers having needs not served well by incumbent companies. The trend towards health and nutrition that began in the 1980s is still going strong, and it continues to create opportunities for entrepreneurs in every country where the trend has taken root.

In the UK, for example, organic and other natural foods now comprise one of the fastest-growing categories in the food industry, and this trend is breeding new ventures like Fresh!, a supplier of fresh, organic prepared foods to supermarkets in England (see www.freshnaturallyorganic.co.uk). Understanding today's macro-trends is one key to discovering where tomorrow's entrepreneurial opportunities will lie. For those looking for a way to leave the corporate nest and start an entrepreneurial venture of their own, thinking carefully about macro-trends can provide the impetus to make such a move possible.

Lessons learned from EMC

For 20 years, EMC rode wave after wave in the high-tech world, successfully identifying and pursuing one opportunity after another. These opportunities, like those pursued by Hero Honda and Whole Foods Market, were driven by macro-trends – technological ones, in this case – that created an unending cascade of new needs for data storage. In an interview at the end of 2000, Michael Ruettgers identified several key practices that had enabled his company to ride the waves for ten years without being swamped.[80] These practices, some of which extend beyond the macro-market focus of this chapter, hold useful lessons for entrepreneurs assessing and pursuing their own opportunities.

■ *Lesson 1:* Speed to market matters, even if all the bells and whistles are not fully in place, a practice that according to Ruettgers was, 'frustrating for engineers, who typically want to refine and refine to ensure that a product is perfect before letting it out the door. But left in their hands, a product might be released too late to catch the wave – if it ever leaves the factory at all.' But Ruettgers tempered this lesson with the next one.

■ *Lesson 2:* Sell the early versions to low-profile customers in out-of-the-way locations rather than to high-profile customers where failure can be costly. As Ruettgers put it, it's like 'having out-of-town tryouts for a Broadway show'. It's not a bad idea for early-stage ventures to iron out the bugs and better understand customers' responses and real needs. Doing so can also be a precursor to raising venture capital, providing hard evidence – as opposed to a mere forecast – that customers will indeed buy.

■ *Lesson 3:* Spend time with prospective customers. 'I talk with about 500 customers and prospects a year, which accounts for maybe 20 per cent of my time,' says Ruettgers. 'They can provide unexpected insights.' Ruettgers' conversation in the early 1990s with the Chief Information Officer of John Deere reinforced EMC's hunch that there was a real need for consolidated data storage in large companies. Some entrepreneurs think the way to perform due diligence on their opportunity is to surf the Web for market and industry data. Doing so is an important start and helps to assess quickly market size and growth rate and identify macro-trends. But it's the tip of the iceberg really. So, pick up the phone or hail a taxi, and build your customer network. It will pay great dividends.

■ *Lesson 4:* Be clear about what business you are in. In a word, focus. 'I think our focus on a single business actually helps us stay ahead of the curve. In some respects, this runs counter to what I learned in business school, where the prevailing wisdom was to diversify,' said Ruettgers.

'But our single-minded focus creates a special lens through which to view and interpret customers' current and future needs.' Budding entrepreneurs should remember how limited their resources are, in terms of time, attention, money and people. It's usually far better to focus on doing one thing exceptionally well than to spread one's efforts all over the map. For entrepreneurs, such diversity increases risk, rather than mitigating it. Focus. Focus. Focus!

Lessons learned from Thinking Machines

It's perfectly fine for the product idea – rather than the customer need – to come first, to then be followed by the necessary work to identify a market that needs what might be offered. We've seen how such a strategy was successful for iMode in Japan. But Thinking Machines never really took the second step. They never really identified who the market was for the machines they would offer, thus they never really understood what those customers needed.

This error is all too common for technology-driven opportunities, where the entrepreneur's love for the technology can blind them to real market needs. As we saw in Chapter 2, without customers there will be no company. Without benefits there will be no customers. Identifying who the target customers are and understanding their needs are important first steps. A key element in doing so, as William Shakespeare noted in introducing this chapter, is riding the tide of macro-trends and taking the current where it leads. Equally important, though, as we've learned in this chapter, is to assess how many customers there are and how much customer spending there is – market size – and how fast these numbers will grow. Thinking Machines ignored all these steps, to their eventual peril.

> **❝ identifying who the target customers are and understanding their needs are important first steps ❞**

The new business road test: stage two – the macro-market test

■ What sort of business do you want? One with potential to become a huge business, or a small 'lifestyle' operation servicing a niche market? Without answering this question first, you cannot assess for your particular opportunity the meaning of the others below.

■ How large is the market you are seeking to serve? In how many ways have you measured it?

■ How fast has it grown over the last one/three/five years?

■ How quickly will it grow in the next six months or two/five/ten years?

■ What economic, demographic, sociocultural, technological, regulatory or natural trends can you identify that will affect your market, and what effect, favourable or otherwise, will these trends have on your business?

This information can be found from secondary sources – library materials or information from the Internet – and from primary sources too. What information on market trends can you glean from talking to your potential customers, suppliers or competitors?

Finally, are you seeking venture capital? If your market's not huge and/or growing rapidly, then forget it.

4

Is this a good industry?

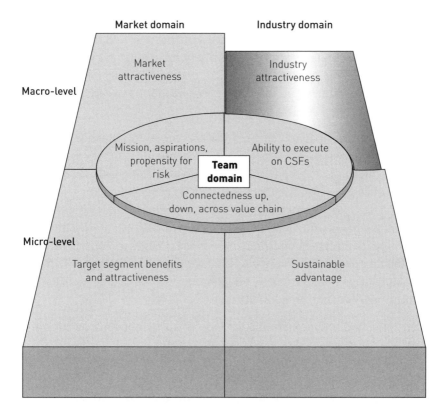

Market domain

Industry domain

Market
attractiveness

Industry
attractiveness

Macro-level

Mission, aspirations,
propensity for
risk

Ability to execute
on CSFs

**Team
domain**

Connectedness up,
down, across value chain

Micro-level

Target segment benefits
and attractiveness

Sustainable
advantage

Your name is Thomas Collins – Tommy to your friends. You are ten years old. You live in a suburb of a city in the UK Midlands where your family has lived since well before you were born. It is a quiet and safe neighbourhood of mid-sized homes. While the neighbourhood was at one time a haven for young families, it has evolved into a community comprised predominantly of retirees. This leaves you and your brother with only a few neighbourhood pals and a lot of surrogate grandparents.

For the past two summers, you have spent your time building a profitable lemonade business. Your lemonade stand is made of a folding card table and a large piece of poster board attached to a wooden post, admittedly not very fancy. Your lemonade recipe is your grandmother Mary's award-winning combination of lemons, sugar, water, ice and a splash of orange juice.

You have a pretty good set-up. Each Monday, your mother goes to the local grocery store to do her weekly shopping. You put in your request for lemons, cups, sugar and orange juice, and you store all of your materials in the unused refrigerator in the garage. Your mother is proud of her entrepreneurial child and does not mark up the cost of goods. To date, she has always been a very reliable supplier – providing you with sufficient lemons, cups, sugar, and orange juice each Monday afternoon. Mum tallies up the cost of your supplies and requests payment when you receive the goods.

With a neighbourhood full of retired folks, very few adults in the neighbourhood work nine-to-five jobs. This is wonderful, of course, for your business, as there are plenty of people taking walks every day. These retirees are, for the most part, middle class – finally enjoying their well-earned pensions. The grandparent-aged adults dote on the few young faces. Yours happens to be particularly cute – with lots of freckles and two chubby cheeks. While you squirm at the thought of having your cheeks pinched ten times a day, you suffer through it, knowing that adults find it hard to say no to a glass of icy lemonade from such an adorable face.

There is really only one reason other kids in your neighbourhood don't start their own lemonade businesses. That reason happens to be your older brother Terry, who weighs in at 150 pounds at the age of 13. You pay him a small retainer – just 10 per cent of your profits – to inhibit others from entering this profitable industry. Your retainer has been well worth it. No kids in your neighbourhood have dared to start a lemonade business.

All in all, you have done quite well for yourself. At the end of last summer, you purchased a brand new mountain bike, and this summer you are saving up for an Xbox. While you attribute your good fortune to Mary's recipe, Terry's domineering presence and your chubby cheeks, the reality is that you have found yourself in a great industry – one that allows you to prosper quite profitably.

Good industries, good businesses

When a management with a reputation for brilliance takes on a
business with a reputation for bad economics, it's the reputation of the
business that remains intact.

Warren Buffett, noted investor[1]

Why is the lemonade stand industry so good to Tommy? As we saw in
Chapter 1, industry attractiveness is determined in large part by the five
forces – threat of entry, supplier power, buyer power, threat of substitutes
and competitive rivalry – so let's take a look at them in Tommy's case.

Threat of entry

With only some lemonade and his stand – made out of a folding card
table and a large piece of poster board – there were no significant start-
up costs that would deter others from entering Tommy's industry. This
is not a knowledge-intensive industry. Just about anyone can figure out
how to make lemonade: no barrier to entry here, either. And, at present,
Tommy has no protection for his intellectual property – recipes cannot be
copyrighted or patented. However, Tommy's big older brother – who takes
a 10 per cent cut of all proceeds – is responsible for scaring off competitors.
So far, he has done a tremendous job. Terry's presence really does put a
dampener on anyone's decision to enter this industry, in his and Tommy's
neighbourhood at least. There appears to be little threat of entry.

Supplier power

Mum buys lemons, cups, sugar and orange juice from the supermarket each week, and does not take a cut on these raw material sales. Not only that, but Mum is pretty fair, asking that Tommy pay for his raw materials upon receipt. Fortunately, the local supermarket carries plenty of lemons, cups, orange juice and sugar, so Tommy never has to worry about a back order. If for some reason Mum didn't want to be his supplier any longer, Tommy is sure that one of his elderly neighbours would gladly fill in on similar terms. All told, the power of suppliers to Tommy's industry is weak, which is favourable for his industry – lemonade stands.

Buyer power

Tommy's customers, the grandparent-aged people who dote on the few young kids in the community, have a decent amount of disposable income and seem to enjoy hydrating themselves with fresh lemonade. With no other lemonade stands in the neighbourhood, Tommy's friendly neighbours have no way of switching to another fresh lemonade provider within walking distance. These buyers are content with the status quo and exert no pressure on sellers like Tommy to change his operations or lower his prices. The power of lemonade buyers is weak. That's good for his industry.

Threat of substitutes

Those who need a caffeine fix can always head to Nancy Lipton's iced tea stand a couple of streets away. Her prices are competitive with Tommy's. Some people are carrying water – either bottled or tap – or fruit drinks on their neighbourhood walks these days. The reality is that many substitutes for Tommy's product do exist. This is the biggest downside for his industry, but so far his winning smile seems to keep the customers coming back.

Competitive rivalry

Thanks to Terry, there are no other lemonade stands in Tommy's neighbourhood. If there were, they would be unlikely to offer better prices than Tommy's. The local grocery store does, however, offer freshly squeezed lemonade, but at a much higher price. That said, Tommy has been selling *Tommy's Own* lemonade for two summers now, and the brand has begun to catch on. Terry's reputation, coupled with the lack of many other children in the neighbourhood, makes this competitive landscape fairly barren. Little rivalry is good news for lemonade stand operators like Tommy.

Overall assessment of industry attractiveness

The five forces analysis indicates that Tommy's industry is quite attractive, as four of the five forces are favourable. The only unfavourable one – threat of substitutes – does not seem severe. Tommy has chosen a good industry in which to play. As a result, Tommy's business is a good one.

In reality, few industries are quite as attractive as this scenario, nor is any industry nearly as neat, simple and easy to analyze. Let's turn our attention to the real world, where we examine industries that are by no means as attractive or simplistic as the one in which Tommy competes. But first, there's the matter of industry definition to attend to.

Defining your industry

Is Tommy Collins in the lemonade stand industry or the food retailing industry? Is easyJet in the airline industry or the transportation industry? Is Ball Corporation in the aluminium can industry or the packaging industry? You cannot assess your industry, of course, without first identifying the one in which you will compete.

> **ff you cannot assess your industry without first identifying the one in which you will compete JJ**

The real question here is whether it's better to define your industry narrowly or broadly. Defining industries narrowly has some merit. It can clarify your focus as to who the principal competitors are, which helps in assessing competitive rivalry. Doing so also can help you think clearly about differentiation, an important issue, as we saw in Chapter 2. easyJet competes with Ryanair, British Airways, Air France and so on. But a narrow industry definition can, if you are not careful, make it easy to overlook relevant substitutes, which, in some industries, are crucially important. Ball Corporation must worry about glass and plastic packaging companies in addition to other aluminium can makers, for example. In wooing its leisure traveller customers, easyJet must consider the car.

> **ff in cash-starved entrepreneurial start-ups, focus is essential JJ**

Defining one's industry broadly also has merit, for it brings substitutes – glass and plastic packaging makers, for Ball for example – directly into the assessment. Doing so may reduce your chance of being surprised by substitutes that might otherwise be overlooked. A broad industry definition also makes it easier to consider changes in your offering that might enhance its marketability. Viewing his industry as food retailing, Tommy might decide to add cookies to his lemonade stand. On the downside, viewing things too broadly may lead to a lack of focus. In cash-starved entrepreneurial start-ups, focus is essential. There simply aren't enough resources to do very many things well.

So, what's the answer? There isn't an easy one. It's generally worth thinking both broadly and narrowly. The key point, though, is that your industry consists of other sellers – not customers, not products – of goods or services that meet the kinds of customer needs that you hope to satisfy.

Does your industry matter?

In Chapter 2, we saw that selling what customers want to buy is important to entrepreneurial success – no great surprise. In Chapter 3, we examined the implications of large, growing markets and smaller niche markets, both of which can be attractive to entrepreneurs under different circumstances. But most of the time, having a product that customers want to buy and an attractive market are not sufficient to build an entrepreneurial venture over the longer term. That's the case because some *industries* just aren't very attractive – the profitability of most companies in these industries is mediocre or, in the worst industries, the failure rate is uncomfortably high.

> **❝ having a product that customers want to buy and an attractive market are not sufficient to build an entrepreneurial venture over the longer term ❞**

As we saw in Chapter 1 and again in the lemonade stand example, industry attractiveness is best assessed using Michael Porter's[2] five forces framework. The key questions are listed in Table 4.1. Chapter 13 addresses each of the five forces in greater detail, and notes the importance of reaching an overall industry assessment once all of the forces have been analyzed.

In this chapter, we examine from an entrepreneurial perspective the case histories of two industries, both of which have seen extensive entrepreneurial activity in recent years. We first examine the global pharmaceutical industry, an industry that has for many years had the reputation of being enormously profitable and having a very favourable competitive climate. Is it still so attractive? Read on. We then look at the digital subscriber lines industry, an industry with a far less attractive competitive landscape. In both examples, we use the five forces model to assess industry attractiveness.

table 4.1   Five macro-level questions to assess your industry

The five forces	Questions to ask	Answers that entrepreneurs want to hear
Threat of entry	Is it easy or difficult for companies to enter this industry?	Entrepreneurs planning a very quick exit are happy if it's easy to enter (so they can get in). Those hoping to build more enduring ventures prefer high barriers to entry (so others cannot follow).
Supplier power	Do suppliers to this industry have the power to set terms and conditions?	Entrepreneurs prefer weak supplier power.
Buyer power	Do buyers have the power to set terms and conditions?	Entrepreneurs prefer weak buyer power.
Threat of substitutes	Is it easy or difficult for substitute products to steal my market?	Entrepreneurs prefer little threat of substitutes.
Competitive rivalry	Is competitive rivalry intense or genteel?	Entrepreneurs prefer little competitive rivalry.

Based on all five forces, what is your overall assessment of your industry? Just how attractive or unattractive is it?

The pharmaceutical industry in the 1980s

In the 1970s and 1980s, the average profit margin (as a percentage of revenues) of the Fortune 500 pharmaceutical companies was two times greater than the median for all industries in the Fortune 500.[3] Each drug introduced between 1981 and 1983 'made at least $36 million more for its investors, after taxes, than was needed to pay off the costs to develop it ... Such profitability was two to three percentage points greater than for comparable industries, even after factoring in the risks of new drug development.'[4] Nearly two decades later, in 1999, the industry was still a star. The pharmaceutical industry ranked at the top in all three of *Fortune* magazine's measures of profitability: return on sales, return on assets and return on equity.[5] What made the global pharmaceutical industry so profitable for so long? Why has its profitability remained so strong, and will the industry remain so attractive?

Threat of entry

For an entrepreneur, high barriers to entry make it more difficult to launch a venture. But happily, for those who are somehow able to enter, these same barriers serve to protect their ventures once they have joined the party. Thus, while barriers to entry can be considered obstacles for the entrepreneur, they also serve to keep competitors out of the industry. A number of barriers mute the threat of entry into the pharmaceutical industry. These include barriers both financial and intangible in nature, ranging from high fixed costs to stringent intellectual property protection. Let's look in some detail at conditions in the pharmaceutical industry in the 1980s.

❝ barriers serve to protect their ventures once they have joined the party ❞

Heavy expenditure on research and development were (and still are) required for the arduous processes of drug discovery, development, manufacturing, and approval through the various regulatory bodies, such as the Food and Drug Administration (FDA) in the USA and the Committee on Safety of Medicines (superseded in 2005 by the Commission on Human Medicines) in the UK.[6] The process of developing a drug was time-consuming, expensive and precarious. During the 1980s, it took an average of 12 years and $194 million to bring a drug to market.[7] And the long and tedious process, which included research and development, clinical trials and government approval, did not guarantee favourable results, as more than 50 per cent of all development dollars were spent on products that never reached the market.[8] The sheer size of an investment like this, coupled with the great uncertainty of whether there would be a payoff, was a powerful barrier to deter those who might have entered the industry.

Research and development were not the only exorbitant costs. Sales and marketing costs were also substantial, as pharmaceutical companies spent large sums promoting their drugs to hospitals and doctors. To compete effectively against the industry's leaders, a new company had to spend millions of dollars annually on large salesforces and other marketing and promotional activities.[9]

Substantial as these financial barriers were, they paled in comparison to the protection that governments placed on intellectual property. Companies generally won patents for their new drugs. These patents were issued on either the drug's chemical structure or its method of manufacturing or synthesis. This highly favourable competitive environment, in which drug companies obtained patents to protect them from rivals, meant that competitors were effectively blocked from manufacturing and marketing drugs with the same chemical composition for 17 years, which equates to between 8 and 12 years once the drug actually gets to market.[10]

The result? In terms of threat of entry, the picture of the pharmaceutical industry in the 1980s was clear. Entry barriers were extremely high, resulting in little threat of entry, a very favourable condition for industry incumbents and for new pharmaceutical start-ups that could find a way to enter.

Supplier power

Pharmaceutical companies were flooded with raw material suppliers anxious to sell to such a strong and profitable industry. In 1982, there were over 12,000 chemical companies in the USA alone.[11] Their products had long shelf lives, were readily available from numerous sources and were bought largely on the basis of price and delivery.[12] These conditions left the chemical suppliers with little power to set the terms and conditions under which their raw chemicals were sold to the drug companies. From the drug companies' point of view, supplier power was virtually non-existent.

> **❝ from the drug companies' point of view, supplier power was virtually non-existent ❞**

Buyer power

How would you like to be in an industry where your buyers are uninformed about your product and almost 100 per cent insensitive to its price? Not only that, but imagine that there are few if any substitutes for your product, and that using it may be a matter of life or death for your consumer. These were, for the most part, the circumstances prevailing in the pharmaceutical industry through the 1980s. The industry enjoyed an almost powerless group of buyers. Drug companies reaped the benefits of unaware doctors who were partial to prescribing brand-name drugs to obtain the most medically effective solution, regardless of price; price-insensitive patients who did not care about the cost of their prescription medications; ill-informed consumers who blindly trusted their doctors' treatment suggestions; and few alternatives to prescription drugs.[13] The weakness in buyer power contributed significantly to the profitability of the pharmaceutical companies.

> **❝ the industry enjoyed an almost powerless group of buyers ❞**

These companies also benefited from consumer trends in Europe and North America towards health and nutrition. Consumers were increasingly eager to do whatever it took to become or stay healthy. Further, consumers had the luxury of being indifferent to drug prices because most of them did not pay full price for their medications. Rather, through the 1980s in most developed countries, government agencies, insurance companies or employers paid the patients' prescription drug bills. And without easy access to information on medications, customers had little say in their treatment plans.

Threat of substitutes

Until the mid-1980s, the global pharmaceutical industry was largely unthreatened by substitute products. If a patient was ill, they took the medicine the doctor ordered. Patent laws prohibited companies from replicating others' brand-name drugs for as long as 17 years, and other regulations deterred the development of chemically equivalent generic drugs. For most conditions treatable by prescription drugs, there simply were no substitutes for the medications the doctors prescribed.

Competitive rivalry

The pharmaceutical industry of the 1980s was populated by hundreds of companies, though none had more than 5 per cent market share. There were two main reasons the pharmaceutical industry was so fragmented.

- Different companies focused on entirely different classes of drugs. These classes included cardiovascular treatments, antibiotics, central nervous system therapy, gastrointestinal treatments, etc.

- The industry's growth rate made it easy for competitors to grow without taking share from each other. There was little pressure to expand beyond one's niche, given abundant opportunities for growth therein.

The result of this fragmentation was that most firms had few direct competitors. The lack of direct competition allowed drug companies to raise prices as they pleased. Couple this lack of competition with a weak threat from substitutes and little buyer power, and the industry experienced little dissent when raising prices to meet profit objectives. Competitive rivalry was almost non-existent.

" the industry experienced little dissent when raising prices "

Summary of industry attractiveness in the 1980s

The result of these industry conditions was impressive profit growth through the middle of the 1980s. With significant barriers to entry, docile suppliers, powerless buyers, almost no threat of substitutes and little rivalry, the pharmaceutical industry in the 1980s was just about as perfect an industry as one could imagine. Given its attractiveness, the industry attracted the attention of genetic and molecular biology scientists and the venture capital community, who saw its appeal and thought their revolutionary approaches to drug therapy could attract enough money to overcome the formidable entry barriers the industry enjoyed.

Thus, as scientific advances in biotechnology took hold, numerous entrepreneurial companies like Genentech and Amgen were founded to commercialize new scientific breakthroughs. Genentech, the first biotech firm to have commercial success, developed a protein that broke up blood clots. Amgen's molecular biology used recombinant DNA to produce erythropoietin, a hormone that increases the supply of red blood cells in anaemic patients under treatment for cancer and other diseases. By 2000, erythropoietin was generating $2 billion in sales and another $3 billion in licensing revenue for Amgen.[14] Both of these new entrants fared very well.

▓ Genentech went public in 1980, and by 2001 its shares had appreciated 2700 per cent since its IPO. In 2004, Genentech earned $785 million in profits and its market capitalization of $83 billion surpassed that of Merck, the longtime pharmaceutical giant.[15] In 2009, Roche, the Swiss pharmaceutical powerhouse, bought the 44 per cent of Genentech that it did not already own for a whopping $46.8 billion, some 22 times expected 2010 earnings and a market capitalization of $106 billion for Genentech. Analysts hailed the acquisition as the best of 2009's big drug deals.[16]

▓ Amgen shares, first offered in 1983, soared more than 16,000 per cent by 2001.[17] In 2004, Amgen earned $2.4 billion.[18] Growth continued steadily and by 2008, Amgen's earnings reached $15 billion.[19]

Was the pharmaceutical industry an attractive industry in which to play? The venture capitalists that backed Genentech, Amgen and other companies like them have not been disappointed, in spite of the fact that the biotech segment of the industry has remained unprofitable as a whole.[20] Saddled with the enormous costs of developing new drugs and the lengthy and uncertain processes required to test new drugs for safety and efficacy, and lacking the cash flow that the older drug companies enjoy from their earlier blockbuster drugs, most biotechs' roads have been much more difficult.

For Amgen, Genentech and a few others whose early discoveries hit the charts, however, the high entry barriers were worth tackling.

Thus, for entrepreneurs who can marshal the resources to overcome high barriers to entry – and who have something to sell that customers want – attractive industries like pharmaceuticals can be rewarding places to play.

The pharmaceutical industry in the twenty-first century

Alas for the drug makers, industries are not static places. Like the rest of the business world, industries are dynamic, subject to ever-changing environments. The pharmaceutical industry has not remained quite as cushy as it once was. Let's look at what has changed.

Threat of entry

Starting in the mid-1980s, the barriers to enter the pharmaceutical industry began to show cracks. New legislation made it easier for generic drug companies to enter the market. In the USA, the 1984 Waxman-Hatch Act, which changed the rules for generic drug manufacturers, reduced the barriers to generic entry. Instead of having to prove the generic drug's safety and efficacy, the act required companies only to prove their formulas were equivalent to that of the brand-name drug. The subsequent growth in generic drugs was profound. By 1996, generic drugs accounted for more than 40 per cent of pharmaceutical prescriptions.[21] In 2003, the Food and Drug Administration (FDA) introduced further regulations limiting the ability of patent-holders to delay the onset of generic competition, so the market share held by generics began to grow even more.[22]

> **in the mid-1980s, the barriers to enter the pharmaceutical industry began to show cracks**

Aside from the influx of generics, the pharmaceutical companies also saw a wave of biotechnology competitors enter their industry – Genentech, Amgen and many others – suggesting that economies of scale meant less than they used to, and that barriers to entry, while still high in absolute terms, were dropping, thanks in part to the availability of venture capital.[23] Further, the biotech companies' new science-focused research model, known as rational drug design, stood the traditional approach to drug discovery on its head. These drug companies worked backwards from known disease biochemistry to identify or design chemical 'keys' to fit the biochemical 'locks' of that disease.[24]

The result of these changes? Barriers to entry crept lower, increasing the threat of entry and making the industry somewhat less attractive.

Buyer power

Beginning in the mid-1980s, three developments gradually began to increase the power of the pharmaceutical industry's buyers:

■ the growing strength of managed care in the USA, the industry's largest market;

■ increased pressure from governments, especially in Europe;

■ a better-informed patient population.

The American transition from an insurance-based healthcare system to one of managed care changed the dynamics of the pharmaceutical industry dramatically. By 1993, 80 per cent of the US population was covered by managed care organizations (MCOs), compared with 5 per cent of the US population covered in 1980. These MCOs typically provided full coverage for prescription drugs. But, because of their sheer mass, these institutions had considerable bargaining power with drug companies, and exerted strong downward pressure on drug prices.[25] Thus, while patients maintained their price insensitivity for drugs, their healthcare payers were far more price-sensitive.

To further increase drug-price awareness in the American medical community, health maintenance organizations (HMOs) set up formularies (lists comparing the prices and benefits of various drugs). HMOs assessed these formularies, deciding which drugs to endorse. If the HMOs did not approve a certain drug, then doctors affiliated with the HMO could not prescribe it. Of course, it is not surprising that HMOs favoured the less expensive generic drugs over brand-name drugs. In 1995, a *Medical Marketing & Media* article claimed: 'Pharmaceuticals appear headed for commodity status, pushed by generics, formularies, and other cost pressures.'[26] The American HMOs were not the only ones putting downward pressure on drug pricing. European governments established price controls, limiting prices at which prescription drugs could be sold.[27] In the UK, a new government agency, the National Institute for Clinical Excellence (NICE), was established to determine the cost-effectiveness of drugs before the National Health Service (NHS) would pay for them.

❛❛ buyer power had increased considerably ❜❜

Finally, by the turn of the century, the coming of age of the Internet generated approximately 100,000 health-related websites. Empowered with more information, patients became more knowledgeable and, consequently, more powerful. And, with new legislation that now permitted prescription drug advertising in the USA, patients there began taking a more active and knowledgeable role in their medical decision-making.[28] Buyer power had increased considerably. The result of this increase in buyer power was downward price pressure on prescription drugs.

In 2009, another source of buyer power emerged: 'comparative effectiveness' studies supported by the new Obama administration. A series of drug comparison trials will reveal whether a specific name brand drug truly has a better effect than a cheaper generic drug: a welcome test for consumers and HMOs, but not for drug makers.[29]

Threat of substitutes

Not only was direct competition from generic drugs impacting the industry, but trends towards more natural therapies also led consumers to try substitutes for prescription drugs. Exercise, nutrition and herbal remedies all began to take market share from the prescription drug makers.

Competitive rivalry

Throughout the late 1980s and the early 1990s, rivalry in the pharmaceutical industry increased. Given the new pressures described above, traditional drug companies felt the pressure to consolidate to take advantage of economies of scale.[30] By choosing to merge, rivalry among the top firms increased, as their areas of expertise began to overlap.

&& the pharmaceutical industry found itself with a whole new set of competitors &&

Additional rivalry stemmed from the flood of more science-focused drug discovery firms. While some biotechs were purchased by the large drug companies, others such as Amgen became strong competitors in their own right.[31] Unlike the drug companies, biotechs were not burdened with high overheads, and they possessed superior product and disease knowledge in their chosen segments.[32] Rational drug design enabled them to discover new therapeutic compounds more quickly and more efficiently than before.[33] While traditionally these biotechs had discovered new drugs and then sold their discoveries to established drug companies, this pattern seemed to be changing, as some began not only to discover but also to develop and market their own drugs.[34] Thus, the pharmaceutical industry found itself with a whole new set of competitors, some of which were more agile and science-focused. New developments in genetics also increased rivalry, as drug companies began developing diagnostic techniques that could predict which drugs could help which people and who was likely to experience potentially life-threatening side-effects. These developments threatened the industry's longtime blockbuster strategy – developing treatments that address large patient markets and can be taken by millions – and led some pharmaceutical companies to drugs targeted more selectively and to patients with specific genetic profiles.[35]

Summary of industry attractiveness in the early twenty-first century

How has the industry fared in light of these developments? A study by the US Congressional Budget Office concluded that, 'since 1984, the expected returns from marketing a new drug have declined by about 12 per cent, or $27 million in 1990 dollars. That decline has not made drug development unprofitable on average, but it may have made some specific projects unprofitable.'[36]

> ❝ while not quite as attractive a place to compete as it had been earlier, the pharmaceutical industry remained more attractive than most ❞

The changing industry environment has had a clearly measurable impact on industry profitability. In 2000, the pharmaceutical industry ranked as the most profitable industry in the USA, with a return on assets of 17.7 per cent.[37] But by 2005, the industry had fallen to ninth position on the *Fortune* magazine list of most profitable industries, with a return on assets of 10.3 per cent, down more than 40 per cent in just five years.[38] From 2006 through to 2009, the industry's average return on assets ranged between 10.5 and 11.5 per cent.[39] Despite this decline since 2000, though, the industry still performed far better than most others, such as airlines at minus 14 per cent return on assets and telecommunications (which we'll see next in this chapter) at 2.3 per cent.[40]

While not quite as attractive a place to compete as it had been earlier, the pharmaceutical industry remained more attractive than most. Why?

- ▨ Threat of entry remained comparatively low, despite the incursion of generic drug makers and biotech firms. Starting a pharmaceutical company isn't nearly so simple as, say, starting a restaurant or an airline.

- Buyer power had increased – a genuine problem.

- But suppliers to the industry still lacked power – good news.

- Substitutes such as exercise, nutrition and herbal medicines were no match for prescription therapies for cancer and other life-threatening illnesses.

- Competitive rivalry remained modest, as the drug companies, having common interests, sought to protect their traditionally high profit margins.

Thus, the pharmaceutical industry remained an attractive place to play, far more so than most industries, including the digital subscriber line industry, which we examine next. Will this continue to be the case, or will the pressure of these trends erode the industry's attractiveness further? Only time will tell.

The digital subscriber line industry

The speed with which Internet usage grew in the late 1990s created a large and rapidly growing market of Web surfers who needed all kinds of things, among them faster Internet access. By 2000, 375 million people worldwide had Internet access, of which a third were in the USA.[41] All indications were that Internet usage would continue to grow worldwide. In the USA, forecasts indicated that by 2004, 75 per cent of all households would have Internet access.[42]

Not only did this market appear attractive at the macro-level, but also a new technology called digital subscriber lines (DSLs) made it possible to deliver data – including Internet data – over ordinary copper phone lines at dramatically higher speeds than the common 56k modems could deliver. At speeds of up to 1.6 million bytes per second – 10–28 times faster than 56k modems – this technology offered dramatic benefits, including the following.[43]

- For consumers, faster downloads, thereby saving the surfer's time. Imagine – no more waiting for the file to load. Stock quotes, airline reservations, movie tickets in seconds.

- For small and medium-sized businesses of every kind, a chance to join the Internet revolution.

- For all, the ability to download audio and video, which was not very practical on slower 56k modems.

With benefits like these and a large and rapidly growing market, DSL technology looked like a terrific entrepreneurial opportunity. Surely, the market was attractive. But how attractive was the DSL *industry?* Let's take a look at the American DSL industry in 2000 from a five forces perspective.

Threat of entry

For an entrepreneur considering the DSL industry, a number of barriers to entry presented themselves. These barriers included logistical hassles,

❝ with market growth like this, how could they go wrong? ❞

turf wars, technical knowledge and equipment costs. All difficult, to be sure, but great to have in place if one could somehow overcome them and enter. And enter they did. Armed with high-flying business plans that attracted buckets of venture capital, executives from telecom firms left their employers to set up DSL firms with names like Covad, Rhythms and NorthPoint Communications. With market growth like this, how could they go wrong?

By the end of 2000, Covad, Rhythms and NorthPoint Communications had won 442,000 subscribers, but they were finding one entry barrier far more difficult than they had imagined. To serve their customers, they needed to send their signals along the proverbial 'last mile' to the customers' premises, the twisted pair of copper wires owned by the incumbent telephone companies, or regional Bell operating companies (RBOCs). But try relying on another company for such access when that same company is a staunch competitor.

❝ they were finding one entry barrier far more difficult than they had imagined ❞

It seemed that the RBOCs also saw the potential for DSL, and they were busily deploying it on their own. How likely were they to allow the newcomers access to their copper and other facilities where the gear of the DSL upstarts had to be co-located? In spite of regulatory efforts to encourage such access, the reality was quite different. As AT&T lobbyist Peter Jacoby said, 'The basic problem, if you're a DSL provider, is you're relying on Baby Bell facilities to deliver your product.'[44]

With little to gain by helping out the new DSL providers and, in some cases, a lot to lose, the RBOCs developed a reputation for being slow and stubborn. To compound the problem, once accessed, the copper wires were not always ready for DSL transmission. DSL was often incompatible with older copper phone lines. But carriers didn't know which lines would be incompatible – and costly to convert – until they started work in each neighbourhood.[45] These problems took additional time to resolve and led to delays of up to six months in getting new customers' services switched on – not exactly what companies poised for high growth had in mind.

A barrier to entry that's high enough to keep out competitors is good. A barrier so high that you can't get over it is a problem. Access to the 'last mile' was such a barrier.

Supplier power

Siemens, Lucent, Nortel, Cisco, Nokia, Ericsson, Alcatel, NEC, Fujitsu – the DSL suppliers read like a laundry list of the most reputable high-technology firms in the world. While some of these suppliers offered highly differentiated products that could command high prices, much of what the DSL companies needed was available from multiple suppliers. The result was that few suppliers had significant clout. In general, supplier power was not a significant problem for the DSL industry.

Buyer power

DSL buyers came in all shapes and sizes. While DSL was an attractive option for residential customers, especially those who were heavy Internet users, it was also an appealing choice for small and medium-sized businesses. It permitted high-speed Internet access at a fraction of the cost of older T1 lines used by large businesses with heavy telecom usage. The good news for the DSL providers was that these kinds of buyers had little power. They knew the advantages of high-speed Internet access and were prepared to pay for it, especially if the service was moderately priced, which it was.[46] Buyer power was not a problem either.

Threat of substitutes

DSL was one of several methods of connecting to the Internet at significantly faster speeds than when using a traditional 56k modem. The most significant substitute for DSL in residential markets was the cable modem, which, like DSL, offered a comparable service at a reasonable monthly price. Unlike DSL, cable modems used coaxial cable, the same cable that carried television to most American homes. Cable broadband providers advertised connection speeds of 1–3 Mbps, 15 or more times faster than a 56k modem and faster, in some cases, than DSL.

ʻʻ with cable television already present in most American homes, cable was a powerful substitute for DSL ʼʼ

In the residential market, cable operators got the jump on DSL due to a variety of factors, the most significant of which was the inability of telecom companies (telcos), particularly in the USA, to provide DSL service in its early days at distances of greater than two miles from the central office.[47] Since cable companies existed long before the advent of broadband Internet connections, cable companies also had the benefit of an established customer base and access to millions of residential homes and neighbourhoods. By the autumn of 2001, there were approximately 5 million cable-modem subscribers.

There were, however, some shortcomings of cable modems. First, the personal computer had to be located near a TV cable, which meant additional cabling in most homes. Second, a cable employee had to hook up the system.[48] And, because cable networks operated on a shared basis, some users were concerned about the safety and privacy of their Internet data and about slower service when the systems were busy.[49] Nonetheless, with cable television already present in most American homes, cable was a powerful substitute for DSL, limiting the prices DSL providers could obtain, with a consequent effect on margins.

For the business market, cable was typically not a viable substitute, as cable often didn't serve commercial areas. Alternative Internet connections, like fixed wireless, were comparably priced and provided a similar speed to DSL, but they required line-of-sight transmission, restricting many businesses from its service. Sharing a high-speed T1 line with one's neighbours was also a possibility, but this assumed cooperation of neighbouring companies and was complicated to arrange. Thus, for the commercial market, the threat of substitutes was relatively low, and this is where most newcomers like Covad, Rhythms and NorthPoint Communications focused their efforts.

Competitive rivalry

Not so long ago, the American telecommunications landscape looked very different. With no competition and a virtual monopoly on telephone service, the Baby Bells and AT&T dominated the local and long-distance markets. All this changed as the trend towards deregulation took hold in the USA. In 1996, US Congress passed the Telecommunications Act, intended to increase competition in the telecommunication industry, encouraging service-provider start-ups and long-distance phone companies to enter local markets previously dominated by the RBOCs.[50] Greater rivalry was the intent, as well as the result.

❝ greater rivalry was the intent, as well as the result ❞

The act set off a stampede of competition. It opened lucrative local telephone markets to new players. At the same time, the Internet was booming, and technology prophets predicted that high-speed networks would be needed to satisfy growing demand for digital traffic. A gold rush ensued. Nearly 400 telecom companies raised $489 billion on the stock market and took on an additional $389 billion in debt.[51]

Without question, however, the incumbent operators had a distinct competitive advantage. The long-distance companies, themselves products of earlier deregulation, and the Baby Bells had abundant resources. They owned most of their infrastructure – including the 'last mile' – and they could offer a comprehensive array of communications options. They also had direct contact with prospective DSL customers. NorthPoint Communications' own research showed that fewer than one-third of consumers even knew there were alternatives to the Baby Bell.[52]

The Baby Bells proved vigorous competitors indeed. In 2000, when Covad, NorthPoint Communications and Rhythms served 442,000 subscribers combined, SBC (a Baby Bell serving the southwestern USA) alone served 767,000 subscribers, Verizon had 540,000, Qwest had 255,000 and BellSouth had 215,000.[53] Rivalry was intense!

Summary of industry attractiveness

Severe threat of substitutes in the residential market. Brutal rivalry for residential and commercial customers alike. To top it off, the entry barrier to the 'last mile' posed by the RBOCs was difficult to breach. Is this the kind of industry where you'd like to play?

The results were not pleasant, especially for users who had subscribed to the DSL services of the new entrants. Investors weren't happy either.

■ NorthPoint Communications, a DSL leader with more than 100,000 customers nationwide, closed in March 2001, leaving its customers scrambling for online access.

■ Soon afterwards, Winstar Communications and Teligent went into Chapter 11 (insolvency).

■ By June of 2001, over 20 major providers of DSL had shut down, filed for bankruptcy or found themselves dangerously short of cash.[54]

The *market* for DSL services was attractive, to be sure. Customers loved DSL, with its blazing speed that was always turned on. But unfavourable forces in the USA had rendered the *industry* so unattractive that many new entrants had gone under. Conditions were less than ideal for the incumbent telcos as well, who faced stiff competition from competing technologies. By June 2005, cable companies enjoyed the largest installed base among broadband users – 21.4 million lines to DSL's 13.8 million.[55] The number of customers was continuing to grow, both for cable and for DSL, but for DSL providers, surviving as a new entrant grew increasingly difficult. By 2009, 95 per cent of the high-speed Internet market was held by cable and telephone companies, with 36.9 million subscribers through cable and 30.7 million through telephone companies.[56]

What investors want to know

A common myth is that investors invest in good ideas and good management teams. While there is an element of truth in both parts of this statement, the essence of venture capital investing, according to Silicon Valley investor Bob Zider,[57] is this:

The reality is that [venture capitalists] invest in good industries – that is, industries that are more competitively forgiving than the market as a whole.

What Zider's statement means, in five forces terms, is little threat of entry (i.e. high barriers to keep future competitors out), weak supplier and buyer power, little threat of substitutes (thereby limiting competition from other industries) and little competitive rivalry. Since these are crucial issues to investors, entrepreneurs seeking capital would do well to have invested some time and effort to understand them fully for the industry they propose to enter.

Most professional investors have already made clear and conscious decisions about the industries they will and will not invest in. Many go so far as to make this information public in various venture capital industry directories or other guides.[58] If the industry you want to enter with your new venture is one that a particular investor has already identified as within their scope, then the chances are good that they will already know a great deal about the industry, perhaps far more than you do. Thus, doing your industry analysis homework, using the lessons of this chapter, can help you establish your own credibility as one who understands the game you seek to play.

Lessons learned

In this chapter, we've looked in detail at two industries, one quite attractive, with profits to show for it, and the other a killing field, where almost no new entrants survived. Case Study 4.1 tells the tale of another industry, cinemas, where unfavourable conditions led to widespread bankruptcies in spite of the large and growing markets it served.

case study 4.1

The cinema industry takes a dive

In 1998, cinemas looked liked money machines. The industry had grown profitably for 20 years, attendance was up and the drinks and snacks they sold generated huge gross margins. Smart people at Kohlberg Kravis Roberts & Company (KKR), a prominent leveraged buyout firm, saw all this and bought the Regal Theater Chain in the USA. Other investment firms saw it too, and bought other cinema companies. Shortly thereafter, according to Perry Golkin, a partner in KKR, their deals 'all went bankrupt'.

Following the debacle, the cinema companies explained their errors by saying, 'We overbuilt after we bought. Regal built in AMC's territory and AMC built in Sony's. We cannibalized each other.' But, as Golkin pointed out, all this 'misses the most important point. What the investment firms had failed to recognize was simply that movie theaters are not a good business. A theater is a commodity. It's a room with a screen. There are no barriers to entry. The consumer decides which theater to patronize based on "what movie do I want to see, where and when". The smart people never stepped back and asked: "What am I buying?".'

What went wrong? Moviegoers may constitute an attractive *market*, but the cinema *industry* is a different story in five forces terms. There are no barriers to entry: anyone can build a cinema, and 'you can get whatever films you want', says Golkin. There are numerous substitutes for the consumers' weekend outing, from restaurants to clubs to sporting events to the great outdoors. And it's hard for cinemas to build customer loyalty, a buyer power problem, since customers choose the movie they want to see and care little about the cinema where they see it.

The lesson for would-be entrepreneurs? Attractive markets are one thing. Attractive industries are quite another.

Source: Knowledge@Wharton, 'A lecture you don't often hear: how smart people lose money', http://knowledge.wharton.upenn.edu/articles.cfm?catid=1&articlelid=546

What can entrepreneurs learn from these case histories? The first and foremost lesson of this chapter is that markets and industries are different things. Don't confuse them! When you see an attractive *market,* don't get so enamoured of it that you forget to ask whether the *industry* is one in which you want to compete. As Warren Buffett noted at the outset of this chapter, the characteristics of the industry are likely to outweigh your prowess as an entrepreneur.

Lessons learned from the pharmaceutical industry

As the pharmaceutical industry example shows, regulatory issues can have powerful effects on industry attractiveness and the profitability of the firms that comprise it. Where regulation makes it difficult for competitors to enter and compete, and other forces are also favourable, it may be worth an entrepreneur's trouble to find a way in, as the biotech companies have done. Both the long-established players and some biotech newcomers have prospered.

The pharmaceutical industry example also shows that high barriers to entry are good. Love and cherish them. And, once you get in, work to keep the barriers high. The same is true of weak buyer and supplier power, and of little threat of substitutes, as we've seen here. While changes in some of these forces have detracted significantly from the drug industry's overall performance, the industry remains, in comparison to many others, an attractive game to play.

Finally, entrepreneurs should note that industry performance data, like those cited in this chapter for pharmaceutical industry performance, are readily available in business libraries in most developed economies. It's well worth a look at such data in the early stages of assessing an opportunity. If an industry is a poor performer overall, you should take a critical look at your opportunity to ask why it should fare differently. Without a persuasively positive answer to this question, I would suggest moving on to something more attractive.

Lessons learned from the DSL industry

We've just said that barriers to entry are good, to be loved and cherished. But one must be sure that there's no barrier that's insurmountable, as was the case for DSL firms' lack of access to the 'last mile' of copper to the customers' premises. It takes only one insurmountable barrier to put you in deep trouble.

❝ it takes only one insurmountable barrier to put you in deep trouble ❞

A second lesson to be taken from the DSL story is that substitutes – in this case, cable modems – can place strict limits on the prices you can charge. Plastic containers cap the prices that aluminium or glass packaging companies can charge, and so on. You must look outside your own industry to see what products other industries might bring to your market. The once stealthy but now dominant advance of digital technology into the realm of traditional silver halide chemistry in the photography industry has not been good news for companies like Kodak, Agfa and Fuji, whose ageing technologies may not last very much longer.

It is also worth repeating that large and fast-growing markets like the Internet population are not sufficient to ensure a successful venture. DSL entrepreneurs were enticed by the predictions that, by 2001, DSL-enabled phone lines would reach as many as 10 million American homes.[59] It's worth noting that research companies make money peddling rosy forecasts in all sorts of markets. Take them with a pinch of salt, and don't forget to examine industry attractiveness too. If it's easy to enter the game you hope to play, then you can be sure you'll have company sooner or later. And if the industry is structurally unattractive, as was DSL, then most entrants will probably fail.

Can one make money in an unattractive industry?

The lessons of this chapter are sobering. The unfortunate reality is that most industries are not nearly as attractive as the pharmaceutical industry, although many are better than DSL. Can one make money in unattractive industries? In the case of DSL in the USA, conditions were so onerous that survival for new entrants was all but impossible. In other cases, where conditions are bad but not *that* bad, can an entrepreneur fare better? Can you make money in a business of the kind Warren Buffett described at the outset of this chapter – one with a reputation for bad economics? We turn to this question in Chapter 5.

The new business road test: stage three – the macro-industry test

■ What industry will you compete in? Define it carefully.

■ Is it easy or difficult for companies to enter this industry?

■ Do suppliers to this industry have the power to set terms and conditions?

■ Do buyers have the power to set terms and conditions?

■ Is it easy or difficult for substitute products to steal your market?

■ Is competitive rivalry intense or genteel?

■ Based on all five forces, what is your overall assessment of this industry? Just how attractive or unattractive is it?

■ If your industry is a poor performer overall, are there (based on the lessons of Chapters 2 and 5) persuasive reasons why you'll fare differently? If not, move on.

How long will your advantage last?

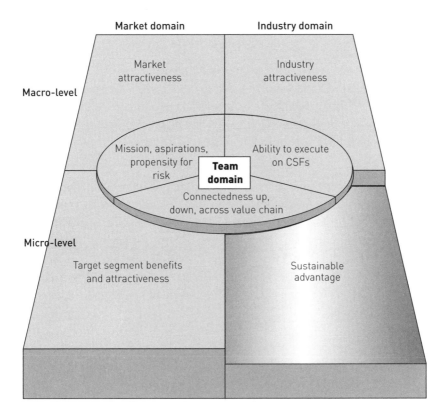

It is 1990, and you and your best friend Simon have just returned to the USA from a holiday in England. While you were there, you did your best to quaff a pint or two of every British beer you could find. The pubs were far more interesting than the museums, in your view, and the robust taste of English bitters made the American beer brewed at home seem lifeless in comparison.

You and Simon decide it is high time someone started selling real beer in the USA, hearty brews like the bitters and ales you enjoyed across the pond. You've dabbled for years at making ales at home, and your friends have always told you just how terrific they taste. With your taste buds to create the beers and Simon's marketing experience, you are fairly certain you have what it takes to make millions in the craft beer industry.

'Hey, look around,' says Simon. 'A few of these microbrewers are starting to get big. Take Pete Slosberg, a seemingly regular guy who came up with Pete's Wicked Ale. He's doing pretty well, climbing his way up in craft brewing. Besides, that oatmeal stout you made last year has been touted as being one of the best-tasting, smoothest brews your beer connoisseur friends have ever tried. Who could replicate such a unique taste?'

Stop there. Had you and Simon chosen to launch your own microbrewery, by the late 1990s you would likely have crashed and burned like some of your rivals or at best been bought by one of your competitors as growth in craft beer consumption in the USA came to a screeching halt in 1997.[1]

Making craft beer is just not that difficult. And, while making a good one does take some time and experimentation, plenty of folks have accomplished such a feat. The reality is that thousands of brewing fanatics had similarly auspicious dreams of hitting it big with their specially brewed, secret-formula beer. Over 1000 speciality brewers had had a go at it in the USA by 1996.[2] But with literally hundreds of microbrews vying for each retailer's limited retail shelf space, it was tough to compete.

Sustainable advantage: winning across time

Best beats first.

Best-selling author and management researcher Jim Collins[3]

Why is it that so many American entrepreneurs tried but did not hit the jackpot in the craft beer industry? Why is it that so many restaurants fail? Most industries aren't like the pharmaceutical industry. There, most companies make money, and lots of it, as we saw in Chapter 4. But in the restaurant industry and the craft beer industry, the threat of entry is extremely high, thus new competitors crop up every day. And there are almost countless substitutes too – numerous ways to satisfy one's hunger or quench a thirst or get drunk. As a result, the failure rate in these industries is enormous and average returns are modest.[4]

> **despite these difficulties many restaurants, craft brewers, grocers and apparel manufacturers get along very well**

Other industries have other difficulties. In food retailing, there's intense competitive rivalry, as competing grocers fight for this week's customers. In apparel manufacturing, there's severe buyer power, enabling the big apparel chains like Gap and Benetton to dictate the terms and conditions under which they will buy. But, despite these difficulties many restaurants, craft brewers, grocers and apparel manufacturers get along very well. Why?

The principal answers to competing in a not-so-attractive industry are found on the micro-level – the lower row of the seven domains model. In Chapter 2, we saw the importance of selling what your target customers want to buy. At the outset of a new venture, doing so can sometimes offset the difficulties inherent in an unattractive industry. If customers flock to your offering because it's faster, better or cheaper, then you'll be off and running.

The hard part, though, is sustaining that initial advantage, since offering superior benefits at the outset is not sufficient to build an entrepreneurial venture that can last over time. Imitation occurs quickly in most industries, both from existing competitors and from new entrants, so initial advantages can disappear in a heartbeat. What many large companies do best, in fact,

❝ first-mover advantage is most often a myth ❞

is act as fast followers, letting entrepreneurial firms like yours take all the risks entailed in bringing innovations to market, and then stealing the show with their superior firepower.[5] Thus, for aspiring entrepreneurs, the second key to competing in not-so-attractive industries is whether factors are present that will enable the company to *sustain* its initial advantage over an extended period of time. The widely talked about first-mover advantage is most often a myth. As management researcher and author Jim Collins puts it, 'Best beats first' almost every time.[6]

Establishing sustainable advantage across time, as we saw briefly in Chapter 1, involves several issues, which are addressed in Box 5.1.

---

box 5.1

The keys to sustaining competitive advantage

An initial competitive advantage arises when the offering provides differentiated benefits to customers that – in the customers' minds – are better, cheaper or faster than those offered by competitors. Such an advantage is likely to be sustainable when:

- there are proprietary elements – patents, trade secrets and so on – that other firms are not likely to duplicate or imitate;
- there are superior organizational processes, capabilities or resources that others would have difficulty in duplicating or imitating;
- the business model is economically viable, i.e. the company won't run out of cash quickly – economic viability, in turn, depending largely on the following factors:
  - revenue is adequate in relation to capital investment required and margins obtainable
  - customer acquisition and retention costs and the time it will take to attract customers are viable
  - contribution margins are adequate to cover the necessary fixed cost structure
  - operating cash cycle characteristics are favourable, including factors such as:

▶

> - how much cash must be tied up in working capital (inventory or other) and for how long
> - how quickly customers will pay
> - how slowly suppliers and employees can be paid.

In this chapter, we explore the concept of sustainable advantage – what it takes for an entrepreneurial company to sustain its advantage over the long term. First, we look at three success stories. With strong patent protection, the British pharmaceutical company Glaxo (now GlaxoSmithKline) found itself in a sustainably profitable situation with its drug Zantac – not surprising, given what we learned in the previous chapter. Nokia, the highly entrepreneurial Finnish mobile phone giant, utilized hard-to-copy organizational processes continuously to innovate, repeatedly staying a few steps ahead of its competitors. Internet auctioneer eBay, one of the dot.com success stories, proved to have one of the most compelling and economically viable business models of any Web-based company.

❝ the industry you'll enter is probably not as attractive as pharmaceutical drugs ❞

We then look at two companies that failed to thrive in the long term. EMI's invention of the computerized axial tomography (CAT) scanner made waves in the medical world. But insufficient patent protection coupled with the company's inadequate organizational processes and resources made EMI's first-mover advantage unsustainable. Finally, in an archetypal dot.bomb story, we examine online grocer Webvan's business model to understand why the company went under.

To conclude this chapter, we explore investors' views on sustainability, we examine the lessons learned and we consider the likelihood that the industry you'll enter is probably not as attractive as pharmaceutical drugs. This closing discussion provides insights for how you can assess whether your opportunity has what it takes to win sustainable advantage, even if your chosen industry isn't so attractive.

Zantac – protected and profitable

One in ten adults develops a stomach ulcer at some time in their lives, a sizeable target market with clearly defined pain in need of relief.[7] In the late 1970s, the leading anti-ulcer medication was SmithKline Beecham's Tagamet, but researchers at Glaxo, the British pharmaceutical firm, had developed a new but chemically different drug in the same class as Tagamet. Both drugs reduced the secretion of stomach acid, thereby allowing the ulcer to heal.

With a huge market in its sights, Glaxo wanted to be sure it offered doctors and their patients a clear advantage over Tagamet. The drug that Glaxo developed and patented was Zantac, introduced in Europe in 1981 and in the USA in 1983. Glaxo's pitch to prescribing physicians was that Zantac was new, had fewer side-effects and was more convenient to take – twice each day, rather than four times a day – than Tagamet.[8]

Glaxo shareholders wanted to know that these advantages could be sustained for long enough to reap sufficient rewards for the R&D investments already incurred. The answer, as we've already seen in this industry, was patent protection.

Winning a patent

Glaxo won a 17-year US patent in 1978 and secured FDA approval to market Zantac in 1983. With patent in hand, Glaxo decided to price the new drug at a 20 per cent premium to Tagamet.

So, how did Zantac fare?

- Just three years after it received FDA approval, Glaxo's sales of Zantac reached $1 billion, making it the largest-selling prescription drug in the world.

- By 1989, Zantac had far surpassed Tagamet, winning 53 per cent of the market for prescription ulcer remedies compared with Tagamet's 29 per cent.

- In 1994, Zantac generated $3.6 billion in sales, $2.1 billion of that in the USA.

- By 1995, 240 million people worldwide had Zantac prescriptions.[9]

By then, however, Zantac's patent was about to expire, and generic manufacturers would be ready with copycat drugs at far lower prices. But Glaxo wasn't finished with Zantac just yet.

Glaxo had prepared itself for the day when Zantac no longer had proprietary protection from generic imitations. To improve its chances of discovering another winning drug, the company had increased its number of research scientists from 2000 in 1986 to 5000 in 1989, funded in part from the profits Zantac generated during the life of its patent.[10]

But betting on new drugs wasn't all that Glaxo did. Any product that delivers genuine value to 240 million customers and enjoys 12 years without imitation is going to develop a very powerful brand. But even a powerful brand won't be enough to protect you when chemically identical products become available at a fraction of the price – especially when the purchasing decision for prescription drugs is taken not by the consumer but by increasingly price-conscious insurance companies and governments. So, in 1996, as Zantac's patent expired, Glaxo won FDA approval to market a milder version of the drug called Zantac 75, available over the counter without prescription. Ulcer sufferers could now purchase a milder version of the drug themselves. Even if an identical generic product became available for a lower price, many consumers were probably less likely to trust an unbranded generic over the powerful and trusted brand of Zantac.[11]

The Zantac case history offers a specific example of why the pharmaceutical industry is so attractive and shows that the music need not stop when the patent expires. Zantac's outcomes – resulting from a superior product that enjoyed 12 years of patent protection and was difficult to imitate – were good for Glaxo employees, good for Glaxo shareholders, and good for patients, who benefited not only from Zantac's ulcer relief but also from subsequent products that the drug's success made possible. Zantac's sustainable advantage is a straightforward story, one that's been repeated frequently in the pharmaceutical industry. Our next case history is considerably more complex.

Nokia: innovator extraordinaire

Nokia, a company that takes its name from a small river outside the Finnish city of Tampere, began life in 1865 as a wood pulp and paper producer. Over its history, it has manufactured rubber boots, tyres and television sets and generated electricity. Nokia found its way into telecommunications in the early 1960s. Since then, over nearly 50 years, Nokia has developed and refined its telecommunications focus, and by concentrating on mobile communications it has become a global technology leader and the world's fifth most valuable brand.[12]

Nokia's results speak for themselves:

■ in 2000, Nokia sold 128 million phones, with sales of $26.1 billion and pretax profits of $5.25 billion;

■ by August of 2001, Nokia had 35 per cent of the worldwide mobile phone market, with almost three times the volume of its nearest rival Motorola;

■ further, Nokia's margins were dramatically better than those of its competitors: Nokia's 20 per cent pre-tax margins – about $28 per phone – put Motorola's 2 per cent margin – less than $3 per handset – to shame;[13]

- despite having missed the consumer trend towards clamshell phones in the early 2000s, Nokia's 2004 market share of 30 per cent was still more than double that of arch-rival Motorola;[14]

- Nokia is the acknowledged leader in supplying low-cost phones to emerging markets in India, its second largest market where it holds more than a 50 per cent share, and Africa – two regions where most of the world's growth in mobile telephone subscribers lies.[15]

Though lower-price phones are still the largest market, one Nokia dominates without significant competition, is the company failing to catch on to the latest higher-end trends, like smartphones, where the Apple iPhone has won upmarket users' hearts and wallets? Not according to Nokia: 'We have an aggressive plan now,' says Kai Oistamo, the Finnish company's Executive Vice-president for mobile phones. 'But if you go back a few years, the market changed suddenly and we were not fast enough changing with it. To a large extent, that is behind us now and we have got our act together.'[16]

How has Nokia thrived in this admittedly cut-throat industry, in which most competitors have fared less well? 'Superior processes,' says telecom expert Andrew Tausz.[17] 'Namely, processes that allow for and encourage innovation.' Nokia's support for innovation comes in two key areas: people (and the capabilities they bring) and corporate venturing.

Acquiring capabilities

In any technology-focused company, having the right human capital is a necessity. Not only did Nokia need clever people with experience and creativity, but the company also looked for people who fit within Nokia's culture. Because the knowledge and capabilities they needed were not available at home, in a country of only 5 million people, Nokia had to attract and develop skills from abroad.[18]

Nokia's human resource policies and processes played a vital role in attracting the best and the brightest. The company's human resource management included a rigorous and extensive interview process and team-based compensation methods. The company's culture, including the organization's structure, learning environment, team focus and job flexibility, also contributed to Nokia's human resource acquisition and retention.[19]

The result, according to Dan Steinbock,[20] whose book chronicles the Nokia revolution, was that Nokia acquired 'the most technologically savvy individuals in all of Scandinavia'. Put simply, Nokia was a great place to work. Nokia's human resources policies and culture worked with its structure and organizational processes to keep new ideas alive.[21]

Nokia also prided itself on being a learning organization. Employees were encouraged to be inventive and to share ideas. 'If you have a good idea at Nokia, it will be hard to find someone who will stop you,' said Marcus Kajanto, Corporate Manager of Strategy Development.[22] Such an environment was attractive to just the types of people Nokia wanted – inventive, motivated, team players.

Exceptional organizational processes

Innovation is imperative to staying afloat in the business world, especially in high-tech businesses. But promoting innovation in a large company can be cumbersome. For Nokia, like other growing organizations, the challenge that faced the company was how to stay innovative as it grew. 'You can't force people to be innovative; you can foster it, encourage it, nourish it, but you can't force it,' said Nokia's Senior Vice-president for Corporate Communications Lauri Kivinen.[23] 'It's a spirit of trying to think outside the box, trying to look around the corner, trying to imagine the outcome of a chain of developments,' says Kivinen, who adds there is no secret formula to the company's success. 'It has to be something that is nurtured all the time; you allow mistakes, allow people to take bold moves, you try to spread energy.'

❝ it's easy to *say* your company will remain innovative, but how has Nokia really done it? ❞

But talk is cheap. It's easy to *say* your company will remain innovative, but how has Nokia really done it? Processes are its key, and some of Nokia's key processes are those in the Nokia Ventures Organization (NVO), the company's formal approach to fostering, encouraging and nourishing innovation. The NVO was created to develop new business opportunities that fell outside the current focus of Nokia's core businesses.[24] The NVO sought to develop both internally generated projects as well as external projects. Once ideas were developed, either they were moved into one of Nokia's business units or they were sold.

To implement such a strategy, the NVO had a collection of corporate venturing tools and capabilities. In particular, there were four specific initiatives for driving innovation and developing new businesses:

- the Insight & Foresight group identified disruptive technologies and developed new business models for Nokia;
- the New Growth Businesses group took business ideas and made them a reality, transforming them into sustainable businesses;

■ the US-based Innovent was a team that collaborated with external entrepreneurs to offer expertise and resources that helped clarify their visions and could accelerate the process between concept development and commercialization in emerging areas of interest to Nokia;

■ finally, the organization's Nokia Venture Partners (NVP) raised capital from Nokia as well as from external investors to invest in mobile telecommunications and related start-ups.

Processes tough to imitate

Nokia's innovation processes were unique to its culture and difficult to imitate. The NVO allowed the company to concentrate on its core businesses while simultaneously nurturing innovation as efficiently as a smaller company. Further, with an organization like the NVO, Nokia could alter its innovative processes easily. If the company felt it should concentrate on internally developed ideas, then the NVO could direct funds to internal projects. On the other hand, if Nokia wanted to look outside the company for ideas, then the NVO could direct monies elsewhere. This kind of flexibility is difficult to establish and maintain in most large, international companies.

Sustainable advantage can result from superior organizational processes and capabilities, as the Nokia case history demonstrates. The results for Nokia have been outstanding performance compared with that of most of their industry peers. Will Nokia's superior performance continue in the topsy-turvy world that is telecoms today? Time will tell, but 145 years of continuing adaptation suggests that Nokia has long been a very good bet.

eBay, one Internet business model that works

We've seen in this chapter how patents and business processes can give companies sustainable advantage – a competitive advantage that lasts for years. But there's one more piece to this important puzzle that we have not examined carefully, that of putting all the pieces together in a way that's economically viable. During the dot.com bust, countless companies went under precisely because the business models they had created were simply uneconomic. One dot.com stood out, however: eBay. Why?

❝ one dot.com stood out, however: eBay ❞

eBay was founded by Pierre Omidyar in September 1995. Omidyar and his team did many things right, but the most dramatic of these was the business model they created. Table 5.1 shows how eBay's business model matches the criteria for economic viability that we saw at the beginning of this chapter.

table 5.1	eBay's ingenious business model
Keys to economic viability	*eBay's answer*
Revenue is adequate in relation to capital investment required and margins obtainable	Plenty of revenue – customers are happy to pay transaction and other fees. Investment is modest
Customer acquisition and retention costs and the time it will take to attract customers are viable	Customers arrive by word of mouth – little marketing expense needed; no shortage of people having items to sell
Contribution margins are adequate to cover the necessary fixed cost structure	Virtually no cost of goods sold, since the customers own them, and transactions are paperless; huge contribution margins, minimal fixed costs
Operating cash cycle characteristics are favourable, including factors such as: ■ how much cash must be tied up in working capital (inventory or other) and for how long ■ how quickly customers will pay ■ how slowly suppliers and employees can be paid	Sellers pay for the listing in advance and for the transaction upon completion; no receivables to collect; no inventory, since eBay's customer – the seller – owns it

Let's direct some attention to each of these items.

Adequate revenue

eBay generated revenue by way of various fees and commissions. 'It's a very clean model. There are not many risks,' said eBay's Chief Financial Officer Rajiv Dutta.[25] To start with, eBay charged an insertion fee based on the opening price of the merchandise. Sellers paid between $0.30 and $3.30 per product listed on eBay's site. An additional fee was charged to those interested in a ten-day auction option. Other fees were charged if a seller wanted to promote their own auction. eBay also allowed businesses to auction merchandise. In this space, eBay charged fellow companies $9.95 per month to have what it called a 'storefront'. For items that were not up for auction (fixed price), eBay charged its sellers another fee. And, in what was called a 'Dutch Auction' scenario, where sellers sold more than one item per auction, eBay established yet another special fee.

While the fees accounted for some of eBay's revenues, commissions were its bread and butter. eBay charged a commission on each sale. The commission percentage was based on a sliding scale, depending on the sale price of the merchandise. In 2001, the company generated $300 million in commissions. In January 2002, the company raised its commission rates, or what it called its 'final value fees'. For items selling for $25 or less, the company charged a 5.25 per cent fee. For items that sold for between $25.01 and $1000, the company charged 2.75 per cent. And for those that sold for over $1000, eBay received a 1.50 per cent commission.[26]

The best news was that sellers and shoppers were plentiful. In 1998, a mere three years after its launch, eBay had 1 million shoppers, some 600,000 items for sale and $6 million in revenues. In 2004, the company conducted over $34 billion worth of transactions and generated over $3 billion in revenue.[27] No longer a site to exchange stuffed dolls, eBay users bought cars, jet planes, computers, printers, cameras and more.

❝ the best news was that sellers and shoppers were plentiful ❞

Customer acquisition and retention costs, time to attract a customer

As good fortune would have it, more than half of all eBay users were referred by other users, which means eBay had to spend relatively little on marketing.[28] Aside from an occasional advertisement and deals with major portals like AOL to deliver customers, it cost eBay little to win a customer and even less to retain them.[29] As tech writer Rick Spence wrote, 'Last fall I fell in love with eBay . . . It's all there. I was hooked.'[30]

Adequate contribution margins to cover the fixed cost structure

Best of all, because eBay is nothing more than a series of software applications placed on servers, the actual cost of doing this business is extremely low – certainly much, much lower than the cost of running Amazon's business. eBay does not buy products that it then has to package and sell. Instead, eBay lets its sellers bear these costs. And it needs no distribution centres with all the fixed costs they entail. As *BusinessWeek*'s Robert Hof notes, 'Customers are eBay's de facto product-development team, sales and marketing force, merchandising department, and security detail – all rolled into one.'[31]

The net result of all this is gross margins above 85 per cent. True, eBay must invest in software, server technology and customer service. But factories?

No. Distribution centres? No. Delivery trucks? Not one. That twentieth-century business model is an expensive one. eBay simply enables the resale of things that others own and takes a small cut of each sale.[32]

Operating cash cycle characteristics

Most entrepreneurs have to worry about how much cash they'll have to tie up in working capital like inventory, how quickly their customers will pay and how long they can wait to pay their suppliers. Not the case for eBay. Since the real transactions were carried out between eBay's buyers and sellers, eBay didn't have to worry about any of these things. Sellers paid to list what was for sale and they paid again when the transaction was done. If they didn't pay, they lost their ability to use eBay again. It's a self-policing

> ❝ **it's a self-policing system, and it works** ❞

system, and it works. These favourable cash cycle characteristics meant that once eBay got started and went public, it was able to grow without needing to raise further capital.[33]

Sparkling results

eBay's business model offered something for everyone: buyer and seller were happy when they reached a deal, and eBay got its cut. And eBay's cut was nothing to sneeze at.

- In 1998, there were 2 million items for sale on eBay. Those 2 million items sold for $746 million, of which eBay generated $47.1 million in revenues. That came to $687,000 in revenues per eBay employee.

- By June 2005, the eBay community included 157 million registered users worldwide, with 64.6 million of them active in the previous 12 months.[34] Revenue hit $1.08 billion in the second quarter alone, up 40 per cent over the prior year, with $10.9 billion in merchandise having changed hands.

- The real story, though, was eBay's profitability. Operating income, up 49 per cent over the prior year, reached $379 million for the quarter, some 35 per cent of sales.[35]

Rivals were in awe: 'These guys have done a killer job,' admits Amazon.com Chief Financial Officer Warren C. Jenson. Financial analyst William Harnisch, President of Forstmann-Leff Associates, says eBay is one of the few companies that can sustain speedy growth even in a sluggish environment.[36]

But was Harnisch right? An economic recession combined with an unwelcome redesign of eBay's auction fee structure battered eBay's earnings – off 31 per cent – for its quarter ending in December 2008.[37] It was the first year-on-year quarterly decline in revenue in eBay's auction and fixed-price business since its inception, and the downdraft continued through eBay's third quarter ending September 2009.[38] Will the people's marketplace fall back into favour with its customers when the economy improves? Or will consumers take their patronage elsewhere? Shareholders and eBay employees have their fingers crossed!

So far, we've seen in this chapter how proprietary protection of one's intellectual property, superior organizational capabilities and processes, and economically attractive business models can lead to sustainable advantage. Sounds easy, right? So what can go wrong?

EMI – advantage lost

The British firm EMI had long been considered a technology pioneer, having developed the first commercial television system that the British Broadcasting Corporation (BBC) adopted in 1937. EMI had product lines in advanced electronics and in the movie and recording industries, where its success with artists such as the Beatles, the Rolling Stones and other top recording artists put it in a strong financial position as it entered the 1970s. Concerned, though, about the fickle nature of the music business, EMI decided to extend its technological prowess and encourage innovation that might lead to opportunities outside of its current businesses.[39]

Godfrey Hounsfield, an EMI senior research engineer, had been carrying out pattern-recognition research. This research and subsequent clinical work showed that something called computerized axial tomography (CAT) could generate and display a cross-sectional view of the human body or parts thereof. Hounsfield's discovery, which was subsequently hailed as the most significant advance in radiology since the X-ray and would go on to win a Nobel Prize in 1979, led to EMI's 1973 entry into the medical products industry.[40] In its first three years, EMI won a 75 per cent share of the global market for scanners, generating £42 million in revenue and £12.5 million in pre-tax profits. The future looked bright.[41]

ff how could such a promising start have gone so wrong? JJ

As the EMI story went on, however, things quickly unravelled. Despite first-mover position in the large and lucrative US radiology market with a cutting-edge product that hospitals needed, and despite patents to protect Hounsfield's technology, within six years EMI had lost its market leadership position. By year eight, it had dropped out of the business entirely. How could such a promising start have gone so wrong?

Patent protection

EMI secured patents on its technology, but patent protection only covers that which is patented. As we saw with Zantac and Tagamet, where Zantac's slightly different chemical composition enabled Zantac to go to market despite Tagamet's earlier patent, EMI's competitors went to work. General Electric Company (GE), the leading producer of conventional X-ray equipment, began a crash programme to develop a similar scanner, without infringing on EMI's patents.[42] Others did likewise. By late 1974, competing CAT scanners hit the American market. In 1975, GE announced its CAT scanner, which it began shipping in mid-1976. EMI's patents had not provided an enduring defence.[43]

Competitors were not only finding their way into the scanner market; they were also finding ways to make improvements in scanner technology. Initially, EMI's scanner had a speed advantage over its competitors. But competitors' machines soon leapfrogged EMI's speed; some could even scan the entire human body, whereas EMI's scanner scanned only the head. In response, Hounsfield developed a second-generation machine, the CT 5000, which offered improved image resolution and could scan the entire body.[44] Would a better machine save the day?

Organizational capabilities and processes

EMI's competitors, all established medical equipment makers, enjoyed significant experience in manufacturing medical products, had established marketing channel access and capabilities, as well as service and support systems, and benefited from an in-depth understanding of the hospital system in the USA, the largest market for scanners.[45] GE, for example, at the time of its scanner introduction in 1976, had a 300-person salesforce and a service network of 1200 people.

EMI had to learn and develop all these capabilities from scratch. The challenge proved too great. EMI, besides lacking sufficient patent protection, lacked the organizational systems, processes and capabilities to compete with its better-established rivals. In 1978–79, plagued by production problems and technical bugs in its scanners, EMI's performance tumbled and its scanner business lost $23.5 million pre-tax. EMI sued GE for patent infringements, but it was

> **in six short years, EMI had gone from an innovative leader in a huge and growing market to exiting the business entirely**

too little, too late. The debacle was so severe that EMI was forced into a merger with Thorn Electrical Industries Ltd in December 1979. Thorn EMI then agreed to settle the lawsuit by selling GE the scanner business for a pittance.[46]

In six short years, EMI had gone from an innovative leader in a huge and growing market to exiting the business entirely. Why?

- Its patent protection proved insufficient.
- It failed to build the necessary organizational processes and capabilities to enable it to compete with its better-established competitors.

EMI had an undisputed advantage at the outset. But it was unable to sustain it.

Webvan's unsustainable business model

Earlier in this chapter, we saw how eBay's business model allowed it to have positive cash flow almost from day one. Having examined that model, we know that Internet-based companies can be profitable. So, why was it that so many dot.coms were unable to survive? For many, the business model was simply not economically viable. Some sold bulky bags of pet food, delivered to the consumer's door for prices far less than the cost of the delivered product. Others spent more on acquiring customers than those customers would ever be worth. Perhaps the most striking example of a dot.com business model that simply was not viable was Webvan, whose demise would cost investors more than $1 billion.

Webvan's idea

In 1997, Louis Borders, a successful entrepreneur in book retailing, saw what he thought was an opportunity to revolutionize American grocery retailing. Borders believed that, by using automated warehouses and computerized scheduling software, he could let customers order groceries on the Internet and have them delivered to their doors at no more cost than if they picked them up at the supermarket.[47] Given his previous track record, Borders was able to attract investment capital from a star-studded roster of blue-chip investors, including Benchmark Capital, Sequoia Capital and Goldman Sachs.

In June 1999, Webvan took its first grocery order in the San Francisco Bay area. The company offered customers access to 24-hours-a-day, 7-days-a-week online grocery ordering. Webvan promised to deliver orders within a 30-minute window, allowing customers to pick a convenient time to receive groceries. For consumers, the story was attractive. No more weekly trip to the supermarket. No more waiting in long lines at the checkout. No more fighting the crowd to select the freshest peaches. Let's take a look at how the business model matches the criteria for economic viability (Table 5.2).

table 5.2   **Webvan's business model**

Keys to economic viability	Webvan's answer
Revenue is adequate in relation to capital investment required and margins obtainable	Huge up-front investment to build high-tech distribution centres; US grocery retailing is a very low-margin business; *requires lots of customers spending lots of money per order to overcome*
Customer acquisition and retention costs and the time it will take to attract customers are viable	Widespread publicity during the dot.com boom means everyone knows about Webvan; *but will they switch? How compelling are the benefits?*
Contribution margins are adequate to cover the necessary fixed cost structure	Ordinary grocery stores benefit from customer labour to select and take home the groceries; *Webvan must incur these labour costs itself, narrowing contribution margins*
Operating cash cycle characteristics are favourable, including factors such as: ▓ how quickly customers will pay ▓ how quickly suppliers and employees must be paid ▓ how much cash must be tied up in working capital (inventory or other) and for how long	No major problems here – customers pay immediately with credit cards, suppliers offer terms; inventory turns quickly, but spoilage can be a problem

Revenue in relation to capital investment and margins

Webvan's initial capital investments were enormous. The company's 300,000-square-foot distribution centres were the most automated in the world. 'Infrastructure is everything,' said David Cooperstein, an analyst with Forrester Research in Cambridge, Massachusetts. 'To do online sales the right way rather than the rush-to-market way, they need to develop a very complex distribution system.' In groceries, profit margins 'are so tight you need to

> **❝ Webvan would need either large numbers of customers spending large amounts per order or great margins ❞**

figure out where the leverage is', said Cooperstein, adding that Webvan had determined that the leverage was in distribution. To make these investments pay, Webvan would need either large numbers of customers spending large amounts per order or great margins. Read on.

Margins in the US grocery business

In the American grocery business, returns on sales of 2 to 3 per cent were considered healthy.[48] One per cent returns were not uncommon. The business works on very high volumes at razor-thin margins. Unless customers were willing to pay substantially more for Webvan's convenience – an unlikely prospect – or unless customers would spend more online than they spent the old-fashioned way – also unlikely given America's traditional weekly trips to the supermarket – then the only route to economic viability would have to be through significant productivity advances. Hence, the highly automated warehouses.

Obtaining customers at affordable cost

With all the fanfare surrounding the dot.com boom, everyone knew about Webvan and other online grocery retailers. But would customers switch? Would they trust Webvan to deliver only ripe peaches, not hard ones? If the green beans weren't fresh, would they arrive anyway, instead of perhaps broccoli for tonight's meal, as one might decide in store? Would one out-of-stock item render tomorrow's dinner plan unworkable, necessitating a trip to the store anyway?

From Webvan's perspective, would enough customers switch their shopping to Webvan to make the huge investments worthwhile? Webvan did $13 million in sales in 1999, its first half-year. By the end of 2000, its San Francisco customer list had grown to some 47,000 households, with fourth-quarter sales totalling $9.1 million. But orders averaged only $81, short of the $103 Webvan's plans required. And sales volumes were far short of what an ordinary high-volume supermarket would generate, despite the far higher capital investment.[49] Online grocery retailers like Webvan had to overcome die-hard shopping habits and a preference among some people simply to squeeze their own melons. In addition, price was a factor for many budget-conscious consumers, who liked shopping for specials.[50] Worse, it was costing Webvan about $210 to acquire each customer.[51]

Contribution margins compared with fixed cost structure

As we have seen, Webvan needed either huge sales volumes or significant operating efficiencies to make its model work. Operating the facilities, marketing the company and delivering the orders were all more costly than Webvan anticipated, however. The process of fulfilling customers' orders was particularly expensive.

Order handling and fulfilment cost the company approximately $27 per order, $18 of which went directly on the delivery process.[52] In ordinary supermarkets, the customer does this work at no cost to the retailer. The company charged a $4.95 delivery fee for orders under $50, a threshold it increased to $75 in November 2000, as delivery expenses exceeded budgets. As Paul Malatesta, a University of Washington finance professor, said later, grocery delivery can work in densely populated areas where grocers offer delivery without building expensive and complicated distribution systems: 'If you have a relatively low-wage delivery person who is pretty much packing grocery boxes and riding elevators, you don't have a large capital investment. But if I have to run $100,000 trucks through the suburbs and pay a driver $25–$35 an hour, when they spend part of the day idling in traffic, that just isn't going to work.'[53]

Webvan also lacked the buying power of Kroger, Safeway and other large chains.[54] Without the enormous economies of scale its competitors enjoyed, Webvan could not easily keep its costs of goods low.

❝ high variable costs put severe pressure on contribution margins ❞

Thus, high variable costs – including higher than normal cost of goods sold and delivery costs – put severe pressure on contribution margins. But this was only half the story. Keeping Webvan's high-tech distribution centres running added a significant fixed cost burden that its thinner-than-thin grocery-industry margins couldn't cover.

Operating cash cycle characteristics

Of the four keys to economic viability shown in Table 5.2, the first three looked gloomy indeed. Only the fourth key posed no real problems. Webvan got the same payment terms that other grocers received, and its customers paid when they placed their orders. Inventory turned at a respectable rate. But these cash cycle characteristics provided little comfort to offset the significant economic disadvantages Webvan faced in the first three arenas.

Results

By July 2001, after just two years in business, Webvan had spent just about all of the $1.2 billion put up by investors. Its audacious plan to reinvent grocery retailing was not going to work. Instead, on 9 July, the company closed its doors. As Miles R. Cook, a vice president at Bain Consulting, said, 'They've got an approach that's profit-proof.'[55]

On the outside, Webvan looked like a new-economy company. On the inside, it was a very old economy, with its high-cost warehouses, its fleet of vans and its labour-intensive delivery system that couldn't compete. As we've seen – and some might have foreseen – its business model simply wasn't viable. The Webvan model wasn't the only way to run a dot.com grocery business, however. For another model that's worked much better, see the Tesco story in Case Study 5.1.

---

case study 5.1

An online grocery model that works

While Webvan's business model was perhaps poorly conceived, Internet grocery retailing was alive and well in the UK. Tesco, the leading British supermarket chain, ran its Internet business model quite differently from Webvan's. What was different?

- No expensive infrastructure: groceries were picked and packed in the company's largest stores.

- Customer acquisition costs: no expensive marketing campaigns, given the already broad awareness of Tesco in the UK.

- Margins: pre-tax profit margins for grocery retailers typically ran at 6 to 8 per cent in the UK, versus 2 to 3 per cent in the USA.[56] Tesco also found that shoppers bought a higher-margin mix of groceries online than in stores, since they were less likely to pick up sale-priced goods. These higher margins, plus a delivery charge, helped offset the costs of picking and delivering orders. And the fixed delivery charge encouraged customers to place larger orders to make the delivery expense worthwhile.

Will Tesco's approach work in the long run? By 2001 Tesco was already making money on its Internet operation.[57] By the first half of 2009, Tesco's online sales, including both food and non-food items, reached the £1 billion mark, serving more than 1 million customers.[58]

What investors want to know

As we've seen, business angels and venture capital investors require returns far in excess of the annual returns on investment that most businesses generate year in, year out. The only way to obtain such returns is to grow the business over time and then to sell it, either to the public or to a trade buyer. But that process takes time – except in exceptional periods, like the aberrant days of the dot.com boom – typically five to seven years or more. Investors want to know that any advantage your new venture possesses will have the staying power to thrive that long. Otherwise, competitors may enter and overtake your company before an exit can be achieved. Sustainable advantage is what ensures the possibility for a successful exit. Of course, the very notion of *sustainable* advantage implies that there's some sort of competitive advantage you possess at the outset. From a seven domains perspective, this means that not only must your product offering resolve some customer pain (as we explored way back in Chapter 2) or offer some new kind of customer delight (as we'll see in the case of Starbucks in the next chapter), but also that in doing so your offering differs in ways meaningful to your customer from those of your competitors. It's better, faster, cheaper, or whatever, from the *customer's* perspective, and you have evidence to prove it. Investors will want to see that you have examined your competitors' offerings with real insight and determined through this competitive analysis how your offering meets this test.

> **investors want to know that any advantage your new venture possesses will have the staying power to thrive that long**

Investors also know that the financial markets are cyclical. Their ability to exit successfully from your venture will depend not only on your company's performance but also more broadly on conditions in the financial markets. Is the IPO window open? Are the prices being paid for acquisitions or IPOs in your industry at cyclical highs? It's impossible to judge, when investing, exactly when the stars will be aligned properly to permit an IPO or trade sale at an attractive price. Thus, sustainable advantage that can last until market conditions are favourable – whenever that may be – is important to investors for this reason as well.

Finally, we saw in the previous chapter that most industries are simply not as attractive as the pharmaceutical industry. Investors know that an industry that they find attractive enough to merit their investment today may change – as we've seen to some degree in pharmaceuticals – and become less attractive tomorrow, perhaps before an exit. Sustainable advantage, through patent protection or superior organizational processes, capabilities or resources – and based on an economically viable business model that protects a company from running out of cash – offers significant protection against such changes and against future competition more generally. Regardless of the level of industry attractiveness, however, such protection, as we've seen, is by no means guaranteed.

Lessons learned

At the end of Chapter 4, I raised the question, 'Can an entrepreneur make money in an unattractive industry?' We've now looked at mobile phones: a great market but a tough industry. As we've seen, despite its recent challenges, Nokia has been very successful and has been able to sustain its success through difficult times. On the flip side of this question, Tagamet – in one of the most attractive industries on earth – lost its market leadership in ulcer medications to Zantac. EMI lost its early market leadership in CAT scanners to GE. Neither of these early successes was sustained. What are the lessons we can take from the case histories in this chapter?

Lessons learned from Zantac

Companies with strong proprietary patent protection enjoy a comparatively benign competitive environment and relative freedom to set prices at levels that generate substantial profits, profits that may be reinvested in developing future winners or simply taken to the bank. Zantac enjoyed 12 generic-free years on the market (the other five were spent getting FDA approval). By 1995, Zantac had been prescribed to 240 million people worldwide and had reaped over $3.6 billion in sales.[59] If you've got a superior product with patent protection that's not easily circumvented, it's a licence to print money.

But entrepreneurs must consider not only whether their product or idea can win patent protection. It's also crucial to know whether that protection will be sufficient to ward off rivals. Doing so typically takes a deep understanding of the technology involved as well as in-depth understanding of how one's industry works.

Lessons learned from Nokia

Entrepreneurs who can build superior organizational processes and capabilities into their companies can, like Nokia, maintain sustainable competitive advantage over their current and future competition *without* patent protection. Nokia's processes for attracting and retaining skilled people and for managing innovation enabled the company to remain innovative and agile, even as its organization grew quite large. Thus, one thing entrepreneurs should think about in assessing an opportunity is whether the opportunity offers ways in which hard-to-imitate processes and systems can be built that can keep the new firm at least a few steps ahead of its current and future competitors.

Lessons learned from EMI

While EMI's CAT scanner was the first of its kind, the patents it received were not broad enough to ward off imitation. Don't assume that a patent means protection. Further, EMI lacked the organizational **❝ don't assume** capabilities to remain at the forefront of CAT **that a patent means** scanner technology, and its lack of medical **protection ❞** marketing and service capabilities put it at a significant disadvantage to its more established competitors. Within six short years, it lost its market leadership, and in eight years it had exited the market entirely.

Thus, entrepreneurs should never assume that their superior, patented product – even one destined to win a Nobel Prize – is sufficient to ensure long-term success. Zantac trumped Tagamet, and GE trumped EMI.

The EMI story is also a poignant reminder that first-mover advantage is often tenuous. Where is VisiCalc, the first spreadsheet software for PCs? Where is Osborne, the first portable PC? Both long gone. Why were Palm Pilots – and now BlackBerrys – everywhere, while the earlier Apple Newton failed? Why doesn't anyone use Sinclair or Commodore computers any more? Most often, it takes something more than patent protection, and something more than a product or service that's new and better, to win in the long term. It takes organizational processes, capabilities and resources that can keep the business at the cutting edge. It takes *sustainable* advantage.

Lessons learned from eBay and Webvan

Put simply, if your business model doesn't add up, your business won't last. If it costs you too much to do what you want to do – regardless of how innovative you are – then your business will die. eBay's economics worked. Webvan's did not. To be sure, numerous other factors, such as great execution, helped eBay. Similarly, poor execution probably hastened Webvan's demise. Given its model, however, Webvan's case history suggests that its demise was probably inevitable.

> **if your business model doesn't add up, your business won't last**

An economically viable business model is not a panacea, but it does serve as table stakes. Without a viable model, you really cannot expect a seat at the table for very long. But discovering a business model that will really work is no simple task. In my work with many readers of this book's first edition, I discovered that the words 'business model' seemed to mean everything and anything and nothing at all. So I set forth on a research project in 2006 to build a framework to enable entrepreneurs and others to think more clearly about business models. The fruits of that labour, along with a process for getting to a business model that will actually work, are overviewed in this edition's Chapter 14.

So, before you write a business plan, put your opportunity through the business model rigour articulated in this chapter and in Chapter 14. If your economics are not looking viable, either find a way to fix them or move on.

Building sustainable advantage in lifestyle businesses

Not every entrepreneur seeks external investors and not every entrepreneur has the resources to build the kind of sustainable advantage that the likes of Nokia, Zantac and eBay have enjoyed. So why is it that many entrepreneurs are able to build businesses of modest size that do business quite profitably over extended periods of time – for years, decades, even generations? With limited resources, how can entrepreneurs whose intent it is to be their own boss protect themselves from voracious competitors who may one day try to eat their lunch?

Often the key to sustainable advantage for lifestyle entrepreneurs or those of modest aspirations is to fly below the competitors' radar, serving niche markets having unique needs that an attentive entrepreneur can understand

and appreciate. In such niches an entrepreneur's ability to tailor what's offered and serve customers exceptionally well can build loyalty that's difficult for larger competitors to erode or dislodge.

Doing so over time typically requires exceptional customer relations and selling skills, which obtains deep insights into changing customer needs that may differ from what mass marketers are likely to address. Without these skills, and without the customer loyalty that can result from their effective application, small business owners are likely to see customers jump at the first opportunity when a bigger, better-known and perhaps more efficient competitor comes calling.

Taking stock of our progress so far

We've now observed in some depth several case histories that bring to life the four market and industry domains:

- ■ we've seen how markets and industries differ;
- ■ we've seen how micro- and macro-level assessments complement one another to tell a more complete story of an opportunity's attractiveness than those told by the macro-level assessments alone;
- ■ we've seen how it's possible to be successful in stagnant markets and in brutally competitive industries if there's sufficient strength at the micro-level, including superior benefits for target customers and a way to sustain the advantage that those benefits bring over a long period of time;
- ■ we've seen that time is not necessarily on the entrepreneur's side and that first-mover advantage is largely a myth.

What we have yet to see are the three domains concerned with you, the entrepreneur, and your entrepreneurial team. There's a saying among venture capitalists that – market and industry considerations aside – successful entrepreneurship comes down to three elements: management, management and management. Is this aphorism true? Is this why Louis Borders, with his strong entrepreneurial track record, was able to raise so much money for Webvan? Can investors – not to mention the entrepreneurs who seek their backing – forget all we've just seen, and simply place bets on capable, experienced entrepreneurs they choose to back? In the next three chapters, we'll take a look at these questions.

The new business road test: stage four – the micro-industry test

- Do you possess proprietary elements – patents, trade secrets and so on – that other firms cannot likely duplicate or imitate?

- Can your business develop and employ superior organizational processes, capabilities or resources that others would have difficulty in duplicating or imitating? Evidence please!

- Is your business model economically viable, i.e. can you show that your company won't run out of cash quickly? That depends upon the answers to these questions:

  - Will your revenue be adequate in relation to the capital investment you need and the margins you can get?
  - How much will it cost you to acquire and retain customers?
  - How long will it take you to attract customers?
  - Will your contribution margins be adequate to cover your fixed cost structure sometime soon?
  - How much cash must be tied up in working capital (inventory or other), for how long?
  - How quickly will customers pay?
  - How slowly will suppliers and employees be paid?

6

What drives your entrepreneurial dream?

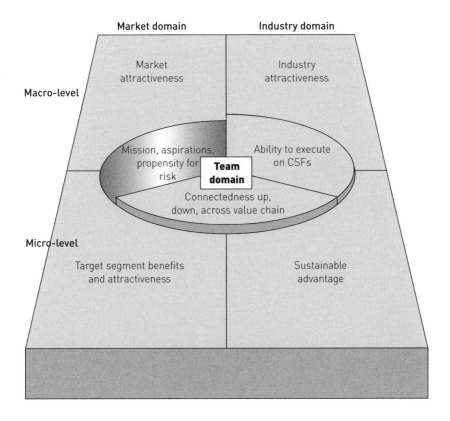

Mahatma Gandhi. Father of the Indian nation. Arguably, Gandhi did more in his lifetime for India and the Indian people than any other human being. The combination of his passion to eliminate injustice and his resolute belief in peaceful solutions led him to establish 'satyagraha'

or passive resistance. He worked tirelessly throughout his 78 years for the rights of low-caste Indian peoples, for peace between Hindu and Muslim Indians and for the independence of India from British rule.

Rather than encouraging violence, Gandhi used peaceful resistance and economic pressure to encourage favourable outcomes. To end violence, he fasted for weeks at a time. To promote independence from the British Empire, he led fellow Indians on the legendary Salt March. He encouraged Indians to spin their own fabrics rather than buy British cloth. His enduring efforts and leadership – and his dream – led to India's independence from Britain in 1947.[1]

What was it that made Gandhi successful? Gandhi was unfaltering in his mission to bring justice to the Indian people. His lofty aspirations to bring about justice for all Indians were ambitious, steadfast and unwavering. And he was willing to take enormous risks – facing imprisonment, even death – to attain such goals.

The mission, personal aspirations and risk propensity of entrepreneurs

Vivre sans rêve, qu'est ce? (What is life without a dream?)

Poet and playwright Edmond Rostand (1868–1918)[2]

It is rare to find someone as committed to a cause and as willing to make sacrifices in the name of his cause as Gandhi. Likening Gandhi's passion to that of an entrepreneur should by no means trivialize Gandhi's efforts and successes. Rather, the intensity and consistency in Gandhi's mission, personal aspirations and risk propensity provides a stirring example of what one person can accomplish.

Each successful entrepreneur brings to their venture an important set of elements that drives their entrepreneurial dream:

■ a mission that determines what kind of business to build or what kinds of markets to serve;

■ a set of personal aspirations that guides the level of achievement to be sought;

■ some level of risk propensity that indicates what sort of risks are to be taken and what sort of sacrifices are to be made in pursuit of the dream.

Phil Knight of Nike had a mission to serve athletes and to help them deliver the best possible performance. He probably would not have been interested in an entrepreneurial venture that targeted any other market. Jeff Bezos, founder of Amazon.com, had aspirations to revolutionize the way people shop for books and to become one of the world's largest retailers in the process. Bezos would not have been content to build a smaller business more limited in scale and scope. As we'll see in this chapter, Howard Schultz, the creator of Starbucks as we know it today, was prepared – twice – to risk a promising career to fulfil his entrepreneurial dream to 'unlock the mystery and romance of coffee. The Italians had turned the drinking of coffee into a symphony,'[3] and Schultz saw an opportunity to recreate the Italian coffee bar culture in America.

The point here is that entrepreneurship – the pursuit of opportunity without regard to the resources under one's control[4] – is a very personal game. *Successful* entrepreneurship requires a clear vision about what you as an entrepreneur want out of the effort. What's your mission? Do you want to serve athletic markets? Do you want to sell coffee? What level of aspirations do you have? Do you hope to be the next Richard Branson, Phil Knight or Howard Schultz, or would you prefer to build a nice little family business that you can run yourself? What sort of risks are you prepared to take? Will you put your own money on the line? How much? Will you go without income? For how long? Must you control your venture, or are you willing to have a smaller piece of a larger entrepreneurial pie at the risk of some day losing control or even being tossed out of the venture you started?

> **entrepreneurship is a very personal game**

Only you can decide these things, and decide you must. Without a clear mission, your entrepreneurial efforts will be fragmented, lacking in purpose and direction. Without understanding your own aspirations, you'll be unable to articulate to others whose support you will need – for money, time, love and much more – why they should support you. Without identifying your own level of risk propensity – it's different for everyone, and in different settings, from business to skydiving – you'll be unable to demonstrate to investors, if you seek investment capital, that you are willing to share in the risks you'll ask them to take. Without sharing the risk you probably won't raise any money.

Equally important, the three elements that drive your entrepreneurial dream – mission, personal aspirations and risk propensity – must fit together in a coherent and cohesive way. You simply cannot aspire to greatness without tolerating some level of risk. You cannot aspire to greatness without a willingness to share ownership and control, since successful entrepreneurship is, most often, a team sport. Going it alone can work for a lifestyle business, but it's unlikely to enable you to become the next Branson or Knight.

In this chapter, we examine the case history of Starbucks, the seemingly ubiquitous chain of coffee bars that now encircles the globe. The visionary creator of what we know as Starbucks today, Howard Schultz, had a mission to bring quality coffee and the Italian coffee-drinking culture to the American public. He aspired to be a part of a company with a vision, a conscience and a powerful energy that could bring about greatness. His personal aspirations were not only to start such a company but also to bring the company to the pinnacle of prominence. To achieve these aspirations, Schultz was willing to take the personal and professional risks necessary to get there.

Howard Schultz and the coffee experience[5]

In 2009, Starbucks operated more than 4500 coffee bars in 47 countries and had grown from its roots as a speciality coffee roaster and retailer in Seattle to one of the world's best-known brands. Howard Schultz made it happen. Here is his story.

Schultz's passion for coffee awakens in Seattle

Schultz grew up a child of 'working poor' parents, as he would say later, in the Bayside Projects in Brooklyn, New York.[6] After finding his way to college on an athletic scholarship, he graduated and began his career in 1976 as a sales trainee for Xerox. Realizing his indifference towards word processors and office equipment, Schultz went after three years at Xerox to Perstorp, a Swedish company with product lines in building supplies and consumer durables for the home. While selling Perstorp's kitchen components in North Carolina, Schultz again found himself less than excited about his product line. It was not until he took the position of Vice-president and General Manager of Hammarplast, Perstorp's housewares subsidiary, that he became more enthusiastic about the products he sold, stylish Swedish-designed kitchen gear.

In 1981, while working for Hammarplast, Schultz noticed that one particular retailer – a Seattle-based company called Starbucks Coffee, Tea, and Spice – consistently purchased large quantities of his drip coffeemakers. With only a handful of small stores, Starbucks was buying more of Hammarplast's coffeemakers than Macy's, New York's leading department store. Schultz wanted to know why. He flew to Seattle to take a look.

Starbucks was a coffee drinker's paradise, selling some 30 different varieties of whole-bean, mountain-grown arabica coffees – from Sumatra, Kenya, Costa Rica and everywhere – as well as high-end coffeemakers. While the store encouraged customers to taste the coffee, they did not sell coffee by the cup.

> **❝ Schultz was hooked, and returned to New York determined to find a way to work for Starbucks ❞**

Schultz was enamoured with the company's coffee, and was even more impressed with the passion that Jerry Baldwin, one of Starbucks' three partners, felt towards his product: 'I had never heard anyone talk about a product the way Jerry talked about coffee.'[7] Schultz was hooked, and he returned to New York determined to find a way to work for Starbucks.

Risk number one

Over the next year, Schultz found ways to spend some time with Baldwin. He believed Baldwin's concept would sell in New York, Chicago, Boston, everywhere. And Schultz had the marketing experience and drive to help grow the business. He wanted in. At last, over dinner in San Francisco in the spring of 1982 with Starbucks' partners, Schultz thought he had won the job. But, on the phone the next day, Baldwin called with bad news: 'I'm sorry, Howard. It's too risky. Too much change.' Schultz was shell-shocked: 'I saw my whole future pass in front of me and then crash and burn.'[8] The next day, Schultz called and reminded Baldwin of his own vision for Starbucks. A day later, Schultz had the job, along with a steep cut in pay and a tiny slice of equity in the company.

> **❝ what we had to do was unlock the romance and mystery of coffee ❞**

In 1983, Starbucks sent Schultz to Milan for a housewares show. During that visit, he experienced the Italian coffee bar culture. This Italian ritual of drinking coffee and socializing intrigued Schultz: 'Coffeehouses in Italy are a third place for people, after home and work. There's a relationship of trust and confidence in that environment.'[9] Schultz discovered that there were 200,000 coffee bars in Italy, with some 1500 in Milan alone. He became fascinated with the idea of bringing such a concept and culture to the USA: 'The connection to the people who loved coffee did not have to take place only in their homes, where they ground and brewed whole-bean coffee. What we had to do was unlock the romance and mystery of coffee, firsthand, in coffee bars.'[10] 'Coffee bars are the mainstay of every Italian neighborhood,' he said. 'That's what I wanted to bring back to Seattle.'[11]

Schultz returned from Milan and pitched the coffee bar idea to the Starbucks partners. Their initial response was a resounding no. They did not want to enter into what they considered the restaurant business, not the best of industries in their view. Schultz finally convinced the partners to add a small espresso bar in their sixth store, which would open in April 1984. Within two months, the store was serving 800 customers a day, compared with the traditional Starbucks stores that averaged 250 customers a day. But even with impressive numbers to support his idea, Schultz could not convince the company's partners to try the coffee shop concept further: 'I felt torn in two by conflicting feelings: loyalty to Starbucks and confidence in my vision for Italian-style espresso bars.'[12]

Risk number two

In 1985, Schultz made one of the toughest decisions in his still-young career. He decided to leave Starbucks to start what seemed to be a very uncertain coffee bar business. At the time, coffee was a seemingly risky game. With the disclosure of health risks associated with caffeine, consumption of coffee had been falling in the USA since the 1960s, hardly the most exciting of markets.

At the time, Schultz's wife was pregnant with their first child and he needed an initial $400,000 in seed capital to open his first store and get the business started – money he simply did not have. As Schultz was planning how to raise the money, Starbucks stepped forward to invest $150,000 in Schultz's venture, and Jerry Baldwin agreed to serve on the board. Gordon Bowker, Baldwin's partner in Starbucks, also agreed to help. Shortly thereafter, Schultz received another $100,000 from a local doctor, who said, 'It appears to me that people who succeed have an incredible drive to do something . . . They spend their energy to take a gamble. In this world, relatively few people are willing to take a large gamble.'[13]

By the time Schultz's son was born in January 1986, Schultz had raised the rest of the money he needed to open the first store. His real goal, though, was another $1.25 million to open seven more stores and to prove that the idea would work on an extended scale. It took an entire year to raise all the money, during which Schultz approached 242 potential investors, 217 of whom turned him away. Over the course of a year, he raised $1.65 million from about 30 investors, enough to open eight coffee bars. Schultz said, 'If you ask any of those investors today why they took the risk, almost all of them will tell you that they invested in me, not in my idea.'[14]

❝ Schultz approached 242 potential investors, 217 of whom turned him away ❞

Schultz opened the first Il Giornale, as his new coffee bars were called, on 8 April 1986. Il Giornale meant 'the daily' in Italian and was the name of the largest newspaper in Italy. On its first day in business, Il Giornale served 300 customers. Within six months, the store was serving 1000 customers a day. Even with just one store, Schultz was dreaming big: 'At the time, our plans seemed impossibly ambitious. Even then, when nobody had heard of Il Giornale, I had a dream of building the largest coffee company in North America, with stores in every major city.'[15]

The first Il Giornale was not a perfect success. Schultz soon realized that Italian opera was not the preferred music of American coffee drinkers. He also learned that the shops should include seating for those customers wishing to relax and stay awhile. Learning from these mistakes, Schultz opened his next Il Giornale six months after the first in a downtown Seattle high-rise office tower. By mid-1987, there were three Il Giornale stores, and each store was generating approximately $500,000 in annual sales.

Risk number three

In March 1987, with the first Il Giornale having been open for less than a year, Jerry Baldwin and Gordon Bowker decided to sell their six Starbucks stores, roasting plant and name. Jerry wanted to concentrate on Peet's, a small chain of stores selling beans and ground coffee that Starbucks had acquired. 'As soon as I heard, I knew I had to buy Starbucks. It was my destiny,' said Schultz. But it would take nearly $4 million to do it. Having seen Starbucks struggle under an excessive debt burden when it bought Peet's, Schultz knew the new money would have to be raised through the sale of equity, in spite of the fact that it would dilute his ownership of and control over the business. Schultz looked again to investors, including those who had invested in Il Giornale and others who had passed, to raise the needed capital. His pitch to investors was one of pure passion:

How many things do people in America drink every day? Coffee is such a social beverage, a personal beverage. There's the romance of coffee, its history. We had an opportunity to utilize the relationship I saw in Italy, the safe haven of the coffee bar, and package it with undeniably great coffee and service that is completely different from most establishments in America. I mean, we can change how people start their day.[16]

Schultz's passion for great coffee and his concept proved successful. By August 1987, at the age of 34, Schultz had raised another $3.8 million, and the original Starbucks was his.

The rest of the story

Schultz realized that taking over a company was not an easy task. His initial goals were twofold: to win the support of the existing Starbucks employees and to hire a winning team of managers. In his first meeting with the Starbucks employees, Schultz announced his mission of building a national company whose values and guiding principles they all could be proud of. Schultz had to make sure the existing employees were on board in order to move forward with his plans. He also recognized that, as his company grew, he would need to rely on the expertise of others: 'I knew I had to go out and hire executives with greater experience than I had.'[17]

ᗪᗪ hire people smarter than you are and get out of their way ᒍᒍ

Schultz did just that. He hired a number of experienced people to lead his management team. He lived by a simple philosophy: 'Hire people smarter than you are and get out of their way.'[18] Finding and retaining top people was one of Schultz's ways to lay a solid foundation for growth.

In October 1987, Schultz and his team opened the first store under the Starbucks name in Chicago. It was their first attempt away from the west coast. In the following six months, three more stores opened in Chicago. The results were less than stellar. With distribution and logistics costs added in, the cost of goods sold was much higher in Chicago than in Seattle. And, Chicagoans showed less interest in the coffee shop experience than their Seattle compatriots. In 1987, the company lost $330,000.

But those financial losses didn't faze Schultz and his team. Schultz could show investors the attractive unit economics at each store to convince them the business model was viable. Overall losses were necessary in order to invest in the people and systems necessary for his company to reach its potential. Investors could also see that the speciality coffee business all over the country, both in supermarkets and coffee bars, was becoming as hot as a freshly brewed cup of espresso.[19] Starbucks kept growing:

- in 1988, Starbucks opened 15 new stores and developed its first mail-order catalogue, but losses grew to $764,000 for the year;

- in 1989, the company opened more stores and lost another $1.2 million;

- in 1990, with another 30 new stores, the company turned profitable.

By that time, the company had received three major rounds of private funding: the $3.8 million to acquire Starbucks; $3.9 million in early 1990 to finance additional growth; and $13.5 million later in 1990 from venture capital investors who saw the potential that the Starbucks story represented.

By 1992, Starbucks' revenues were rising at approximately 80 per cent per year. In June of that year, Starbucks went public, raising $29 million to support even faster growth in new stores. At the time of its initial public offering, Starbucks had 2000 employees and 600,000 customers weekly. That year, 53 additional stores were opened, bringing the grand total of Starbucks coffee bars to 140.

By 1993, Starbucks ranked among the 40 fastest-growing companies in the USA according to Fortune magazine. And the company was not just a model for growth. In 1994, Schultz received an award from the Business Enterprise Trust for courage, integrity and social vision in business.[20] And the growth continued:

- in 1997, Starbucks' revenues exceeded $1 billion;

- a year later, the company had 1500 outlets and 25,000 employees, and was beginning to sell its coffee in supermarkets;

- by 1999, stores were averaging $800,000 in annual revenue and there were 80 Starbucks stores in Great Britain and 53 stores in Japan.

In 2000, Schultz decided to cede his CEO position to his President and COO, Orin Smith. Not ready to leave Starbucks, Schultz remained as Chairman and Chief Global Strategist. The company didn't miss a beat:

- by the end of 2001, Starbucks was serving 2 million customers a week from its 5000 outlets worldwide, and had delivered 121 consecutive months of positive comparative store sales;

- that year, profits grew by 92 per cent to $181.2 million on sales of $3 billion;

- by 2002, Starbucks operated 1200 stores outside the USA in 20 countries, up from 281 international stores in 1999.[21]

Starbucks' stock had soared more than 2200 per cent over the past decade, outpacing Wal-Mart, General Electric and Microsoft in total return. Schultz's shares alone were worth $400 million. By 2004, Starbucks' annual revenue had passed the $5 billion mark, with comparable store sales still growing, up 10 per cent on 2004, and with overall net revenue up 30 per cent on the previous year.[22] The company ranked 11th in *Fortune* magazine's '100 Best Companies to Work For' list.[23] The lad from the Projects in Brooklyn had done quite well.[24]

Starbucks' incredible growth continued over the next four years, breaking $9 billion in revenues in 2008.[25] But all was not as well as it seemed: there was talk of over-expansion in the US, and the company's long-time focus on the customer experience, the very thing Schultz had been so passionate about, was getting lost as the megabrand grew in scale.

Schultz was asked to take back the top job. His task was not made any easier by the recession, a difficult environment in which to sell $4 lattes. In 2008 and 2009, outlets were closed and staff numbers reduced. There was renewed focus on the customer. By 2009, operating margins began to increase, though sales continued to disappoint. 'The entire Starbucks organization is committed to continually improving our customer experience as the roadmap to renewed growth and increasing profitability. At the same time, we will continue to innovate and differentiate, two perennial hallmarks of the Starbucks brand,' said Schultz.[26]

Can the lad from the Projects deliver an encore? As Schultz reminds those who question his company's future, 'The pundits said we were saturated in Seattle in 1992. Since then we have opened 340 stores in the state of Washington. We sell less than 10 percent of the coffee consumed in the US and less than 1 percent outside the US.'[27] Clearly, Schultz has not yet forgotten his entrepreneurial dream.

What investors want to know

Some entrepreneurs need no investors. They are able to pursue their entrepreneurial dreams without external capital. Others, like Howard Schultz, cannot expect to reach their aspirations without more capital than they and the three Fs (family, friends and fools, remember?) can bring to the table. What roles do an entrepreneur's mission, aspiration and risk propensity play in attracting investment capital?

First, most professional investors – business angels or venture capital investors – have missions of their own, often driven by what they already know or what's made money for them before. Some invest in certain industries, like telecommunications or media. Some invest in certain markets, like companies serving medical practitioners. Matching your mission to their mission is critical, for only rarely will investors invest outside their chosen arenas. Had Howard Schultz chosen an initial mission of coffee manufacturing and wholesaling – as some companies did once they saw Americans' growing fascination with better coffee – instead of coffee retailing, then his investor group would probably have looked quite different. Most investors want a clear understanding of the kind of company you plan to build.

Second, professional investors' aspirations are usually quite simple – to make loads of money for themselves and their own investors. Doing so involves growing and *ultimately selling* the ventures they invest in – reader, take note – either to the public or to a trade buyer. The day you accept venture capital is the day you've agreed to sell your business. If your aspirations are less lofty – something that's true for many entrepreneurs – or if your dream is to run your business independently for a long time rather than selling it, then seeking investors, other than the three Fs, is probably not for you.

Third, professional investors understand the risks they take. They know the odds run against any single venture meeting its goals. Only one or two out of every ten deals in a typical venture capital portfolio will make big money. A few more may return their capital but earn no return. The rest will lose most or all of the capital invested.

Given these difficult odds, angels and venture capitalists want to know that the entrepreneurs they back will make extraordinary efforts and commitments to beat the long odds. To ensure such commitment, they want to know that you have something to lose if you fail, just as they do.

> **❝ investors want to see that *you* are willing to risk your capital, just as they are risking theirs ❞**

What this means, in practical terms, is that investors want to see that *you* are willing to risk your capital, just as they are risking theirs. Typically, they measure your willingness to share in the risks by the relative amount you'll risk compared with what you have. If you don't have much money, then your cash investment can be modest. If you've already made it big once, then you'll be expected to risk some of your gains alongside the capital you ask others to put at risk.

In summary, you need to be clear about your mission, aspirations and risk propensity *before* you write your business plan and before you approach prospective investors. Approaching them sooner is a waste of time or – worse – a potential disaster. There's no faster way for investors to remove you from your leadership role than to have them discover that your goals are incompatible. This is far more common than most nascent entrepreneurs would believe. Building an NLO business – a nice living for the owner – is not something most investors have in mind.

Lessons learned

Not every entrepreneur can start a company and lead it to greatness in just 15 years. Some are good at the start-up stage and pass the leadership baton once things are well under way. Others grow their businesses slowly and steadily, sometimes taking decades to reach their dreams. Only a few can take the business all the way from conception to stardom as quickly as did Howard Schultz. What can would-be entrepreneurs learn from Schultz's story?

ff his clear sense of purpose helped him focus his energies 打打

- Schultz was clear about his mission: to build a company that brought the Italian coffee bar culture to the USA, to serve only the finest coffee and to run an organization that valued its employees. His clear sense of purpose helped him focus his energies.

- His personal aspirations were audacious: to build a large, prominent and profitable company that would change how Americans started their day. Simply running a few coffee shops in Seattle was not his cup of tea.

- He was willing to repeatedly take risks to achieve his goals.

Mission

Howard Schultz didn't choose coffee because coffee was hot. As we have seen, American coffee consumption had been declining for years before Schultz and other espresso entrepreneurs came along and reversed its direction. He chose coffee because he was hooked. Hooked on the taste and aroma of dark-roasted arabica coffee, so different from what he had known as coffee before. Hooked on learning about coffee and different ways to roast it. And hooked on the idea of introducing the Italian coffee culture to the USA and, thereafter, the world.

Schultz's passion for coffee served him – and Starbucks – well. It helped him attract committed employees like coffee aficionado Dave Olson, who came to personify the company's passionate attitude towards coffee.[28] It helped him win investors, without whom his story never would have played out. It helped him win believers among suppliers who would go on to benefit greatly from Starbucks' growth.

While for many investors the mission is simply to make money, for entrepreneurs a burning desire to make money is not enough on its own. It's almost impossible for an entrepreneur to be wildly successful in a business they don't care about deeply. Without a greater purpose than money, the battles are simply too tough to tackle simply for money's sake. As Jeff Hawkins, founder of Palm Computing and Handspring (whom we will hear about in the next chapter), says, 'Do something you believe because you believe it.'[29]

Early in his career, Schultz was successful in selling copiers and housewares, but he could never have matched what he achieved selling the coffee experience if he had tried his own venture selling, say, office supplies. Schultz's story suggests that if you don't feel passionate about your opportunity, then you might be better advised to find a venture that does light your fire. We'll have more to say in Chapter 10 about where good opportunities come from, but simply looking at what's hot – whether plastics, software, biotech or whatever – isn't the answer.

There's another mission-related aspect of Schultz's story that offers lessons to learn. At the beginning, Schultz was focused clearly on a single direction that his business would take – coffee bars in urban settings. Would-be entrepreneurs sometimes lack Schultz's single-minded mission, seeing multiple paths that they might pursue. For Schultz, his passion for great coffee could have been pursued in other ways. Coffee speciality stores like Jerry Baldwin's original Starbucks stores were one possible choice. Roasting better coffee for the supermarket trade was another. What makes more sense for a would-be entrepreneur – a laser-like focus on a single direction, or hedging one's bets?

> **❝ what makes more sense for a would-be entrepreneur – a laser-like focus on a single direction, or hedging one's bets? ❞**

Experienced entrepreneurs know there are two serious drawbacks to the latter approach. First, attempting multiple things with the typically scarce resources that most entrepreneurs have at hand results in doing none of them well. Less is more. It's usually far better to devote all one's energies to the most promising path. If the path turns out to be blocked, then something will likely have been learned that can identify a more promising one. Probably one of the reasons you're reading this book is that you're trying to identify just what your best path is and whether it's good enough to be worthy of placing your bet.

A second drawback is that having multiple paths in mind can detract from your ability to attract employees, investors and suppliers to your cause. If you lack the confidence and commitment to choose the best path for your business, then why should these other stakeholders get on board? Single-minded focus wins every time with these groups.

Personal aspirations

Different entrepreneurs have different aspirations. For some, their entrepreneurial dream is simply to make a satisfactory living for themselves and their family, or to escape the humdrum world where they work today. Others, like Hero Honda's Brijmohan Lall Munjal, India's Mahatma Gandhi and Starbucks' Howard Schultz, want nothing less than to change the world in some way. There are three questions every aspiring entrepreneur should ask.

▦ How big do I want this business to become – in sales, profits, number of employees, number of locations or by some other measure?

▦ What role do I want in this venture: do I want to *do*, to *manage* or to *lead*?

▦ For how long do I want to remain involved with it?

Some entrepreneurs or entrepreneurial teams have aspirations to run a business just large enough to meet certain objectives: to provide a living for their family, to provide multiple roles in which two or more partners can work and so on. Others, like Schultz, want to build something big. In Schultz's words 'If you want to build a great enterprise, you have to have the courage to dream great dreams. If you dream small dreams, you may succeed in building something small. For many people, that is enough. But if you want to achieve widespread impact and lasting value, be bold.'[30]

Reaching the kind of scale that Starbucks has reached is not something a single individual can ordinarily do. Entrepreneurship played for these kinds of stakes is a team sport. Not every entrepreneur has the capacity, courage and willingness to do this. And with size comes complexity. Some simply don't want this sort of complexity in their business lives, or they may prefer to devote significant energies to their personal lives – family, avocations and so on. Building a fast-growing venture takes all one can give. As Schultz says, 'You have to work so hard and have so much enthusiasm for one thing that most other things in your life have to be sacrificed.'[31] It's not for everyone. Is it for you?

The question of roles is also worth some thought for a would-be entrepreneur. As small businesses grow into large ones, the roles of those who lead them must inevitably evolve. At the outset, what entrepreneurs do is *do*. Schultz roasted coffee, made espressos, raised capital and found locations for his next stores. But it simply was not possible for him to do these things himself for ever. As it turned out, Schultz was happy bringing on 'people smarter than me' and letting them do what they'd been hired to do. As Schultz puts it:

There's a common mistake a lot of entrepreneurs make. They own the idea, and they have the passion to pursue it. But they can't possibly possess all the skills needed to make the idea actually happen. Reluctant to delegate, they surround themselves with faithful aides. They're afraid to bring in truly smart, successful individuals as high-level managers.[32]

> ** what is it that you really want out of being an entrepreneur? **

But managing and delegating is not what every entrepreneur wants. If you are an architect whose work is admired, then do you want to do architecture and keep designing interesting buildings, or do you want to grow your business and manage architects and let them exercise their own creativity? It's an important choice, and one not to be taken lightly. Make it consciously, not by default.

Then there's the question of how long you want to manage or lead your business. Do you want to stay the course for many years to build your business yourself? Or are you happy to get it started, exit early if possible and move on to something else? Is it creating, i.e. the early-stage work, or the managing, i.e. the later-stage work, that turns you on? It's another choice to take seriously. What is it that you really want out of being an entrepreneur?

Risk propensity

Most successful entrepreneurs do not regard themselves as risk-takers. Managers of risk, yes. But risk-takers, no. Their job is to offload the inherent risk in their ventures to suppliers, investors, landlords and whoever is willing to bear it. In their hearts, most entrepreneurs see little risk – naïvely, perhaps – given their belief that theirs is one new venture that will buck the long odds and succeed.

But, as Schultz's story points out, there are repeated risks to be taken along the way. The obvious ones include money – yours and others' – and months or years of your life and the opportunity costs of doing something else with that time. There are other risks that are less obvious. There's the risk that your investors may at some point decide that you should go. Is this a risk you are willing to bear to raise investment capital, or is maintaining control, even at the cost of limiting the scale of what you can accomplish or the resources you can assemble, a crucial factor for you? And what about the risk propensity of those you love who are sure to bear some of the costs of your entrepreneurial pursuits? Marriages have been broken as entrepreneurs and their spouses fail to agree on what should be risked. Dinner with the family? The house? The security of a regular salary? What level of risk are you willing to bear? Is that level of risk acceptable for the upside your opportunity offers? As Schultz tells it:

> ** there are risks that are less obvious **

For me, the thrill of business is in the climb. Everything we try to achieve is like climbing a steep slope, one that very few people have managed to scale. The more difficult the climb, the more gratifying the effort put into the ascent and the greater the satisfaction upon reaching the summit. But, like all dedicated mountain climbers, we're always seeking a higher peak.[33]

Risk and reward, constant companions. How much of each will you choose? What's the nature of your entrepreneurial dream? And what, indeed, is life without such a dream?

The new business road test: stage five – the mission, aspirations and risk propensity test

▓ What's your entrepreneurial mission?

- To serve a particular market?
- To change a particular industry?
- To market a particular product?
- Is the passion really there?

▓ What level of aspirations do you have for your entrepreneurial dream?

- To work for yourself?
- To build something small or something big?
- To do? To manage? To lead?
- To change the world in some way?

▓ What sorts of risk are you and are you not willing to take?

- Will you risk a secure salary and the things that go along with your current employment? For how long?
- Will you risk losing control of your business?
- Will you put your own money at risk? How much?
- Will you risk your home or time with your family or loved ones?
- Do those you love accept the risks you'll take?

7

Can you and your team execute?

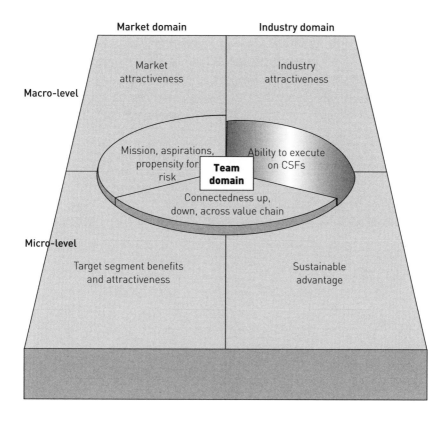

What makes a sports team successful? It depends upon the sport. For most teams, the need for talented, conditioned, well-trained athletes and a competent coaching staff are obvious requirements. Yet, beyond these fundamental criteria, no two sports have the same critical success factors.

Take for example basketball, football and polo. Successful basketball teams must have players with the hand–eye coordination to shoot the ball accurately. Having tall players doesn't hurt, either, of course.

On the other hand, football (soccer) is played largely with the feet, so hand–eye coordination doesn't matter very much. Agility and an ability to control the ball while keeping one's head and eyes up are critical, however.

A polo team's success depends on both the athletes and the horses. As in basketball and football, the athletes need to have a good shot, but they must also be able to make this shot while riding a horse at high speed.

In all three sports, endurance also matters – the fittest team often wins. In each of these sports, different factors are critical to success. Height and shooting ability make a big difference in basketball. Foot skills and the ability to maintain possession of the ball are important in football. Well-trained horses and skilled equestrians separate winners from losers in polo.

The sport of entrepreneurship

In the People was my trust,
And in the virtues which mine eyes had seen.

William Wordsworth (1770–1850)[1]

Just as nearly every sport requires its athletes to be physically fit, so every entrepreneurial venture needs to have the fundamentals – a superior product or service, an efficient supply chain, motivated people and so on. These are the basics without which no business can survive for long. Returning to sport for a moment, all the world's top tennis players, all the footballers in the World Cup, all the runners on the start line of an Olympic marathon are superbly fit. Fitness is a basic requirement. But it takes more than fitness, of course, to win a Wimbledon title or an Olympic medal.

So, what separates the great athletes from the very, very good ones? The great ones are the ones who consistently meet the critical success factors for their chosen sport, whether that be speed, strength, balance, tactical savvy or whatever. An ability to execute on these critical success factors is the difference between great and almost great. As in the World Cup or on the tennis circuit, where there's significant difference in performance between the winners and those who don't place, so the same is true in the business world. In mobile phones, Nokia thrived while Motorola and others struggled. In athletic footwear, Nike grew while the traditional athletic footwear makers just muddled along. What is it that causes such variation in performance within an industry?

We've already seen some sources of variation, such as patent protection and organizational processes and capabilities that are not imitated easily. But there's something else that can account for such differences. That 'something else' is a management team's ability to execute against the few critical success factors – no more than a handful, usually – that tend to account for much of the difference in performance from one company to another within an industry. Just as in each sport there are a few key attributes that separate the winners from the losers, the same is true in entrepreneurship. A common difference between winners and losers is that the winners figure out the factors critical to succeeding in their particular industry, and then stack their team accordingly. The losers either do not identify these critical success factors or do not possess a team capable of delivering on them.

❝ just as in each sport there are a few key attributes that separate the winners from the losers, the same is true in entrepreneurship ❞

So, what if your industry is extremely competitive, with one or more of the five forces conspiring against you and your prospective competitors? Can you still be successful? The answer to this question is 'Yes, *but* . . .'. This chapter speaks directly to the 'but'. Even in relatively unattractive industries, at least some companies typically perform quite well. Others are left in the dust. So, the 'but' is this: yes, entrepreneurs can succeed in difficult industries, *but* they must be able to:

- identify the critical success factors specific to their particular industry;
- assemble a team that can execute on these factors.

Getting things right on the rest of the seven domains doesn't hurt either.

In this chapter, we'll first discuss how you can determine the critical success factors for your industry. Then we'll examine the case histories of two companies: Palm Computing, a highly successful start-up in handheld computing, and Schwinn, a long-time bicycle manufacturer. In each case, the stories identify the factors critical to success in the relevant industry and look at the degree to which the company's team – the key people in whom investors had placed their trust – was able to execute on these factors.

We then consider what investors look for in the entrepreneurs and entrepreneurial teams they invest in, and we examine the lessons an entrepreneur should learn from this chapter. In doing so, I remind you that the industry you may enter is unlikely to be as attractive as pharmaceutical drugs. The lessons of this chapter, in concert with those already learned in Chapter 5, can provide a way around any shortcomings your opportunity may have in industry attractiveness terms.

Identifying the critical success factors

How do I work out what the critical success factors (CSFs) are for my industry, you may ask. Are the answers found in the trade press, on the Internet or in strategy textbooks? Unfortunately, no. Knowledge of the CSFs for any industry resides in the experience of those who have learned – often the hard way – which things absolutely must be done right. Whether you have such experience or you must access that of others who have it, there are two key questions to ask to identify your industry's CSFs.

■ Which few decisions or activities are the ones that, if you get wrong, will almost always have severely negative effects on company performance, even when other things are done well?

■ Which decisions or activities, done right, will almost always deliver disproportionately positive effects on performance, even if other things are done less well, or even poorly?

In retailing, the industry where I spent much of my business career, the CSFs are, as they say, location, location, location. Retailers in great locations can get other things wrong and still perform well, at least for a time. Those in poor locations, despite doing most other things right, will struggle to survive. That's how powerful CSFs are. As Starbucks' Howard Schultz said, 'Our process of site selection was enormously time-consuming, but we couldn't afford a single mistake. One real estate error in judgment would mean . . . a minimum of a half million dollars at stake.' The Starbucks team demonstrated such skills, for 'Of the first 1000 stores we opened, we opted to close only two locations because of site misjudgments.'[2]

❝ in retailing, the CSFs are location, location, location ❞

To identify the CSFs in your industry, ask the two questions above of 15 or 20 thoughtful, successful entrepreneurs and executives in your industry. You'll get various answers, of course, but some will converge on the same few themes. That's what you are looking for.

Palm Computing: Jeff Hawkins' innovation catches on

It is rare today to sit in a business meeting and not see at least one person checking their email, calendar or contacts on a BlackBerry, an iPhone or another mobile device. While these little battery-operated gadgets have been on the market since 1993, it was not until 1996 that the concept really caught on. Introduced to the public in April 1996, the Palm Pilot was a near-instant success, selling 1 million units in its first 18 months. Palm's little invention had been accepted faster than any other computer – even faster than televisions, video recorders, mobile phones or almost any previous consumer electronic product.[3] In just two years, the company sold more than 1.5 million Pilots. What made Palm so successful, beating out the earlier Apple Newton and Microsoft Pocket PC?

Learning the hard way

The Palm story began with Jeff Hawkins, an electrical engineer and inventor who was more interested in the human brain than starting a multibillion-dollar company. In the late 1980s, Hawkins was working for GRiD Systems, a computer company in the San Francisco Bay area. It was at GRiD that Hawkins worked on pen computing. With this new technology, users could write directly on the computer screen with a stylus (it looked like a pen but contained no ink); theoretically, the user's handwriting could be recognized. The key word was 'theoretically'. The concept depended heavily on the computer's handwriting-recognition capability.

Hawkins had already developed PalmPrint, a software program that could recognize hand-printed characters. In 1989, with Hawkins' software under licence, GRiD developed and marketed a tablet computer called GRiDPad. While it was a modest success as the only pen computer available commercially, it was too big and heavy, at 4.5 pounds, and too expensive, at $2500, for use outside the specialized markets for which it had been designed.[4]

In 1991, Hawkins set out to create a pen computer that would be more appealing to everyday consumers. He pitched the idea to Tandy, GriD's parent and the operator of some 7000 consumer electronics stores. As Hawkins saw it:

Palmtop computing devices will be as ubiquitous as calculators by the end of this decade . . . To get an idea of the market size for these computers, consider the possibility that most high school students, nearly all college students, and most professionals will own one. With prices starting at $200, it is entirely conceivable, and I believe likely, that 50 per cent of those people will own or use a portable handheld computer at some time in their life.[5]

Tandy and two venture capital firms liked Hawkins' idea, and in January 1992 Palm Computing was financed with $1.3 million in exchange for 40 per cent of Hawkins' company. Hawkins' proposed product, the Zoomer, would consist of hardware and an operating system that allowed the computer to serve as an address book and a diary. Hawkins knew he could not develop the Zoomer alone, so in early 1992 he hired three talented engineers and set to work.

Hawkins and the Palm Computing team immediately faced pressures from the project's various partners. By autumn 1992, there were six partners on the Zoomer project, including Casio, Tandy, AOL and Intuit. Palm was a living example of too many cooks in the kitchen. These partners wanted everything and the kitchen sink included in the product. Palm's Engineering Director Monty Boyers said, 'They had the longest, longest list of features they wanted to put into the device. And it would not make any difference to them at all whether these things made sense or not. Our point of view was: "Gee, we don't need all these things. Let's make this other stuff work really well".'[6] With Hawkins at the helm, the Palm team tried to stave off the idea that 'more is better', focusing instead on simplicity and functionality. But the battle wasn't easy.

> **❝ Palm was a living example of too many cooks in the kitchen ❞**

In August 1993, Apple began shipping its Newton. Palm's Zoomer followed in October. Neither of the two products was terribly successful. Of his own product, Hawkins said, 'When I personally used the product, I felt it was usable, but a lot lacking.'[7] At $700, this somewhat heavy and cumbersome handheld device was equipped with only a mediocre handwriting-recognition tool. And by then, the Palm team realized the need for PC connectivity, which the Zoomer lacked. They wanted to find a way to move data back and forth from the Zoomer to the PC.

Working quickly, Palm brought to market in November its PalmConnect, an add-on to the Zoomer that allowed information to be moved from the handheld to the PC, and vice versa. While PalmConnect was a useful and successful add-on, it did not save the fate of the Zoomer. Both the Newton and the Zoomer failed to gain momentum. After selling 20,000 units in its first two months, Zoomer's sales slowed to a crawl.[8]

What does it take to win in high-tech?

Hawkins, a tenacious sort, was not about to give up hope after the less than successful Zoomer project. The first thing he did was to strengthen his team by hiring Donna Dubinsky as his CEO. She had a proven track record of managing high-tech teams and delivering results. More importantly, her appointment also released Hawkins from a managerial role he had never wanted to play, leaving him free to concentrate on learning from the mistakes made on the Zoomer in order to develop a handheld that had real market appeal.

Hawkins and Dubinsky learned some important lessons about what it takes to be successful with high-tech innovation.

- First, they learned that developing new technology was the easy part. Many high-tech entrepreneurs could do that.

- Second, and far more important, they learned that what was crucial in the high-tech world was linking the promise of technology with genuine customer needs so that real customer problems are solved.

As we've already seen in Chapter 2, satisfying customer needs is nothing new – it's important in any industry. In high-tech, though, doing so or not doing so turns on three CSFs. Getting these CSFs wrong dooms the business. Getting them right gives it a good chance of success. What are they?

- Anticipating and understanding customers' real problems or needs – or, more graphically, the customer pain.

- Understanding deeply an area of technology and what it can and cannot deliver, both today and tomorrow.

- Finding ways to harness the technology to resolve these problems or needs. Can the customer's pain be relieved?

For high-tech ventures, sometimes the technology comes first and customer pain must be found that can be relieved by the new technology. At other times, the customer need comes first, driving the engineers to develop a solution. Either sequence works, as long as the meeting of the two – the third CSF – occurs. Let's look at each of these CSFs and see how they played out at Palm.

What did customers really need?

With Dubinsky now on board, Hawkins and the Palm team went to work on understanding what needs customers had that could be resolved by a handheld device. But which customers?

The Palm team decided to target the growing number of PC users. Within this large market, their target was professionals who were not necessarily experts in computers but who were unafraid of technology. Refining the target market further, the Palm team focused on the segment of professionals who worked away from their offices, whether locally or at large distances. What did these mobile professionals who were comfortable with technology really want in a handheld device?

Let's ask the customers what they really want, thought Hawkins. Their answer was clear: don't try to replace our desktop computers; just replace our

❝ let's ask the customers what they really want ❞

pocket and desk calendars. People wanted an accessory to their PCs, some means of carrying around some of the data already on their hard drives – especially contact and appointment data. Eureka! 'I realized my competition was paper, not computers.'[9] Most of the PC functions that Palm had painstakingly built into the Zoomer served only to clutter the screen with options that the customer didn't need.[10] Hawkins' realization allowed him to focus his attention on the features and functionality that his prospective customers really wanted. Instead of developing a handheld PC, Hawkins and Dubinsky pushed their engineers to design a straightforward, portable, easy-to-use organizer.

Hawkins knew what was on the drawing boards at other companies and was sure that every one of them was missing the boat. What everyone was doing was not what the customers wanted.

Peter Skillman, who worked with Hawkins as a consultant for IDEO, the engineering firm that teamed up with him on several of the Palm products, said: 'Jeff understands the user experience and instinctively knows what's important to them. He has a real empathy for customers.'[11] In other words, he was able to execute on the first of his industry's CSFs.

Hawkins identified the characteristics most important to his market. Customers required simplicity, small size, reasonable price, attractive design and connectivity: 'We knew people would want something that's reliable and intuitive and quick, very quick. Faster and easier to carry than paper. Products can do complex, sophisticated things. But the user experience has to be simple.'[12] A Forrester Research study concurred, finding that people used their handheld organizers to manage calendars and to-do lists far more than they used them for complex tasks like retrieving and sending emails.[13] 'It had to be easy to use for the average consumer,' said Hawkins, 'not a product for techno geeks, but as easy and fast to use as the millions of Day-Timer and Filofax paper organizers that were sold each year.'[14]

What could (and couldn't) technology deliver?

In order to keep the product small, fast and convenient, Hawkins realized that Palm would need great handwriting-recognition technology. The problem was that, at the time, the technology was not good enough. More importantly, Hawkins, who knew this technology arena intimately (CSF number two in high-tech), knew it would not be good enough any time soon. He needed to come up with a better handwriting-recognition tool. His invention was ingenious. Instead of asking the computer to recognize everyone's handwriting, as Apple's Newton and Palm's Zoomer had tried to do – ineffectively, as it turned out – Hawkins decided to create a standard alphabet and characters that people could learn to use. He would train people in a new, but easy way to write.

Graffiti, Hawkins' new alphabet, mimicked traditional Roman letters with just simple modifications. The result was a near-perfect technological solution with two key benefits. First, anyone could learn to print characters that the product could recognize, thus eliminating the handwriting-recognition issue. Second, the handheld no longer needed a keyboard, thus facilitating a smaller product.

Yet another problem with technology was the limited screen space. When writing long words or sentences, the user would run out of room on the small screen. Hawkins' solution was to have users write one letter on top of another, forcing the software (rather than the user) to display the letters and characters in sequential order. Again, Hawkins came up with an inventive and practical solution that was technologically feasible.

The team also realized the importance of data exchange between the handheld and the PC. Palm engineers wrote software that could import and export data to and from a number of desktop software programs, like Microsoft Outlook and Lotus Organizer. With this functionality, pertinent daily information usually stored on a PC suddenly became portable.

Matching the two – harnessing technology to meet customer needs

With Hawkins' criteria in mind and the key technologies in place, the Palm crew set out to develop a superior handheld organizer. The team was meticulous when it came to the product's features and functionality. They knew the machine had to be simple to operate. Keeping it simple meant fewer features. When deciding what features to include in Palm's handheld, Vice-president of Marketing Ed Colligan asked, 'Is this feature going to sell one more unit?'[15] If the answer was no, then the Palm team dropped it. Colligan's discipline was a key factor that helped execute on CSF number three. What the engineers designed would be what the customers wanted – no more, no less. In the end, the team decided on four basic features: a calendar, an address book, a to-do list and a memo pad. Palm's competitors, on the other hand, missed the boat, cramming far too much functionality into their little handhelds.

Hawkins also realized that existing operating systems wouldn't work for the simple and sharply focused device he had in mind. A better operating system was needed, and Palm's Ron Marietti was the engineer who delivered it, another instance of Palm's ability to execute on harnessing technology to meet customer needs.

While the Palm team was busy sticking to its simple features, the company did allow for software add-ons for customers who might want them. The company relied on outside software developers to provide these applications. Independent software developers could obtain a Palm software development kit and create add-on shareware and commercial programs for Palm's handheld. Anxious to get their hands on a big audience, these developers designed everything from financial calculators and video games to astrological charts and news updates.

Results – a hit from day one

Palm Computing demonstrated its new Palm handheld at a trade show in January 1996. Half of the more than 400 trade show attendees took Palm up on its $149 pre-order offer. In April of that year, Palm began shipping.

❝ the company knew it had a hit when computer columnists failed to return its review units ❞

PC Computing magazine wrote: 'The Pilot 1000 is an outstanding product: It's fast, easy to use, and inexpensive . . . If you're searching for the ultimate palm-size organizer, look no further.'[16] The company knew it had a hit when computer columnists failed to return its review units.[17]

Throughout the remainder of 1996, Palm's Pilot organizer gained popularity. By the end of the Christmas season, Palm's Pilot won over 70 per cent of the US handheld market. That year, the Pilot received 21 'best product' awards from the press, consistently beating Microsoft's handheld launched in the autumn of that year.[18]

It took Palm only 18 months to sell 1 million Pilots. But Hawkins and Dubinsky refused to rest upon their laurels. To maintain momentum, Palm worked vigorously to develop newer, better versions of its handheld. Palm III hit the market in March 1997. This version was slimmer than the original Pilot, and weighed only 6 ounces. Gartner Group said, 'The product delivers exactly what existing users want.'[19] A still thinner version, the Palm V, was next. While the Palm V had no functional difference from the Palm III, it was a far more attractive product. As Hawkins said, 'The goal was beauty. Beauty, beauty, beauty. I didn't want any distraction with other things.'[20] The Palm V sold for $449, weighed 4 ounces, and was equipped with rechargeable batteries. Palm VII took a jump into the wireless world. Equipped with an antenna, it could send and receive emails and Web clippings. In 1998, however, Hawkins, Dubinsky and Colligan departed to form a new company, having struggled for years under corporate oversight that, in their eyes, limited their progress.

For a time, the rest of the Palm team continued to deliver impressive results. During its fiscal year ending May 2000, Palm reached over $1 billion in sales. During the next six months, it sold another $922 million. It had taken Palm three and a half years to sell 5 million handhelds.

But profits were another story. Amid rampant innovation across the category and fierce competition – including the new Visor from Hawkins' and team's new company, Handspring – PalmOne, the portion of the old Palm that marketed devices, had by mid-2003 chalked up nearly $900 million in losses over three very difficult years.

In October, Hawkins and team returned to Palm, bringing together Handspring's engineering and design prowess with Palm's manufacturing and sales expertise. The reunited companies launched the Treo 600 to rave reviews, as combination devices like Treo and the BlackBerry, which combine PDAs and mobile phones into a single unit, became the next must-have device for on-the-go businesspeople. In 2005, with Colligan holding the reins as CEO, Palm announced its first annual profit since 2000.[21]

Despite the positive outlook in 2005, hot new products from BlackBerry as well as Apple's iPhone presented Palm with serious challenges in the ensuing years. By 2009, revenue was falling sharply, off a whopping 44 per cent from 2008; Palm incurred $732,000 in losses for its year ending June 2009.[22] Colligan, after 16 years at the company, stepped down from his CEO post and Palm's Executive Chairman Jon Rubinstein, an Apple veteran, took the reins. In mid-2009, Palm introduced its Palm Pre to compete with the iPhone and a new webOS operating system, again to rave reviews from technology pundits.[23]

Will Palm be able to get back in the game against the likes of Apple and the ubiquitous BlackBerry? Rubinstein believes it can. 'With Palm webOS we have ten-plus years of innovation ahead of us, and the Palm Pre is already one of the year's hottest new products. Due in no small part to Ed's courageous leadership, we're in great shape to get Palm back to continuous growth, and we plan to keep the trajectory going upward.'[24]

What made Palm a high-tech success in its early years? Palm's success did not result from proprietary technology that was patent-protected, although Palm did win some patents and it did develop its own operating system. The story wasn't superior organizational processes that others could not match. The key element in Palm's ability to win in a business where other companies and products – including Palm's own Zoomer – had failed was the ability of the entrepreneurial team to execute on the three factors that were – and still are – critical to high-tech success. Let's recap how Palm's entrepreneurial team – Hawkins, Dubinsky and Colligan – executed on these three CSFs.

- *Understanding customers' real problems or needs:* Hawkins, Dubinsky and Colligan focused relentlessly on building the small and simple product that they knew customers wanted. 'Delight the customer', was Colligan's mantra for design decisions.[25]

- *Understanding deeply an area of technology and what it can and cannot deliver, both today and tomorrow:* Hawkins knew the limitations of handwriting-recognition technology and what it could and could not do well. With Graffiti, he found a better way to resolve the technical problem.

- *Finding ways to harness technology to resolve these problems or needs:* 'He was really anal about a lot of stuff,' recalls Karl Townsend, who designed the electronics for the first Palm Pilot. 'He said, "Look, it's really important how thin it is; it's really important how the buttons feel." All the other products I had worked on, people didn't have the same passion that Jeff had, and the product then becomes a huge gigantic compromise.'[26]

Of these three CSFs, the first and third are often overlooked in technology-driven companies, where engineering elegance sometimes takes precedence over customer needs. The Palm team, however, executed superbly. At the end of the day, it's execution – not design brilliance or engineering elegance alone – that counts. Hawkins and his team executed. They delivered cutting-edge products that worked and that customers wanted and would pay for – all things easy to say but difficult to do in the high-tech world. And, as the last few years have shown for Palm, increasingly difficult to continue to do in the face of innovative, fast-moving and capable competitors.

❝ at the end of the day, it's execution that counts ❞

Schwinn hits the skids

We now turn our attention from a company that executed superbly on its industry's CSFs to a company that succumbed in the bicycle industry by failing to do so. In the USA, Schwinn is a brand that evokes nostalgia. American baby boomers remember the classic Schwinn models and reminisce fondly about riding their Schwinns around town. So, what was it that caused a venerable company with a widely recognized brand to fail? The sad reality is that the company's team did not execute on its industry's CSFs.

Before we begin the Schwinn story, let's first identify the CSFs in the bicycle industry. Sometimes, those factors depend on the nature of the strategy a company pursues. In bicycles, as in most mature manufacturing industries, there are three broad strategic approaches, as Treacy and Wiersema[27] point out.

- *Operational excellence*, i.e. 'providing customers with reliable products or services at competitive prices and delivered with minimal difficulty or inconvenience'. Such a strategy seeks to lead the industry in price and convenience.

- *Customer intimacy*, i.e. 'segmenting and targeting markets precisely and then tailoring offerings to match exactly the demands of those niches'. This strategy is focused on individualized service to each customer, based on an intimate understanding of what that customer needs.

- *Product leadership*, i.e. 'offering customers leading-edge products and services that consistently enhance the customer's use or applications of the product, thereby making rivals' goods obsolete'. Product leadership companies seek to provide a continuing flow of state-of-the-art products or services to remain at the cutting edge of their industry.

What CSFs are required to carry out each of these strategies effectively? According to Treacy and Wiersema,[28] here's what each strategy requires.

- Operational excellence:
  - minimize costs in every regard;
  - optimize business processes for extreme efficiency and effectiveness.

- Customer intimacy: gather detailed information about each customer so that they may be assigned to a micro-segment in which the offering is tailored carefully to that segment's needs. Sometimes, the segmentation is so precise that offerings are tailored to market segments of one.

- Product leadership:
  - creativity, to recognize and embrace ideas that may originate outside the company;
  - optimize business processes for speed, in order to bring these creative ideas to market quickly;
  - relentlessly pursue new solutions that may render obsolete those that the company has just introduced. If anyone is to render the product leader's technology obsolete, then the product leader prefers to do so itself.

In addition to the one or two CSFs pertinent to each strategy, another CSF applies to manufacturers regardless of strategy.

- Effective, efficient value-chain relationships: without effective and mutually beneficial relationships with suppliers and resellers, any manufacturer will face an uphill battle. From suppliers, manufacturers need reliability, quality and on-time delivery at an affordable price. From resellers, they need commitment and sell-through – a commitment that a manufacturer wins by being a reliable supplier of quality products itself.

Let's see if Schwinn executed on any of these CSFs.

A changing American market for bicycles[29]

One day in the late 1970s, a group of Schwinn engineers paid a visit to a small California bicycle factory called Fisher MountainBikes. Back in 1974, Gary Fisher had built a dozen 'klunkers', as he called them, bikes cobbled together from sturdy bike frames found in thrift shops, but fitted with the latest European parts – fancy ten-speed gears, thumb shifters, motorcycle brake levers, knobby dirt-grabbing tyres and so on. The purpose? To enable Fisher and his buddies to ride their bikes up and down the dirt tracks among the hills along Northern California's dramatic coast.

Fisher, though still not 30 years of age, now had a real company, and he and others like him were building bikes like none built before (see Case Study 7.1 overleaf). The engineers from Schwinn, long the leading bicycle brand in the USA, were there to take a look at the mountain bikes Fisher had crafted, including one made from an old Schwinn Excelsior. As Fisher recalled the scene some 15 years later, 'This guy in his 50s was looking down at me like I was some jerk kid who didn't know anything. The Schwinn engineers are going, "We know bikes. You guys are all amateurs. We know better than anybody".'[30]

It was Fisher who knew bikes, not Schwinn. As had happened in the 1970s, when Europe's lightweight ten-speed road bikes invaded the American bicycle market, and later with motocross-inspired BMX bikes, Schwinn was left in the dust. By the end of the 1980s, mountain bikes like Fisher's would account for 60 per cent of a booming American market for bicycles, and Schwinn would be on its way towards bankruptcy court. Was the Schwinn team able to execute on the CSFs entailed in any of the Treacy and Wiersema strategies in the 1970s and 1980s? Consistently not. Let's see how Schwinn fared on the success factors that characterize it.

---

case study 7.1

Entrepreneurial newcomers remake the bicycle business[31]

In 1979, ten years after the mountain bike craze began in earnest, Gary Fisher's Fisher MountainBikes was selling 15,000 bikes annually at prices up to $1200 each. Fisher was on his way towards being a millionaire. There were more than 5 million mountain bikes on the trails in the USA alone.[32] Fisher's was among the best-known of the new companies that had built thriving businesses from what Schwinn had overlooked. Steve Potts, at the smaller but high-priced end of the scale, offered tailor-made bikes built to order for customers willing to pay $3400 for his signature craftsmanship.

Specialized, another newcomer, having seen the mountain bike trend and knowledgeable about low-cost manufacturing in Asia, sold a broad line of mountain bikes at half Fisher's prices. Even the European makers like Raleigh finally got into the game.

Like Phil Knight of Nike, John Mackey of Whole Foods Market and Pierre Omidyar of eBay, these entrepreneurs had changed the way consumers live and play. That's what entrepreneurs do.

Trouble at Schwinn

While Schwinn had been a trendsetter in the bicycle industry for 80 years, by the 1970s the family-run company had lost its ability to gauge the market. In October 1979, Ed Schwinn, aged 30, took over the presidency of Schwinn Bicycle Company from his uncle Frank V. Schwinn. At the time, Schwinn had a 12 per cent share of the American market and was by far the most trusted name in bicycles.

After just a few months in his new job, Ed decided that the long-time executives who had led Schwinn for years weren't what the company needed. In April 1980, he arrived unexpectedly at Schwinn's western sales office in California and said to Max Scott, Schwinn's Vice-president for Sales and Marketing, 'Max, I'm here to ask for your resignation. We'd like for you to leave the company right now. You can come tomorrow to get your belongings. That's all I have to say.'[33] Marketing Director Ray Burch was also replaced. The veteran number-two man, Al Fritz, was banished in 1980 to Excelsior Fitness, a small Schwinn division selling exercise equipment. As the veterans left, in came younger family members lacking in business experience. Schwinn's old guard may have lacked the ability to develop cutting-edge products but they had presided over decades of operational excellence. Would the new team be able to match them?

The year that Ed Schwinn took over, Schwinn's Chicago factory employees voted to unionize. Rather than continue to work with his experienced but now unionized factory workers, Ed decided to close Schwinn's Chicago factory. In its place, the youthful Schwinn decided to open a new factory in Greenville, Mississippi. Things went downhill quickly from there.

As Chris Travers, one of Schwinn's California dealers, said later, 'Greenville was quickly branded as having an inferior product.' Other dealers complained that the Greenville-manufactured bikes had parts that did not fit together, wheels that weren't true or frames that had mismatched colours.

❝ some bikes even arrived without seat posts ❞

For a while, some bikes even arrived without seat posts. There were delivery issues as well. Long-time Schwinn dealer Joe Russell said, 'We just couldn't get the right bikes when we needed them.'[34] Clearly, Schwinn failed to execute on the CSFs for an operational excellence strategy and in doing so was beginning to do irreparable damage to the company's relationships with its resellers, a major shortcoming on one of the CSFs.

The manufacturing problems in Greenville led to significant operating losses, exacerbated by write-offs of obsolete inventory, equipment and buildings in Chicago. The severance costs associated with laying off all the Chicago factory employees also proved financially damaging to Schwinn, as did the habitually free spending of Schwinn's management team, itself a further difficulty in maintaining operational excellence. The result was that the Schwinn Company's net worth plunged from $43.8 million in 1980 to $2.7 million just three years later.

Seeking to resolve its continuing manufacturing problems, Schwinn transferred most of its production to Taiwan-based Giant Manufacturing Corp. Ed Schwinn was soon captivated by doing business in Asia, even bringing to Chicago a Chinese junk that he would sail on Lake Michigan. The odd-looking boat was a reminder to all of Schwinn's free-spending culture. Schwinn's globetrotting executives enjoyed other finer things in life, too: 'It doesn't cost that much more to eat well,' commented Vice-president of Finance John Barker, after one of his regular trips to China.

❛❛ the odd-looking boat was a reminder to all of Schwinn's free-spending culture ❜❜

Despite the free spending on overheads, the lower Asian manufacturing costs boosted unit profit margins from losses of $5–20 per bike to gains of $20–30. Margins on Al Fritz's exercise bikes were even better, in the 50 per cent range. Sales of Fritz's new Air-Dyne exercise bikes doubled, but Schwinn's corporate team didn't believe the optimistic forecasts that Fritz was making. As a result, according to Fritz, 'We never had enough exercisers.'[35] This time it was the new management team who proved unable to deliver on the CSFs required for product leadership. Indeed, the fact that Schwinn didn't miss the exercise craze completely was due largely to the experienced Al Fritz.

In 1984, Schwinn turned its first profit in four years, earning $3 million on sales of $134 million, due mainly to the booming exercise business. By 1986, Schwinn's earnings peaked at $7 million, its best in a decade, on sales of $174 million, and it opened swanky new offices.

Schwinn's troubles go global

Alas, the good news was only temporary. Schwinn's network had grown to include suppliers in mainland China and Hungary, leading to reduced reliance on Giant, their established Taiwanese supplier, which in 1986 had been producing some 80 per cent of Schwinn's bikes. What did those decisions do to their value-chain relationships? Giant retaliated with higher prices, cutting into Schwinn's margins and forcing it to raise prices. Schwinn bikes were suddenly priced $10–20 higher than competing models. 'When people came in here and saw the price – boom, out the door they went,' said John Pelc, a Schwinn dealer for more than 40 years.[36] To compound the problem, Schwinn had quality problems once again, this time with its new Chinese supplier. Both efficiency and effectiveness had gone out the door.

❛❛ both efficiency and effectiveness had gone out the door ❜❜

Once again, Schwinn's manufacturing and supply problems showed up on the bottom line. In mid-1989, Controller Don Gillard came to Ed Schwinn with an analysis that showed Schwinn was losing money on bikes, and that only the Air-Dyne cash cow was keeping it afloat. Gillard was asked to resign soon after. Ed Schwinn just didn't like hearing bad news.

Meanwhile, Giant decided to expand its own brand and reduce its reliance on Schwinn. When Schwinn bought a $2 million stake in its Chinese supplier, China Bicycles Company, Giant's President Tony Lo was furious. Lo hired Bill Austin, Schwinn's recently departed marketing chief. Austin shrewdly offered dealers a better profit margin than Schwinn was offering, along with a compelling story – Giant bikes were made by the same factory that made Schwinn! By 1992, Giant would sell more than 300,000 bikes in the USA, more than half of Schwinn's 543,000.

The end of Schwinn's road

By the end of the 1980s, Schwinn was back in the red, losing $2.9 million in 1990 and $23 million in 1991, when it shut down the Greenville factory. The Air-Dyne cash cow disappeared, as its sales plunged by one-third due to lower pricing by competitors. Al Fritz, after complaining of the lack of payrises for his division's staff, had been dismissed years earlier. By 1991, Schwinn's lenders were applying pressure once again and Schwinn family members, long accustomed to fat dividend cheques, were growing restless. In 1992, Schwinn's banks began sweeping cash from Schwinn's revolving line of credit to pay overdue loans, leaving Schwinn with little money with which to pay Giant and China Bicycles. Schwinn's debt to these two suppliers ballooned to some $30 million, and Schwinn's net worth was wiped out. 'It was like being on a runaway train,' said Dennis O'Dea, Schwinn's attorney in the bankruptcy that soon followed. 'It was horrific.'[37] In October 1992, Schwinn filed for bankruptcy. Soon after, its remaining assets were sold to a group of investors. The most respected name in the American bicycle business brought a paltry $2.5 million.

> ❝ **the most respected name in the American bicycle business brought a paltry $2.5 million** ❞

Execution, not

At the beginning of this section, we identified the CSFs entailed in the strategies that Schwinn might have chosen. Let's summarize how the Schwinn team executed on the industry's CSFs.

- Did it minimize costs? Hardly. A free-spending culture. A Chinese junk on Chicago's Lake Michigan. And a swanky new office building.

- Were business processes optimized for efficiency and effectiveness? Certainly not. Severe quality and delivery problems were recurring events.

- Were there detailed customer data for targeting small or expanding segments? None. We saw no evidence of any attempts to tailor the offering to meet small segments' individual needs.

- Creativity and a willingness to accept new ideas like mountain bikes and bring them to market quickly? No way. From all appearances, Schwinn's leadership appears to have been about as backward-looking as a management team can get.

- What about organizational processes? Relentless pursuit of new solutions? Were they geared to speed, to support a product leadership strategy? Except for Air-Dyne, Schwinn's days as a product leader were long gone.

- Value-chain relationships? Cutting out a reliable supplier? Supplying its dealers with faulty products. Inadequate product delivery. Not exactly what most observers would call effective execution.

Sadly, the Schwinn story is a textbook example of 'management missteps, global mishaps and the pitfalls peculiar to family-owned businesses by third- and fourth-generation executives'.[38] There are lots of phrases one could use to describe the Schwinn debacle, but effective execution on CSFs is not among them.

What investors want to know

££ what does great management look like? ??

Do investors care about execution? Absolutely, they do. It's what keeps them awake at night. It's the best protection they have after they've made a decision to invest in a nascent entrepreneurial venture. Once they've made the decision to invest in your venture, your ability to execute on your CSFs is the best – maybe the only – protection they have for their money. No wonder they'll fixate on it before they settle up.

We really dig into the management team. We want to be totally confident that this team can deliver on the promises they have made. We do that by looking at their experience, by assessing how well they understand their industry and their customers. We want to know about their leadership in terms of the CEO and the heads of engineering, R&D, and marketing [or whatever the most important functions are for any given opportunity].

OD, USA

Execution is why the refrain 'management, management, management' is heard so often in venture capital circles. But what does great management look like, when viewed from up front, before events have unfolded? Is it about character? Chemistry? Drive or motivation? Perseverance in the face of adversity? Is it industry experience? Is it glib salespersonship? Is it technological expertise? Is it 'having done it before', as Louis Borders had done in book retailing before his ill-fated Webvan adventure?

In the research that led to this book, I learned that great management is about all of these things and something more. Do character, drive and perseverance matter? Sure. Is industry experience relevant? Of course. But not just as a line on a CV. Does the ability to sell matter? Absolutely: it's what successful entrepreneurs do with much of their time. But successful selling is not to be confused with a dynamic personality, as the naturally introverted Jeff Hawkins will attest. Most of these elements are like fitness to the athlete. Necessary, but not sufficient for greatness. What do astute investors look for?

What astute investors look for in people they back – and 'people', plural, is the right word here – is simple, really, but not very obvious to most aspiring entrepreneurs.

■ Investors want to know that the lead entrepreneur has identified and understands the CSFs in the industry they propose to enter, as well as the market and competitive environment they will encounter. A credible understanding of the seven domains can provide the evidence here. That's step one.

■ Step two, the crucial one, is that the lead entrepreneur has then assembled a team that can demonstrate – in past *deeds*, not words – that its players taken together can execute. 'On what?', you may ask. Execute on each and every one of the handful of CSFs that the venture's industry and strategy therein will require. Or, alternatively, and equally satisfactorily, the entrepreneur has identified what's necessary and also what's lacking on their team and acknowledged the need to fill that gap, perhaps with the investor's help.

So, if you want investors' backing for your new venture, make the effort to understand the CSFs that your venture will face. If you've not worked in the industry you plan to enter, you'd better find someone who has. There

❝ look in the mirror and ask what you bring to the party ❞ are always just a few factors that are crucial. It's the ones that make the difference between who wins in your industry and who are the also-rans. Next, look in the mirror and ask what you – demonstrably, in past deeds, not just words – bring to the party. Finally, fill out your team with people who can deliver what you yourself do not have or cannot do. Fill it with people who are different from you – diverse teams generally perform better than look-alikes.

Lessons learned

As I noted in the first pages of this book, the majority of entrepreneurial ventures fail. They do so for many reasons, lots of which are opportunity-based. Some pursue poor markets. Others choose unattractive industries where almost no one can win. Some offer no real benefits to their prospective customers, offer benefits no better than what is already available or have no way to sustain their initial advantage. At least some of these errors, however, can be overcome through effective execution.

If you were to ask the successful entrepreneurs whose case histories have graced the chapters in this book about the mistakes they have made, they would smile. Then they'd probably ask with a chuckle, 'How long have you got?' My research team and I chose each of the stories in this book to bring to life just one of the seven domains. In reality, though, most of these world-class entrepreneurs got more than just one domain right. They got most of them right, but not always on the first attempt, as we saw with Jeff Hawkins' Zoomer. But they would be the first to tell you that they also made lots of mistakes along the way. Having the right team – a team that can execute on the important things, the CSFs – is a crucial element in recovering and learning from those mistakes. Let's see what we've learned from this chapter.

Lessons learned from Palm Computing

In the case of Palm Computing, Jeff Hawkins not only knew what it took to succeed with a high-technology firm; he also made certain that his company had the right people to fulfil these necessary criteria. When Hawkins resolved that Palm would produce a simpler handheld, he knew 'the most critical employee to the project . . . was Ron Marietti'.[39] He needed an engineer of Marietti's calibre to write the operating system, otherwise the product simply would not work.

> **❝ execution mattered – contrast Palm's execution with that of other early entrants into handheld computing ❞**

Earlier, Hawkins had agreed with his venture capital backers that he should hire a CEO to run the company. It took about a year, but when the time was right that's exactly what Hawkins did. Donna Dubinsky, Hawkins thought, could execute, and she could do things he could not.

To his credit, Hawkins knew his strengths and weaknesses, having never claimed to be a good manager.[40] He knew the CSFs that his business faced, and he built a team that could meet them. Execution mattered. Contrast Palm's execution with that of other early entrants into handheld computing – Apple's Newton and Microsoft's Pocket PC – which simply failed to understand the limits of the technology and to marry it with customer needs.

Hindsight tells us that, at least at its early stages, the handheld computing industry was a tough game to play. There were numerous entrants and quite capable substitutes – pen and paper, principally – that led most entrants to fail. Arguably, Palm's superior execution – Hawkins, Dubinsky, Colligan, Marietti and the rest of the team – made the difference.

Lessons learned from Schwinn

To be fair, the bicycle industry when Ed Schwinn took his family company's helm was not all that attractive. But there were segments – like mountain bikes – where the prospects were bright. But unlike the new mountain bike pioneers like Gary Fisher, Schwinn failed to respond to the trends sweeping the industry.

And, unlike Palm's Jeff Hawkins, Ed Schwinn seemed not to understand the importance of a good team. Instead of surrounding himself with the best and the brightest, he eliminated key veterans (flawed to be sure, but the newcomers didn't shine either) and replaced them with young relatives. Al Fritz, who latched on to the fitness trend, was demoted. Don Gillard, the bearer of bad news, was terminated. Family ties are no substitute for a team's lack of ability to execute on the CSFs.

> **❝ one's team includes more than one's employees – bankers, suppliers and dealers count, too ❞**

Worse, Schwinn antagonized key partners – Giant and, later, China Bicycles – apparently not realizing that one's team includes more than one's employees. Bankers, suppliers and dealers count, too. Arrogance, rampant at Schwinn, does not breed cooperation and team-work.[41]

Business – as with entrepreneurship – is a team sport, and Ed Schwinn was not a team player.

As we'll see in the next chapter, there's one more dimension of your entrepreneurial team we've yet to deal with, and it addresses an important issue in completing your team. The team issues are crucial ones, especially if your venture requires external capital. As William Wordsworth noted in opening this chapter, it's in you and your *people* – not your *idea* – that investors will ultimately place their trust.

The new business road test: stage six – the 'can you execute?' test

- What are the few – only a handful, please – critical success factors in your industry? What support can you provide to show that you've identified them correctly?

- Can you demonstrate – in past deeds, not mere words – that your team taken together can execute on each and every one of these CFSs?

- Alternatively, have you identified which CSFs your team is not well prepared to meet, for which you need help in filling out your team?

8

Your connections matter: which matter most?

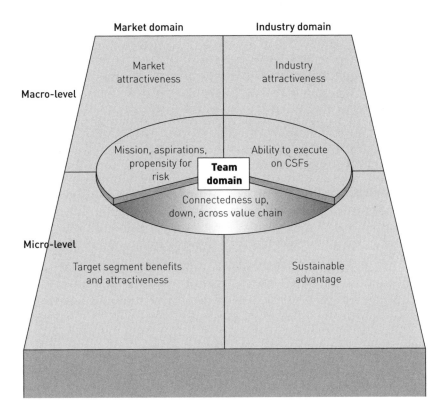

Littered with used oxygen tanks and rubbish, the Mount Everest base camp has played temporary host to the numerous climbers wishing to reach the summit of this 29,000-foot peak. Base camp serves many purposes, one of which is to acclimatize climbers to the high altitude.

Another purpose is to act as a central information hub for the climbing teams perched high above on this Himalayan monster. With the advent of wireless technology, climbers can stay in close contact with their base camp brethren. Not unlike an air traffic control station, climbers attempting to climb Everest can communicate with others at the base camp to learn of incoming inclement weather.

As a climber, communication with base camp can be a lifeline. Knowing that a storm is approaching can be the deciding factor for whether or not to attempt the summit. Not knowing that a storm is approaching can change a potentially successful ascent into a deadly adventure.

Put yourself in this situation ... you and a team of climbers are perched at nearly 28,000 feet above sea level, with winds whipping around you and temperatures that haven't seen zero for days. You have just spent your thirtieth night on Mount Everest. It has taken you just over two weeks to get from base camp to this, your last overnight site before reaching the summit. You awaken at 5 a.m. with a pounding headache and spells of dizziness that have become the rule rather than the exception over the last several days. More than anything, you want to find your way to the summit and then quickly (albeit safely) make your way off this brutal mountain.

As has become the daily ritual, your team leader uses his satellite telephone to speak with base camp. Base camp is in contact with various teams of climbers at several locations on the mountain. Each team on the mountain has another vantage point of the cloud and storm systems. Each team can provide critical information about changing weather. For the first time in seven days, your team leader hears that the weather appears to be stable – for at least a few hours – enough time to get to the summit and back to safety. Your leader signals your team to prepare to ascend. You pack your gear and take off for what will be a long, tiring, but safe last 1000 feet of this climb.

Entrepreneurial connections

It's not *what* you know; it's *who* you know.

Business wisdom from an unknown source

Choosing to communicate with base camp before attempting a summit seems like the obvious choice. With precious little oxygen and difficult climbing a given, why risk adding fierce weather to this already daunting mix? While lack of oxygen doesn't play much of a role in starting new ventures, the fierceness of competition can make you just as dizzy. The pace of technological change can create new markets in a heartbeat. Companies with strong networks of contacts having varied vantage points – including those of customers, suppliers and others in the industry and related industries – are more capable of anticipating and understanding forthcoming changes and are therefore better prepared to deal with them. Likewise, entrepreneurs who surround themselves with a strong network up, down and across the value chain are well positioned to gauge the ever-changing market and modify their offerings, operations, organization and processes to meet the needs of a changing business climate.

Put another way, the ability to combine the tenacity for which entrepreneurs are legendary with a willingness to change course – typically due to changes in the marketplace – can make all the difference. Sometimes, such market changes are favourable ones. Good luck can sometimes help an entrepreneurial venture. But good luck is most likely to pay off when those in charge have the right connections that provide the information required to help them respond to market changes quickly and adroitly. Otherwise, it is unlikely that the company will be able to take advantage of good luck when it shows up. Without the information sources to tell you when mid-course corrections are necessary, all the willingness in the world will do you no good.

Thus, you should ask how connected you and your team members are up, down and across the value chain as shown in Figure 8.1 – with suppliers and customers, as well as competitors in your industry – to address this concern. Connections with suppliers (up the value chain), with competitors (across the value chain) and with distributors, customers, consumers or end-users (all down the value chain) can provide crucial leading-edge information that could spell the difference between success and failure at an important juncture in the life of your business. If you're not yet sufficiently connected, start building your network now!

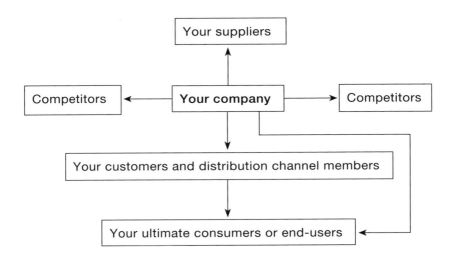

figure 8.1   Connections in all directions

In this chapter, we'll examine the case histories of two companies. As we'll see, Virata's connections in the UK and Europe enabled it to change its business completely to take advantage of a new application for which its technology happened to be extremely well suited. Digital Equipment corporation on the other hand, simply failed to adapt to several marketplace changes – including the PC revolution – and found its minicomputer business obsolete. In both of these case histories we examine how just having connections is not sufficient – it's having the right ones and having the ability to understand and act on the new information, even if it's not what you want to hear. We then examine this domain from an investor's perspective, so that you may understand better what investors will look for in your entrepreneurial team. Finally,

❝ you should ask how connected you and your team members are up, down and across the value chain ❞

the chapter closes with lessons to be learned from these two case histories for assessing your opportunity and the team you've assembled – or need to assemble – to pursue it.

Virata gets lucky. Why?[1]

Virata is not exactly a household name. We don't sip Virata coffee. We don't shop in Virata stores or ride in Virata cars. We don't book our meetings on Virata PDAs. We don't talk on Virata telephones. Or do we?

If you dialled up your high-speed DSL connection today to bid on that special something on eBay, then your data probably passed through a Virata chip. If you bought a book from Amazon via a DSL connection, then you probably used Virata hardware and software. If you checked your email using a high-speed DSL connection, then it went a lot faster because of Virata.

Virata, a British company that grew out of technology developed in the research labs of Cambridge University, provides communications processors and the relevant software that enable the world's telephone companies to compete for the growing demand for high-speed digital access. But getting there wasn't easy.

With roots dating back to 1986, Virata was an offshoot of the Olivetti Research Laboratory in Cambridge, UK, where Andy Hopper and Hermann Hauser had been leading research into a new technology called Asynchronous Transfer Mode (ATM). ATM had what Hopper and Hauser thought was an important advantage over other competing technologies: it could simultaneously handle voice, video and data transmission over local area networks (LANs) and wide area networks (WANs), and it did so at high speed. With technology valued at $6 million and seed capital from Olivetti, 3i and private investors, Virata was spun out of the Olivetti lab in 1993. With premises in Cambridge, UK, it was given a chance to make its name developing and marketing equipment for LANs.

> **❝ Virata was an offshoot of the Olivetti Research Laboratory ❞**

Ethernet, an older LAN technology that dated back to the 1970s, was not well suited to video and voice, since these time-dependent applications required information to be delivered in a constant stream. Ethernet separated data into packets that were distributed through different routes and reassembled at the receiving end. Ethernet worked fine for data, but not for voice or video. Garbled conversations or jerky images were the result.

A better mousetrap

Hopper and Hauser thought the need for voice and video would grow, so their new company soon began marketing video servers, switches and network interface cards that together comprised a complete ATM solution for LAN networks. Their ATM25 switch was the fastest in the world at the time, operating at 25 megabits per second compared with the 10-megabit products that the Ethernet providers offered. In 1994, with its new headquarters and sales office in California, to tap what was expected to be the first market for this new technology, Virata was off and running.

Like many technology companies, however, the cost of developing the technology outpaced the meagre early revenues. Thus, in 1995, with ATM all the rage in the venture capital community, Virata secured a first round of venture capital led by two prominent Silicon Valley firms, Oak Investment Partners and New Enterprise Associates, raising another $11 million for about 30 per cent of the company. As Hauser put it, 'Venture capitalists are basically "sector lemmings". When a sector is as hot as ATM was at the time, venture capitalists have got to have some ATM investments. We had one of the best ATM teams in the world and we had a product that was outstanding compared with all the other switches on the market.'[2]

With others developing similar technology, Virata staked its competitive advantage on its ability to enhance the software functionality of its ATM products. Unfortunately, however, by late 1995 it was clear that, in the words of Virata's Vice-president of Marketing, Tom Cooper, 'The dog was not eating the dog food – not just Virata's brand, no one's brand.' As one of Cooper's former colleagues from Hewlett-Packard pointed out, 'Tom, your problem is that you have a technology in search of a problem. No one has a problem yet!'[3] Tom's former colleague was right. The vast majority of traffic over LANs was data, not voice or video. Multimedia networking simply wasn't a mainstream application just yet.

But an absence of a real customer need was only part of the problem. Companies like 3Com, whose livelihoods were invested in Ethernet technology, were not about to let some upstart technology eat their lunch. These companies had deep pockets and large numbers of customers who had made significant investments in Ethernet networks.

> **companies like 3Com were not about to let some upstart technology eat their lunch**

These customers were happy to pay for upgrades and enhancements as further developments in Ethernet technology occurred. Even though Virata's ATM switches ran at more than twice the speed of Ethernet switches – at twice the price – customers just were not buying. 'It was the classic better mousetrap phenomenon,' said Cooper.[4] The better mousetrap, however, is not always the one that sells.

By 1996, morale at Virata was heading south. Virata's CEO tried to rally his troops, arguing that Virata was just slightly too early with its technology. He believed that, 'When this market takes off, Virata will be a leading player and will ride on its successes far into the future.'[5] Fortunately, there was continued faith among investors that ATM was a technology for the future. After all, ATM *was* a better mousetrap. As a result, Virata obtained another round of $13 million in June: $3 million from the original investors and $10 million from Oracle, whose CEO Larry Ellison had invested in another of Hauser's companies some years earlier. Ellison had faith in Hauser and it took only a 30-minute meeting to seal the deal.

Stay the course or change direction?

With a fresh injection of cash in hand, Virata renewed its efforts to sell its line of network products. Significantly, and as a result of connections built earlier in his career, Tom Cooper had had some success in licensing the software and semiconductors used in Virata's LAN equipment to companies interested in Virata's technology for applications in quite different areas. One recent approach had come from Alcatel, a French communications equipment company.

Alcatel was pioneering asynchronous digital subscriber line technology (ADSL), which it thought might make possible the upgrading of old-fashioned twisted-pair copper telephone wires to handle the growing interest in broadband applications. Alcatel wanted to use Virata's ATM LAN products as part of its ADSL demonstration, license the technology, and perhaps build it into its own hardware devices. These devices would handle high-speed data in the so-called local loop – the 'last mile' of copper that reached from telephone companies' facilities to their subscribers' homes and premises. As we saw in Chapter 4, the market for high-speed data applications like DSL looked promising even in 1996, and Virata's technology was worth a look, Alcatel thought.

Some at Virata were intrigued with the forecasts of rapid growth of online ADSL subscribers and wondered whether this market might be a more attractive one than the LAN markets Virata had been pursuing. But Virata's CEO would have none of this thinking: 'It would be disastrous to divert our attention to the licensing market as you suggest.'[6] The company soon found itself split into two camps and, barely one month after Virata received Ellison's cash, the CEO left the company.

In the summer of 1996, the Virata board asked Charles Cotton, the General Manager of the Cambridge operation since mid-1995, to become COO and acting CEO. Cotton's charge was to determine which direction Virata should take in the short term. Pulling his team together for a late summer strategic retreat in California's Napa Valley and fuelled by the California sunshine – and some of the world's finest wines – Virata management decided to pursue both directions concurrently, at least for the time being. It was too early to know whether the licensing strategy – or DSL itself, for that matter – would bear fruit, and it remained unclear whether the networking market might turn profitable. Although networking sales had grown to nearly $1.5 million per quarter, the direct selling and distribution costs exceeded the gross margin. Virata was burning cash rapidly and more would be needed soon.

That same month, Alcatel won a large contract with four regional Bell operating companies in the USA to deploy its DSL architecture. This broad-based deal covering a significant portion of the American telecom terrain focused the market on ATM-based ADSL solutions. At last, there was a light at the end of Virata's tunnel. By 1997, Virata had licensed its technology to other telecom suppliers and to Com21Corporation, a leader in bringing high-speed data capability to American and European cable television operators, who also saw the potential for an ATM-based solution for their applications. Notwithstanding these deals, Virata's licensing revenues were still very small.

As the company pursued both the licensing strategy and the networking market, the Virata team remained badly divided. A new CEO – the third in just 15 months – was convinced that networking products – not DSL – were the bread and butter of Virata's future. The licensing business was just too different and required different skills. Licensing deals were sold to original equipment manufacturers (OEMs) that would add Virata's software technology and chips to their own products. Sales cycles were certain to be long and there was no assurance that the extensive selling effort required would actually result in purchase orders. The licensing business would also hitch Virata to the DSL wagon, and it was by no means clear that DSL would win the battle with other competing technologies.

> **❝ Virata's better mousetrap would lose ❞**

Cotton and Cooper, however, were of the mind that Ethernet was going to win the battles *and* the war for networks, and that ATM – Virata's better mousetrap – would lose. Licensing looked to them like the better bet. The debates over Virata's direction became increasingly divisive, and in September 1997, after only five months at the helm, the new CEO departed and Cotton was promoted into the position. As he saw it, the two-pronged strategy was no longer tenable: 'We were straddling a chasm that was starting to widen. Sooner or later we had to jump to one side, otherwise we risked falling into the chasm never to recover.'[7] His first move was to dismiss Virata's entire networking product sales staff. The house would be bet on DSL.

The new direction required that Virata would have to develop new capabilities in chip design. It also meant that Virata's customer base would shrink sharply in number, as it focused its efforts on large OEMs. By 1998, three customers accounted for 40 per cent of Virata's revenues, and its total customer base numbered less than 20. The long sales cycle also meant that cash losses continued.

A happy ending

Fortunately, there was not a day that passed in 1998 when someone wasn't reporting the red-hot growth of the Internet and its follow-on effect for broadband access. The Internet frenzy enabled Virata to raise, with the help of Index Securities, a Swiss investment bank, another $31 million from existing and new investors to fund the company until a planned public offering in 1999. In November 1999, with Virata showing growth in the licensing business – no profits just yet, however, but declining losses – Virata shares started trading at $14 on NASDAQ and jumped to $27 by the end of the first day. Broadband access and the Internet were hot. Virata's technology was playing a key role, and technology investors wanted to get on board. By early 2000, Virata's share price reached $100.

In the year after its IPO, in an effort to broaden its market and its technology base, Virata made four acquisitions. In doing so, it soon became evident that Virata was headed for a competitive collision with Globespan, an American fabless semiconductor company with a similar strategy. In December 2001, the two companies merged to create the world's leading provider of integrated circuits, software and systems designs for DSL providers.[8]

What endowed Virata's long struggle with its happy ending? To be sure, the coming of the Internet age had a lot to do with it. Hermann Hauser's ability to raise a sorely needed $10 million from Larry Ellison in a 30-minute meeting didn't hurt either. But, as Hauser recalled, 'Without a doubt, the thing that carried us through was the quality of the team and all of its connections.' When Cooper told the story about Alcatel's interest in the Virata technology at a board meeting, 'The board seized upon the story and talked to some people that they knew. It turned out that the board had spotted an early trend, and this is where we made all of our money.'[9]

Virata's connections mattered. Call it luck or serendipity if you like. But Tom Cooper's connections down the value chain to potential customers in markets not then being served led to the Alcatel enquiry. The board's connections up and across the value chain – to suppliers and other players in related industries who could confirm what was happening with DSL – enabled Virata to place a very risky bet with more confidence than would otherwise have been possible. It's been said that lady luck comes to the well-prepared. As we've now seen, she also comes to the well-connected.

❝ lady luck comes to the well-connected ❞

Digital Equipment Corporation: missing the boat[10]

'Customers don't want a computer that sits on a desk. Customers want computers that sit on the floor.'[11] That's what Ken Olsen, co-founder of Digital Equipment Corp (DEC), said in a speech in the late 1970s. Most of us, of course, now have computers on our desks, with processing power that surpasses DEC's computers that sat on floors at that time. And DEC itself and most DEC computers are long gone, having been replaced in the 1980s and 1990s by PCs and servers from the likes of Dell, HP and Sun.

DEC founders Ken Olsen and Harlan Anderson set out in the late 1950s to provide functionality similar to large mainframe computers – mostly IBMs, in those days – but in a smaller, more bare-bones machine. In 1959, the company came out with its first computer – the Programmed Data Processor (PDP-1). Olsen described this computer as a console 'with all the instruments and lights, very much like you see in a power plant'.[12] The PDP-1 cost the customer $125,000–$150,000. By 1965, DEC had sales of $6.5 million, with profits of $807,000.

In 1966, DEC started selling the PDP-8. While considerably less expensive than its predecessor, each of these machines still sold for $18,000. DEC marketed the PDP-8, with its high-quality video display terminal, to businesses, universities, newspaper offices and publishers. It was also a particularly attractive computer for third parties who bought the PDP-8 machine from DEC, customized the hardware and software to meet the needs of their customers, and sold the enhanced computer as their own product. DEC's third-party business soon accounted for 50 per cent of its sales. By 1970, DEC was the most successful minicomputer manufacturer in the world.

Through the early 1970s, DEC remained a leader in the minicomputer industry. Olsen said, 'For many years we made the same two computers, the PDP-8 and the PDP-11. We kept that design consistently so that software the customers wrote would continue to work on newer models and the software we wrote would continue to work and get more and more robust.'[13]

Quite deliberately, rather than join the competition for the PC market as it emerged in the late 1970s, DEC avoided it and concentrated on networking issues: 'We made some PCs designed to be part of the networking but the general PC market was not for us. There were too many people in it . . . You could build them in your basement. That was not for us.'[14] The VAX was DEC's product line that offered networking capability. It connected several minicomputers in a LAN. One of the company's most popular networking products, the VAX 8600, allowed a system of minicomputers to function like a mainframe. But targeting the mainframe market, with its sales trend heading south, flew in the face of the rapid growth in the capability of PCs.

Finally, in 1980, DEC did begin developing personal computers, but Olsen insisted that the new machine be called an 'application terminal and small system' rather than a PC.[15] 'We believe in PCs. We encourage them. We network them. We use them in large numbers. But we still believe that most people in an organization want terminals. With terminals you don't have to worry about data management, you don't have to worry about floppy disks. You just sit down and it does the work for you automatically.'[16]

DEC's late decision to enter the PC market, and to enter with three different product lines (Rainbow, Pro and DECmate), proved both confusing and damaging. In 1984, the effects began to show. In the third quarter of that year, earnings were down 72 per cent from the previous year. And that was only the beginning.

In 1988, Sun Microsystems introduced computers that ran the UNIX operating system. Hewlett-Packard soon followed with its own UNIX-based Apollo computers. All these systems had far more computing power than DEC's minicomputers and were much less expensive. Moreover, they ran on UNIX, which was rapidly becoming the de facto standard in operating systems, thereby encouraging third parties to write innovative software that would run on these platforms. Ironically, much of the UNIX software was developed on DEC machines. DEC, however, had been doing so well with its proprietary VMS operating system that it gave its UNIX offering little support. As UNIX took hold, no longer were DEC's minicomputers, with their proprietary operating system, the best alternative. They were no longer in the race.

By the dawn of the 1990s, DEC found itself in dire trouble. Tens of thousands of employees' jobs were lost. By 1994 DEC, once 126,000 people strong, was a company of only 63,000. Finally in 1998, DEC, by then no longer a computer maker, was sold to Compaq.

What did DEC miss?

There were many things that DEC did right in its heyday. It fared well for a quarter of a century – a veritable eternity in the high-tech industry. And, while it did post some impressive financial results along the way, it was plagued repeatedly by an inability to stay in front of the technology curve, missing the mark on some sweeping trends.

> **" it was plagued repeatedly by an inability to stay in front of the technology curve "**

In the late 1960s, a group of DEC engineers led by Ed de Castro was assigned the task of designing a 16-bit computer that would replace the then-current 8-bit technology. Their final plan contained a basic 16-bit system that could be grown to 32 bits as well as a series of compatible products that would allow users to upgrade their existing machines rather than replace them. But what de Castro's group was suggesting amounted to scrapping the entire DEC product line and replacing it with the new 16-bit machines. DEC's management soundly rejected it. So in April 1968, de Castro and two other engineers left DEC, raised their own venture capital and started their own company, Data General Corporation, to produce 32-bit computers. By 1969, Data General was one of the hottest new companies in minicomputer manufacturing, tapping a market that could have been DEC's.

Then in 1972, a DEC team working on the PDP-11 recommended that DEC develop a product that combined a computer (the PDP-11/20) with a terminal and a printer. According to the PDP-11 group, this 'Datacenter' would appeal to a broad market of individual users, including scientists, technicians and others in administrative positions. DEC's leadership rejected this individual computer idea. Had DEC pursued the datacenter, could it have been the PC pioneer? We'll never know.

By 1980, with Apple and other personal computers beginning to make waves, and a year before IBM's PC introduction, DEC's product managers, those individuals who face the customer, suggested that DEC begin to play in the personal computer space. Olsen and his team refused. The rest is history.

Why?

Why did DEC repeatedly miss key changes in its marketplace? It's difficult to know with certainty without having been in DEC's meetings or inside Ken Olsen's head. The contrast with Virata, however, is striking. Virata had extensive connections up, down and across its value chain. When Virata got new information, it fanned out its other connections to help it interpret what it had heard. DEC, too, may have had some of these connections, but if it did, its top management wasn't very good at listening to them or leveraging other connections to take advantage of the information those connections provided. DEC leadership, like the ostrich, had its head in the sand.

The vibrancy of DEC's connections was perhaps encumbered by DEC's focus on and belief in its own technology and its faith that its solutions were superior to others. 'They believed [their] operating system was simply the best and would remain so into the new millennium,' said Jean Micol, a former DEC marketing executive.[17] If this is the case, why bother to develop connections for keeping track of external developments? Call it corporate arrogance or simply naïveté. DEC missed 16-bit computing. It missed PCs – not once, but twice! It missed UNIX. And now DEC is gone.

> **❝ DEC leadership, like the ostrich, had its head in the sand ❞**

Markets and industries do change – especially high-tech ones. Success in changing markets requires well-developed connections to keep abreast of the changes, and it requires a top management team that's open-minded enough to consider changing course when conditions so indicate. Had Olsen spent time talking to and building a wider set of informational relationships

– with DEC's sales channel and distributors, with its OEM manufacturers, even with its own marketing department – then he would have heard the resounding push towards PCs in the early 1980s and towards UNIX in the late 1980s. Hindsight suggests that the DEC team simply wasn't up to this task. Are you?

What investors want to know

Connections up, down and across the value chain are important to investors for a variety of reasons. In the short term, your connections with potential customers, especially large or strategically significant ones, enhance the likelihood that your new venture will meet its revenue targets. Connections up the value chain – with suppliers – enhance the likelihood that your new venture will be able to obtain the inputs it needs at favourable costs and on favourable terms. Connections across your industry will enhance your understanding of the competitive situation that your venture will face, helping you differentiate and position your products in ways that will stand apart from those of your competitors. These short-run roles are important, and investors will want to know how your team measures up on such connections.

In the long term, however, the value of connections like these is more subtle, perhaps, but extremely important, especially in changing markets. Investors know from experience that most of the money they've made has been made from plan B, not from plan A. 'Surprises are not deviations from the path. Instead they are the norm, the flora and fauna of the [entrepreneurial] landscape, from which one learns to forge a path through the jungle', says Saras Sarasvathy,[18] based on her research into entrepreneurial decision-making. But there's a problem here, because when an investor decides to invest in your venture, they do not really know what plan B will look like. How can investors insure themselves against the risk that your plan A will not work and that you might not come up with a suitable plan B? The best answer? Your and your team's connections.

> **investors know from experience that most of the money they've made has been made from plan B, not from plan A**

Without such connections, you won't have the market and competitive information that you'll need to revise your strategy when the need arises, as Virata was able to do at a crucial juncture but as DEC was not. You won't be able to take advantage of a favourable change in market needs that could benefit your venture substantially. You won't have the ability to judge quickly – and quickly may be important – which of several alternatives to a failing plan A ought to be your plan B. These are crucial investor concerns that will influence their view of the attractiveness of your opportunity and your entrepreneurial team, because they reduce the risk that your venture will fail. These concerns should be of similar concern to you.

Lessons learned

The fact that connections matter will not surprise any astute entrepreneur. But some of the ways they matter, in both the short and long run, are issues to which many entrepreneurs give little thought. What can we learn from the Virata and DEC stories to help you assess your opportunity?

Lessons learned from Virata

Virata was fortunate that a confluence of technological trends created a market – telecom providers seeking to provide dial-up broadband access to their telephone customers – for which its technology happened to be extremely well suited. It's been said many times that luck can play an important role in entrepreneurial success. Being in the right place at the right time, as Virata was, can turn a struggling company into a blockbuster.

The lesson from Virata isn't, however, about luck. The lesson is that connections – the right kind of connections – can deliver to an entrepreneurial firm three important outcomes:

▓ identifying fortuitous trends or changes in the marketplace that the company might take advantage of;

▓ doing so early, before other would-be competitors can do so;

▓ obtaining a broad-based assessment of such a development, from a variety of perspectives outside the firm, in order that a decision to pursue it can be an evidence-based one rather than a risky guess.

What kind of connections will your venture want to have?

▓ Connections *up* the value chain to suppliers who deal with the leaders in your industry and with firms in other industries that might serve as substitutes for the products you provide.

▓ Connections *down* the value chain to potential customers in target markets that you might serve one day in addition to the markets you plan to target at the outset.

- Connections *across* your industry with competitors – and with firms from other industries that offer substitutes – so that you can gain some perspective to gauge accurately changes in market conditions. When your sales increase, it's good to know if they are doing so because you are gaining market share or if you are simply benefiting from a rising tide that floats all boats. The same is true when your sales are soft.

Connections across your industry also help you understand its CSFs, an important issue in helping you assemble an entrepreneurial team that can deliver the kind of performance you and your investors seek. These connections can also identify and build relationships with skilled people who know your industry and whom – now or later – you may wish to attract to your company.

Lessons learned from DEC

As we have seen, DEC failed to adapt to trend after trend in the computing industry: 16-bit computing, the rise of PCs and UNIX. The problem for DEC was not that they had no connections or that no one in DEC saw these things happening. Indeed, some did. Of the three outcomes listed above that the right kind of connections can deliver for an entrepreneurial firm, DEC's difficulties seemed to be with the third issue, i.e. obtaining a broad-based assessment of these developments from a variety of perspectives outside the firm. As a result, DEC's decisions not to pursue these developments in a timely and aggressive manner appeared to have been based on DEC's blind faith in its own products and solutions – arrogantly and naïvely, some would say – rather than on the basis of the marketplace evidence that was there to be seen and understood.

An inward-looking culture, especially in a rapidly changing industry like computing, adds additional risk to what we've seen is an always-risky game of entrepreneurship. As Andy Grove,[19] long-time CEO of Intel, wrote, 'only the paranoid survive'. The same is true for those assessing new opportunities. Yes, this means *you*. Being inward-looking, focused on your *idea* rather than on the market and industry where it might take root, and focused on building the right team to help you achieve your dreams, is a pathway to impending disaster. Having a broad set of the right kinds of connections – *who* you and your team know – does matter, not only in running your business once it starts, but much earlier as well, in assessing and shaping your opportunity and developing your business plan. Don't go too far without them. Entrepreneurial success is not just about *what* you know. It's about *who* you know and your ability to use your network productively.

The new business road test: stage seven – the connectedness test

■ Who do you and your team know *up* the value chain in the companies that are likely suppliers to your proposed business and to your competitors? In suppliers to companies in other industries that offer substitute products for yours? Be sure you have names, titles and contact info.

■ Who do you and your team know *down* the value chain among distributors and customers you will target, both today and tomorrow? Names, titles and contact info., please.

■ Who do you and your team know *across* the value chain among your competitors and substitutes? Names, titles and contact info., please.

9

Putting the seven domains to work to develop your opportunity

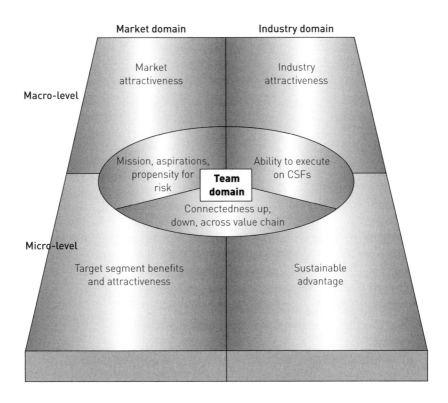

Market domain   Industry domain

Macro-level

Market attractiveness

Industry attractiveness

Mission, aspirations, propensity for risk

Team domain

Ability to execute on CSFs

Connectedness up, down, across value chain

Micro-level

Target segment benefits and attractiveness

Sustainable advantage

It's not simply a checklist

A moment's insight is sometimes worth a life's experience.

Writer Oliver Wendell Holmes (1809–94)[1]

We've now explored all seven of the domains in the model. If you already have in mind an opportunity that you might pursue, then you've probably considered how well it fares in each of the seven domains as you've been reading this book. Most likely, your idea fared well in some domains and not so well in others. What should you make of this result? How should you interpret what you learn about your opportunity as a result of a seven domains analysis?

> **using the model is not a simple matter of constructing a scoresheet**

In this chapter, we address the practical realities of working with the seven domains model. As we pointed out in Chapter 1, using the model is not a simple matter of constructing a scoresheet that adds up the scores for the seven domains, because they interact and their relative importance can vary. Thus, a simple checklist will not suffice. The wrong combination of factors can kill your new venture, and enough strength on some factors can mitigate weaknesses on others.

To help you interpret the results of your seven domains analysis, we first examine the extent to which highly attractive or unattractive conditions in any of the seven domains can make or break a deal. Next, we look at situations where things on the surface don't look so attractive, but where committed and insightful entrepreneurs can 'make lemons into lemonade'. It's important to know the circumstances under which not-so-perfect opportunities can still be attractive. We then examine situations that are likely to be favourable for niche-market entrepreneurs who seek to start businesses having modest aspirations. Finally, we identify five common traps entrepreneurs should avoid, where entrepreneurs before you have been led unwarily down a primrose path to disaster.

As is the pattern throughout this book, we close the chapter with some key things that investors look for – issues that reach across the seven domains, including some red flags that can be the kiss of death if you don't address them carefully. Then we identify several final lessons learned.

Why will or won't this work?

In Chapter 1, we raised a simple but all-important question that the best entrepreneurs ask regularly about their opportunity: 'Why will or won't this work?' Now that you understand the seven domains, it's time to apply this model. One way to use the seven domains framework would be to score your opportunity – say, from one to ten on the seven domains – and add up your opportunity's score, with 70 being perfect. But that's not exactly what I suggest you

> ❝ this is the 'moment's insight' that could make your life's experience! ❞

do. Score them, but don't add them up. (Actually, you should score only six of them – you can skip the mission domain, for it's not really something to score.) Instead, do the following.

1 Consider your mission, aspirations and propensity for risk, so you'll know what sort of opportunity you are looking for. Take another look at the test at the end of Chapter 6 as you do so.

2 Look for the one (there may be more, but it's unlikely) domain where your opportunity's score is off the charts – a 12 on a 10-point scale. If you find one or two of these scores located in certain sectors of the model (see below), then you may have a high-potential opportunity. This is the 'moment's insight' that could make your life's experience! If you are looking for a niche business, one that can fly under the competitors' radar, then this criterion is not so critical. We address what niche opportunities require later in this chapter.

3 Look for any domain where your score is low – say, below five or six on a 10-point scale. Then, using what you'll learn in this chapter, ask yourself whether a strong score in another sector effectively mitigates this problem. If so, that too can be another 'moment's insight' on which the feasibility of your opportunity is based. If not, then you'll

have discovered that your opportunity needs more work. In this case, you'll need to put some effort into further developing and reshaping your opportunity, because you don't want to go to investors – nor to market – with a crucial flaw in your opportunity. If you can't mitigate this score by reshaping your opportunity, then perhaps you should abandon it now and move on to something more attractive. Finding your Achilles' heel *before* you write your business plan is not a bad outcome.

4   For the other domains with more intermediate scores, use what you'll learn in this chapter about how the domains work together to see whether some further shaping may be required for these reasons.

Deal makers, deal breakers

In what domains can a sufficiently high score – a 10, or even 12, on a 10-point scale – make an opportunity a winner, regardless of scores in the other domains? Let's consider them.

■ *Macro-market*, in the upper left corner: as we'll see later in this chapter, the large market fallacy shows that a winning score here is not sufficient alone. Large and growing markets are, by themselves, *never* sufficient reason to pursue any opportunity.

■ *Micro-market*, in the lower left corner: for a niche-market opportunity, a strong score here may be all that it takes. For a high-potential proposal to win venture capital backing, a strong score here is necessary but by no means sufficient. A strong team is also essential, as is either an attractive industry at the macro-level or a source of sustainable advantage at the micro-level.

■ *Macro-industry*, in the upper right corner: if an industry is overwhelmingly attractive – though few really are – in which nearly all players are successful, then a high score here may suffice for a niche market venture, even if scores at the micro-level are not all that strong or the team isn't stellar. To win venture capital funding, however, a me-too venture in a good industry won't cut it. The attractiveness of the industry will need to be supplemented by differentiated benefits (micro-level, lower left corner) and by a strong entrepreneurial team.

■ *Micro-industry*, in the lower right corner: the ability to sustain one's advantage is important, of course, but only if that advantage is sufficient to start with. Thus, a strong score here is good news, but only if the customer benefits – in the lower left corner – are sufficiently differentiated and attractive to be of value over the longer term.

- The team's *Mission, aspirations and propensity for risk*: this team sector isn't one to score. Rather, it acts as a screen to see whether a particular opportunity fits with what the members of your entrepreneurial team – as well as investors – seek.

- The team's *Ability to execute on* the industry's *CSFs*, the team's *Connectedness up, down and across the value chain*: as we'll see later in the 'hubris trap', having done it before is no assurance of successfully doing it again. Louis Borders did very well building Borders books into a retailing giant, but Webvan, his next venture, had quite a different outcome. As the noted investor Warren Buffett said in opening Chapter 4, 'When a management with a reputation for brilliance takes on a business with a reputation for bad economics, it's the reputation of the business that remains intact.'[2] Thus it takes more than a good team. It takes strong scores on some combination of the market and industry domains.

So, is there any single domain where a strong score can, by itself, be a deal maker? From the discussion above, the answer is clear. No! Unfortunately, while an outstanding score in just one domain can take you a long way and can mitigate against weaknesses elsewhere, with the exception of small, niche or 'lifestyle' businesses in extremely attractive industries, a single high-scoring domain will never be a deal maker on its own.

However, given the long odds against entrepreneurial success, it will come as no surprise that a poor score in certain domains can be enough to kill your new venture before it even gets off the ground. So, what are the domains of certain death, where a weak score becomes a deal breaker on its own? Let's examine the options.

- *Macro-market*, in the upper left corner: a weak score here need not be a problem. Innovation in stagnant markets – Nike and Starbucks are just two striking examples we've seen in earlier chapters – can overcome this weakness.

- *Micro-market*, in the lower left corner: this one's a deal breaker. If your opportunity offers no clear benefits, if it's not differentiated from what's already in the market and if you cannot find a way to reshape it to resolve these shortcomings, then put it aside and move on to another more attractive opportunity. The only exception is where the industry is overwhelmingly attractive and you seek to build a small niche-market business, in which case you might just stand a chance. The micro-market domain is the first and most important test among the seven domains, and it's why I began the book's seven domains journey with its chapter.

■ *Macro-industry*, in the upper right corner: not a deal breaker. Good opportunities can be found in unattractive industries, as we'll see with the examples of Zara, Wal-Mart and Gap later in this chapter. They and others have done well in retailing, one of the least attractive industries around. The keys to success in unattractive industries are found at the micro-level, through careful targeting, delivering differentiated benefits and building complex, hard-to-imitate processes that can provide a basis for sustainable advantage.

■ *Micro-industry*, in the lower right corner: what if you've got an otherwise attractive opportunity, but there's no patent protection and no way to build superior processes and capabilities that competitors can't match? Should this shortcoming alone scare you off? Not necessarily, but it will raise the bar for what you must accomplish as your venture grows. This is the classic tale of first-mover advantage. If you are able to continue to innovate to stay ahead of later entrants, or build a strong enough reputation that wins customer loyalty, you can still win. eBay continues to dominate the online auction industry despite competition from QXL, Amazon and others. So, innovating to retain product leadership and establishing and retaining a loyal customer base are two ways to cope with shortcomings here. A third way to cope with shortcomings in this area is simply to plan to sell your business before others catch up. Thus, a poor score on the sustainability of your advantage is not necessarily a deal breaker.

■ The team's *Mission, aspirations and propensity for risk*: as was noted for deal makers, this team sector isn't one to score. These issues by themselves won't kill your deal. But if your mission, aspirations or propensity for risk are not aligned with those of the investors you seek or with the level of resources you will need, then your chances of obtaining venture capital will be nil. We'll address this issue later in this chapter.

■ The team's *Ability to execute on* the industry's *CSFs*: if you and your team cannot show that you can execute, then you'll have difficulty raising capital, although if you can somehow get started and your execution skills pan out, you may well be successful. The only exception is during cyclical peaks in the capital markets – like the one that created the dot.com bubble – when almost anyone with a pen and a cocktail napkin could raise new venture finance.

One attractive option for would-be entrepreneurs whose ability to execute is not proven is to buy a franchise business, where the franchisor's systems, support and brand awareness may compensate for your inexperience or shortcomings. If in reality, though, you don't have and cannot learn what it takes to execute in the industry you choose, then even a franchise system may not make you successful. The ability to execute is crucial.

■ The team's *Connectedness up, down and across the value chain*: is this a deal breaker? Not likely, by itself. Where this factor is most useful is in generating early sales and in seeing market signals that may indicate a need to change course, as we saw in the Virata case history. Thus, not having useful connections is a risk factor, but it won't break your deal. This is also an area where investors often bring more than just money. Their connections can make up for those you lack.

So, to summarize, which are the deal breakers for low scores on just one of the seven domains?

■ *Micro-market*, in the lower left corner. If your opportunity does not provide a differentiated solution to a customer's pain – better, faster or cheaper – forget it and move on to something else. Life is simply too short to be a me-too entrepreneur.

■ Your *Ability to execute on CSFs*, in the upper right third of the circle. If you cannot deliver results, then becoming an entrepreneur is not for you!

Making lemons into lemonade

Some opportunities look unappealing on one or more of the seven domains, but they may nevertheless be attractive to certain entrepreneurs, given the presence of either:

■ sufficient innovation to cause a stagnant market to grow substantially;

■ differentiation that is either proprietary or complex enough to provide sustainable advantage in spite of unfavourable industry conditions.

Sufficient strength in these micro-level domains – especially when combined with a strong, well-connected team – can offset weakness on the macro-level factors. Let's consider some examples.

Product innovation in stagnant markets

As we saw in Chapter 2, Phil Knight's passion for building a better athletic shoe, combined with his company's ability to differentiate its shoes on a segment-by-segment basis through product design and effective marketing, eventually made Nike a household name and one of the world's best-known brands.

Even more, it turned the previously boring athletic shoe market into a growth machine. What Nike took advantage of – in the lower left corner of the seven domains model – was an opportunity so compelling, in terms of customer benefits (both tangible and psychological, as the Nike brand developed), that the benefits of building a better product (and doing better marketing) outweighed the then-stagnant market conditions, measured in macro-terms.

> **❝ compelling customer benefits can provide sufficient reason to proceed on an opportunity whose market looks otherwise unattractive ❞**

Compelling customer benefits like Nike's can provide sufficient reason to proceed on an opportunity whose market looks otherwise unattractive. Another such example is Starbucks, where Howard Schultz's insights into why customers might welcome a lively respite where they could enjoy better coffee led to unabated growth for 20 years, in spite of the fact that American coffee consumption had been declining in pre-Starbucks days. Here, innovation that produced an enjoyable customer experience and a better product, combined with effective execution, offset what might have appeared in the 1970s to be an unattractive market. Starbucks, by selling an experience has achieved spectacular and very profitable growth.

Differentiation and careful market targeting in unattractive industries

A five forces analysis of the retailing industry would show that retailing is an unlikely setting in which to build a high-growth enterprise able to withstand imitation over the long term. Barriers to entry are simply too low, affording easy entry to imitators; supplier power, at least at the outset for a new entrant, is typically high; and consumers usually have many choices of where to shop. This unfavourable industry structure is reflected in average industry profitability that ranks far lower than that of many other more attractive industries.

Zara, Wal-Mart and numerous others, however, have managed to build profitable, growing retail businesses whose competitive advantage has lasted, in spite of these unfavourable industry conditions. What did they see in the opportunities they pursued? Fundamentally, they saw opportunities to build competitive advantages – advantages that benefited customers and proved to be sustainable – over other retailers.

Zara, the Spanish apparel retailer with stores throughout Europe and elsewhere, offered classic styles of clothing in high-street locations at very competitive prices. By keeping its range of apparel limited and its supply chain short, Zara was able to achieve buying and operating efficiencies that it could pass on to consumers in lower prices.

In Wal-Mart's case, Sam Walton saw an opportunity to extend discount retailing to the small towns and cities of rural America and offer vastly superior selection at sharply lower prices than small-town, main-street merchants were able to offer. Unfortunately for the main-street merchants, Wal-Mart's relentless efficiency drove many of them out of business. This competitive advantage became sustainable over time, as Wal-Mart built complex, hard-to-imitate information and distribution capabilities (real-time sales data transmitted daily to headquarters via satellite, and low-cost, cross-dock merchandise handling in its distribution centres, to name just two) that made it among the most efficient of retailers.

Gap, seeing growing demand for Levi's jeans and other casual clothing in the early 1970s, identified an opportunity to base its competitive advantage on superior systems that ensured an in-stock position every day on the wide selection of sizes and styles Levi offered.

&& the combination of three factors enabled these retailers to create successful entrepreneurial ventures 🗦🗦

This was what customers wanted but did not reliably get from other retailers. In the 1990s, Gap's transformation into a prominent global brand and fashion leader changed the basis of its customer proposition. However, having the right fashions, in the right colours, at the right time in each market – Gap's apparent strategy at the turn of the millennium – is a far riskier and easier-to-imitate game to play than Gap's original one. Its inability to make the right fashion decisions from 1999 to 2002 led to a significant downturn in its performance.[3] In 2009, Gap was still struggling to get back on course.

Notwithstanding Gap's recent troubles, it was the combination of three factors – genuine benefits to customers, clear differentiation for competitive advantage and teams that could deliver results – that enabled these retailers and others like them in other merchandise categories to create successful entrepreneurial ventures in an otherwise daunting industry context. All three companies grew successfully for long periods of time. Thus, unfavourable industries – at the macro-level – need not be deal-killers, provided other pieces of the puzzle are strong enough.

Opportunities for niche-market entrepreneurs

Not all entrepreneurs want to make their businesses large ones. Not all entrepreneurs want to exit. Many prefer to operate the business for many years or pass it on to subsequent generations of family or management. Local car dealers, small manufacturing firms, some franchised businesses and other businesses in fragmented industries or very small markets are examples. Can the seven domains model help these entrepreneurs assess and shape their opportunities?

> **❝ not all entrepreneurs want to make their businesses large ones ❞**

Commonly, when such businesses are successful, it is partly because they fly below the radar of larger, more established firms, and target relatively small niche markets where larger companies choose not to compete. What makes a good opportunity for entrepreneurs having these kinds of objectives?

My research suggests that for those who want to build sustainable businesses of modest size, the macro-level factors aren't nearly as important as one particular micro-level factor: target segment benefits and attractiveness. If you can find a small market segment whose needs are not currently being served well, and – due to the sharply targeted nature of your business – you can deliver the benefits these customers need in a superior fashion, then that may be all you need to succeed. Thus, compelling customer benefits and clear differentiation in a carefully targeted market segment – in the lower left quadrant in the seven domains model – are the keys to assessing these kinds of opportunities.

Sometimes, as time unfolds, such niche businesses can grow into very large ones. Enterprise Car Rental, which focused for years on the neighbourhood market as opposed to business travellers, is an example of one such business that grew relatively slowly but quite persistently. Surprisingly to some, it's now the largest car rental company in the world, in spite of the modest early objectives of its founders.

Five common traps to avoid

In this section, we identify five common traps – common opportunity patterns revealed by my research – that look attractive by some criteria but often are fundamentally flawed.

Trap 1: the large market fallacy

Investors often hear entrepreneurs say something like this: 'My market is huge. If I get just 10 per cent of it (or 5 or even 1 per cent), we'll all be rich!' The problem with large markets, especially large markets that are growing

❝ the problem with large markets is that others like them too ❞

fast, is that others like them too. Large markets attract competitors, often large established ones with deep pockets. Such markets can be very difficult places for entrepreneurs to play, especially in industries where the threat of entry is high. Equally importantly, if your product doesn't offer genuine benefits to your targeted consumers, then the largest market in the world will not save your business. Thus, serving a large market offers no assurance of entrepreneurial success.

For example, nearly two decades ago, Nestlé's refrigerated foods division examined the American market for pizza, worth $18 billion at the time. They decided to enter this huge market with a refrigerated pizza product sold in supermarkets; they needed less than three-tenths of 1 per cent of the market to be successful.[4] Their entry failed. Why? Fresh-baked pizza, delivered to their homes for an easy family meal, was seen by consumers as superior in taste and was no more expensive than Nestlé's pizza. It was convenient too. Cheaper frozen pizza was adequate for a fast meal for the kids. Nestlé's refrigerated product offered no clear benefits to either market segment.

What's the lesson for avoiding this trap? For entrepreneurs, large markets are good news only when their offering delivers genuine benefits for some segment thereof. For new ventures serving large markets, it's generally far better to pursue a large share of a small but carefully targeted segment rather than a small share of the overall market. Nestlé failed to do that with its refrigerated pizza entry. In large markets, targeting is crucial. If entry into the initial segment provides entry to other segments later, so much the better.

Trap 2: the better mousetrap fallacy

Especially in technologically driven industries, entrepreneurs often try to capitalize on technology for its own sake. Doing so rather than asking what the technology can do that benefits some target segment of customers is a trap. Better technology – a better mousetrap – does not necessarily equal a better solution for the customer. The key question for technology entrepreneurs, where there's typically uncertain demand for the technology, is 'Who wants it and why?' Nestlé, as the story above shows, fell into this trap. Thus, the trap can occur in the low-tech world and in smaller markets too.

In 1999, a British start-up called Navigation Zone[5] had developed a novel and patented method for searching and navigating very large websites. The

> **who wants it and why?**

market for search engines and Web navigation tools was large and growing rapidly, and the company was readily able to raise seed funding. A year after funding, the company had still not made any sales, and the money was running out. Crucially, the company had not identified exactly who wanted what they had to offer. Was it site owners, other search engine suppliers, or developers? While they had developed a technology that demonstrated small but real improvements over existing approaches, the gain was not sufficient to warrant any potential customer changing his or her current buying behaviour. The company was forced to downsize and survived only by refocusing entirely on the site developer market with a specific tool that improved the site developer's productivity by a factor of two.

How can you best avoid this trap, especially if your opportunity is technology-based? Re-read the case histories of OurBeginning.com in Chapter 2, Palm Computing in Chapter 7, and Virata and DEC in Chapter 8. Remind yourself that entrepreneurial success is not about you and your technology. It's about identifying the right customers and using technology to satisfy their needs.

Trap 3: the no sustainable business model trap

Many failures in the dot.com bust had business models that were simply unsustainable. We've already seen the example of Webvan in Chapter 5. Pet supply e-tailers were another example.[6] While large, attractive markets of pet owners and compelling customer benefits were present (who likes carrying heavy bags of dog food home from the store?), the raw economics of acquiring new customers and shipping dog food one bag at a time were simply unsustainable. Put another way, the relationship between the two micro-level factors, i.e. benefits for which a group of target customers are willing to pay and a cost structure that makes the intended product or service economically viable, must be sustainable. If not, the business will not last long, as we saw in the demise of most pet supply e-tailers in 2000.

How might you avoid this trap? Build your network so you understand your industry and its economics. Then do the mathematics on your opportunity. Grand concepts are no substitute for running the numbers, including those specified in Chapter 5 in the lower right corner of the seven domains model.

Trap 4: the me-too trap

The combination of high threat of entry (a macro-level industry factor) and lack of sustainable advantage for new entrants (a micro-level industry factor) can cause a large number of competitors to pursue an opportunity, only to be winnowed in a hurry. In the early days of the Winchester disk drive industry, for example, so many me-too entrants entered the industry that capacity of more than 40 times the total market size was funded by venture capital investors.[7] Thus, the combination of low barriers to entry (revealed in the upper right corner of our model) and a lack of sustainable advantage (lower right corner) should be a red flag to would-be entrepreneurs. The only ones who should tolerate this combination are niche-market entrepreneurs who can fly below the competitors' radar.

> **the combination of low barriers to entry and a lack of sustainable advantage should be a red flag**

How to avoid this trap? This one's easy. If barriers to entry are low and you have nothing on which to sustain your initial advantage, stop before you start. If you've already started, sell now, unless you are happy to run a niche-market business that does not compete with the big guys. That's what Jack and Andy Taylor did in starting Enterprise Car Rental. Hertz, Avis and the others couldn't be bothered with the neighbourhood segment, and the Taylors had it almost entirely to themselves.

Trap 5: the hubris trap

Some people build careers as serial entrepreneurs. They start venture after venture, seemingly always successfully. Those who are successful usually succeed by choosing opportunities without crucial flaws and by executing effectively. In Chapter 2, however, we saw Michael Budowski, a successful entrepreneur in his previous ventures, stumble with OurBeginning.com. Louis Borders stumbled with Webvan, in spite of his earlier success in bookstores, as we saw in Chapter 5.

> **having done it before does not obviate the need for attention to the seven domains**

How can you avoid this one, if you've already done it before? Having done it before is a great advantage when it comes to fund-raising, but it does not obviate the need for attention to the seven domains. Don't rest on your laurels. Do your homework. Even you are not invincible!

What investors look for

❝ professional investors do make mistakes ❞

Professional investors – those who invest for reasons other than that they love you – understand intuitively the seven domains, even though they, like entrepreneurs and the rest of us, do make mistakes.

■ They confuse markets and industries, mistaking the attractiveness of one for the attractiveness of the other.

■ They overlook the distinctions between the macro- and micro-levels. Like lemmings, they sometimes follow one another into large and growing markets, falling into the large market fallacy.

■ They fail to ensure that what their portfolio companies bring to market offers clear and differentiated customer benefits – falling into the better mousetrap trap.

■ They forget to examine whether the initial advantage brought by those benefits can be protected and/or sustained.

■ They mistake personality, chemistry or a few lines on a CV for an entrepreneur's ability to execute on the CSFs. They fail to determine an entrepreneur's connections, or lack thereof, up, down and across the value chain.

In short, professional investors, like the rest of us, are human. Nonetheless, professional investors – angels and venture capitalists – do know what they want in the deals they back. In general, they like to see:

■ large, growing markets supported by favourable macro-trends;

■ attractive, competitively forgiving industries – four or five favourable forces;

■ market offerings that resolve real customer pain, by delivering clear and differentiated benefits not available elsewhere;

■ innovations that can be defended over time through patents or superior organizational processes and capabilities, having economically viable business models;

■ entrepreneurial teams whose missions, aspirations and propensities for risk are compatible with their own;

■ entrepreneurial teams who can execute on their industry's CSFs;

■ teams well connected up, down and across the value chain.

Can they have it all in any particular deal? Exceedingly rarely, otherwise their success rates on individual investments would be far higher than the one or two in ten that most venture capital portfolios achieve. So, what do they do? They take risks in pursuit of greater rewards. They bet that a shortcoming on one domain or another will be compensated for by strength on another. That a strong enough team will meet the challenges that will inevitably be encountered. That others won't soon see the opportunity you and they see.

In contemplating these risks, however, investors have identified certain red flags or warning signs that tell them when the risks are too great, regardless of how exciting the opportunity's other elements may appear. They've done this the hard way, through unpleasant experience. Among these signs are the following.

> **investors have identified certain red flags**

- Lightweight (or even non-existent) market research. 'What are the customers saying?' asks Joseph Bartlett, a partner at Morrison and Foerster LLP. 'This kind of interchange has no substitute; it has to happen before you solicit money from venture capitalists.'[8] True, there were a couple of years in the late 1990s when ideas scribbled on cocktail napkins somehow won funding. But those days are long gone.

- Better than market research, even, are hard data that customers have actually bought or will buy. Actual orders from a website, letters of intent or other indications of real demand are powerful testimony. What people say, in a market research setting, is not necessarily what they will do.

- Overly confident assessment of competition. 'It always puzzles me when I come across plans that claim they have no competition,' says Daniel Kim of Circle Group Internet.[9] Virtually every customer need is being satisfied presently, in some way, however imperfectly. Your competition may not look like you or what you plan to offer, but surely as day follows night, it's out there. If there's no competition, there's probably no market either!

Entrepreneurs who have carefully assessed the seven domains don't make the above mistakes because:

- the research has been carried out;

- evidence of genuine demand has been gathered;

- competition – direct competitors as well as substitutes – has been identified and assessed.

Thus, in dealing with investors, the seven domains framework gives you the tools to speak their language of risk and reward. It takes you beyond blind faith – that everything is wonderful about your opportunity – and enables you to understand deeply your opportunity, warts and all. It enables you to answer for prospective investors your two key questions, which happen to be their key questions, too.

- Why *will* this work? What are the one or perhaps two domains that lend to your opportunity a compellingly positive story?

- Why *won't* this work? Where do the risks lie, and what is there about your opportunity and your team that effectively mitigates them?

> **the seven domains analysis puts you and your investors on the same page**

In short, the seven domains analysis puts you and your investors on the same page. It aligns your perspectives. It gives you a common language with which to discuss and debate the merits and flaws that each of you sees in the opportunity you wish to pursue. And, as we'll see in the next chapter, it provides a solid, evidence-based foundation on which to build a compelling business plan.

Lessons learned

In this chapter, bringing together the seven domains, what additional lessons have we learned?

Not a checklist

As we've now seen, using the seven domains framework is not as simple as constructing a checklist and adding the scores. The seven domains work together in complex and sometimes surprising ways. Different entrepreneurs with different missions, aspirations and propensities

> **assessing and shaping a market opportunity is no simple task**

for risk will reach different conclusions about opportunities that may be quite similar in market and industry terms. This point has important implications for crafting your business plan, an implication we'll explore in the next chapter. It should now be clear, however, that assessing and shaping a market opportunity is no simple task. It takes thought, evidence, hard work and insight.

The all-important micro-level domains

It should also be clear by now that, of the four market and industry domains, the most important, by far, in assessing your opportunity are the two micro-level domains. The importance of understanding customer needs and shaping your opportunity so that your offering delivers valuable and differentiated benefits in a sustainable way is difficult to overstate. Unfortunately, though, in this Internet age, many aspiring entrepreneurs (I trust you are not among them!) won't get out of their chairs and away from their computer screens to talk first hand with prospective customers to uncover the real problems inherent in their opportunities and to work out in advance how to resolve them. We'll have more to say in Chapters 10, 11 and 15 about how to conduct the research you must do, but surfing the Web is only step one.

Management, management, management

As we've now seen, there's an element of truth in this adage, though making the case for what you bring to the entrepreneurial party isn't as simple as updating your CV and turning on your charm. The lead entrepreneur – and more importantly the entrepreneurial team as a whole – is important. Get the team right. Entrepreneurship, if you're playing to win, is a team sport.

Lessons for the family and friends of aspiring entrepreneurs

As we've now seen, while most professional investors understand intuitively the ideas inherent in the seven domains, it's true that most investors – like the rest of us – do make mistakes. They do so more often than most like to admit. In researching this book, I learned that most investors are hungry for ways to think more clearly about their investment decisions. The same is true for informal investors including the three Fs – family, friends, but no fools among you, having read this far.

Informal investors may also find the seven domains model useful for dispensing, along with money, another kind of love – tough love, as it's sometimes called. Your objective, independent and dispassionate questions and an occasional moment's insight – in the words of Oliver Wendell Holmes, who introduced this chapter – for the entrepreneur you love are always welcome.

10

What to do *before* you write your business plan

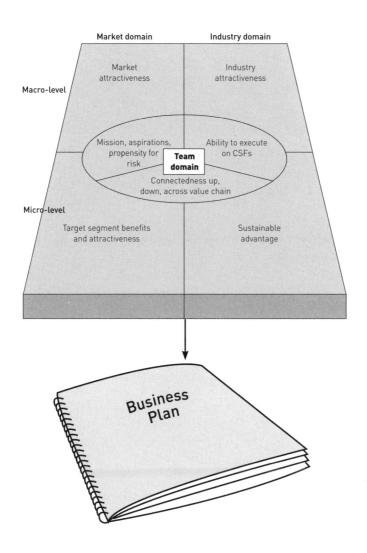

Why do most business plans not raise the money?

Never doubt that a small group of thoughtful, committed citizens can change the world®. Indeed it is the only thing that ever has.

Margaret Mead[1]

Planning is important. But results are what count. And who delivers the results? Entrepreneurs. Entrepreneurs like you can change the world. Why, then, is there so much fascination with business *plans* in today's entrepreneurship community? Why are there dozens of books with titles like *How to Write a Business Plan*? Why are there software packages to automate the business *planning* process? Why do most leading business schools offer courses in which teams of students write business *plans* for hypothetical or real new ventures? As we noted at the outset of this book, the vast majority of business *plans* are unsuccessful in raising any money. Of those ventures that do win financing, many if not most will fail. What's wrong with this picture?

At least three things are wrong here.

▓ First, most business plans are written for opportunities that are fundamentally flawed. Why write a business plan for a no-hope opportunity? It's a waste of entrepreneurial time and talent. *Your* time and talent. Instead, put your opportunity through a stringent new business road test by doing the seven domains homework. If necessary, reshape your opportunity or invest your time in finding a better one.

▓ Second, the inherently persuasive nature of business plans, a principal purpose of which is often to raise money, forces their proponent entrepreneurs into the 'everything about my opportunity is wonderful' mode. As we saw in Chapter 9, the likelihood – at least for attractive opportunities – is that everything is not wonderful but there are one or two things that are quite wonderful that outweigh those that are not.

The would-be entrepreneur who prepares and pitches an 'everything is wonderful' business plan – like the ones many books and software describe – risks their credibility with investors, who know the real risks that entrepreneurial ventures entail. This naïveté makes it harder, not easier, to raise the money that's needed. Worse, such a positive slant risks blinding the entrepreneur to the very real risks that may lie in wait in one or more of the seven domains (even though a risk section in the typical plan identifies what might go wrong and explains why it won't).

- Third, most business plans are focused on the entrepreneur, their idea and why the idea is wonderful. They are me-focused or my-idea-focused rather than customer-focused. People do matter – true – but investors don't really care very much about you and your idea, at least not at the beginning. What investors care about is solving significant customer problems or needs that offer significant profit and growth potential. If you have a solution to such a problem, then their ears will perk up. If you've shown that you can deliver results in solving this kind of problem, then you'll have their undivided attention. Thus, the importance of people lies in the context in which they operate. Set the context first. Let the people story – of you and your entrepreneurial team – close your sale.

So what should you do before you write your business plan?

- First, come up with an idea that you think might fly, one that solves genuine customer problems or needs.

- Second, assess and shape it, using the lessons of the seven domains framework with which you now are familiar. Doing so requires data, and lots of it, as we've seen.

- Third, write what I call a customer-driven feasibility study – a memo to yourself, really – that lays out the conclusions you've reached from your data and analysis.

Having taken these steps, you'll then be well prepared to write a truly great business plan, one that acknowledges the merits and shortcomings of your opportunity, develops a strategy and shows that your team is the right one to pursue it.

In this chapter, we cover the nitty-gritty how-to that completes the research foundation for these tasks, to prepare you to write that great business plan. First, we see where most great ideas for new ventures come from. Then we explore where and how you might best gather the data that your analysis requires, and we offer practical tips on how to conduct cost-effective research on your idea. We also examine the different approaches for tackling perhaps the toughest of your challenges – forecasting the demand you'll get for what you propose to sell. You'll need this forecast to craft your business plan. For the many entrepreneurs whose business plans are never funded, a whistle-in-the-wind forecast is what sends the ill-prepared business plan directly to the rubbish bin. Without a solid, evidence-based sales forecast, your business plan will be little more than a house of cards.

We bring these themes together, outline the customer-driven feasibility study and show how it's similar to and different from a business plan. The chapter then closes with a set of final thoughts.

▒ Why bother? Is it really worth all this trouble? Why shouldn't you simply get started on writing your business plan without all the feasibility fuss?

▒ Considering a business planning book? How should you choose a book to guide you in writing your business plan?

▒ Software or not? Should you use business plan software, or should you create your business plan from scratch?

▒ What will investors be looking for in *your* business plan?

Great opportunities – where do they come from?

Everyone who aspires to be an entrepreneur has ideas. For some, ideas arise on a daily basis. The real challenge, though, is to find *good* ideas. Good ideas are more than just ideas – they're opportunities. Where do great opportunities come from? How are they born? In the case histories in this book, we've seen four common patterns, patterns that you too can use to find your opportunity:

▒ opportunities created by macro-trends;

▒ opportunities found by living and experiencing the customer problem;

▒ opportunities created through scientific research;

▒ opportunities proven elsewhere that you can pursue where you hope to do business.

Opportunities created by macro-trends

We live in a changing world. Trends of all kinds are swirling around us every day. Studying these trends and anticipating their impact on the lives we live, on the industries where we work and on the markets we serve is a rich source of opportunities. In Chapter 2, we saw Miller identify social trends towards fitness coupled with the demographic trend that moved baby boomers through and beyond their early twenties beer-buying age. The result: Miller Lite. We saw iMode take advantage of developments in technology to offer new services that took Japanese mobile phone users by storm. In Chapters 3, 4, 7 and 8, we saw similar responses to macro-trends:

- Brijmohan Lall Munjal of Hero Honda saw the growing but still modest buying power that would fuel a growing need for motorized two-wheeled transportation in India;

- John Mackey of Whole Foods Market saw the trend towards health and nutrition that would spur rising demand for natural and organic foods;

- Roger Marino and Richard Egan of EMC saw that companies were moving away from mainframe computers to minicomputers, resulting in an increasingly decentralized minicomputer environment that would create customer needs for additional memory and, subsequently, data storage;

- the long line of innovative leaders at Nokia had a vision of the possibilities in mobile communications, which led them to the leading position among mobile phone manufacturers;

- Pierre Omidyar of eBay saw in 1995 the potential that something new called the Internet might hold for individuals who wanted to clear out their garages and attics – or at least trade their old stuff for other people's old stuff;

- the insight of Jeff Hawkins at Palm Computing into developments in pen-based computing technology led to the PDA, one of which – or a smartphone – is probably in your pocket right now;

- the connections of Hermann Hauser, Charles Cotton and the team at Virata enabled them to see that Virata's technology meshed nicely with the emergence of broadband communication.

Whether the trends are demographic, sociocultural, economic, technological, regulatory or natural, there's nothing more important for the creation of opportunities just waiting to be discovered by entrepreneurs. In the words of management guru Peter Drucker, 'The overwhelming majority of successful innovations exploit change.'[2] According to Drucker, identifying opportunities is about 'a systematic examination of the areas of change that typically offer opportunities'. And it's people – people like you – who spot them. If you want to find a good opportunity, study today's trends systematically, as Drucker suggests, and ask yourself how those trends will influence the life you and others lead, the markets you serve or the industry where you work.

Living and experiencing the customer's pain

Phil Knight and Bill Bowerman, Nike's founders, had lived the customer problem and felt the pain – literally. As distance runners themselves, they had subjected their bodies to mile after mile of feet meeting ground, suffering shin splints and sprained ankles that better shoes might have eliminated. Equally important, they had sometimes been edged out at the finish line, wondering whether lighter shoes might have given them a competitive edge. Knight and Bowerman knew first hand of these customer problems and were well placed to solve them.

66 fixing what's inadequate or broken is another rich source of opportunities for watchful entrepreneurs 99

If we think about it, most of us can also recognize opportunities where something can be improved – products, services, processes or whatever – in the lives we lead or the work we do. Fixing what's inadequate or broken is another rich source of opportunities for watchful entrepreneurs.

The fertile ground of scientific research

In many institutional settings – university research labs, industrial R&D groups and so on – extensive efforts are under way to create new knowledge that can, intentionally or otherwise, spawn commercially viable new products. That was the case for EMI, where Godfrey Hounsfield's research led to the breakthrough that made CAT scanning possible. The same was true for SmithKline Beecham's Zantac, developed through the extensive research for which the pharmaceutical industry is famous.

The challenge of turning basic scientific research into viable new ventures is the challenge we saw in Chapter 7 for turning new technology into viable products. Linking the promise of scientific discovery with genuine customer needs – sometimes latent ones – so that real customer problems are solved is the key. Unfortunately for consumers, research scientists often lack the market and industry understanding to identify the commercial applications that may be present in their science, and their principal interests sometimes lie more in the knowledge itself than in its commercial application. If you are – or know – a cutting-edge scientific researcher, then give some attention to how your – or their – research might solve some customer's problem.

It works in Italy – let's try it here

Starbucks' Howard Schultz didn't invent the espresso bar. The Italians did more than a century ago. Schultz was, however, alert enough to see the coffee bar culture in Italy and its societal role, and insightful enough to believe that it might translate well to American shores. Many opportunities, especially those of the niche variety, arise because an entrepreneur sees something new in one place and brings it home. Italian coffee bars were replicated in Seattle. European fashions hit Los Angeles. Cable television invaded Europe. QXL mimicked eBay in online auctions.

In a study of the fastest-growing companies in the USA, Amar Bhidé found that most of the founders simply replicated or modified an idea they encountered through previous employment or by accident.[3] Looking for opportunities in one place and bringing them home can be a great source of opportunities that are already market tested. And they're a great excuse for taking a holiday away!

But I'm not a market researcher – where should I start?

So, you've got an idea – a real opportunity, perhaps – and you've decided you'll assess it. But examining the seven domains seems daunting. Where should you start? First, give some thought to your mission, aspirations and propensity for risk. These factors will help you screen out lots of ideas that may not be right for you, given who you are and what you want to achieve. Once that's done, the market and industry domains are the first to address – since knowing something about market and industry attractiveness tells you a lot about how differentiated your solution must be, and how important it is that your advantage be sustainable.

The fastest way up the market and industry learning curve is to use what market researchers call secondary data – data that someone else has already collected and reported. All you have to do is find the data. There are three good places to look:

- trade magazines and trade associations for your industry, usually the most direct route to relevant information;
- business libraries with a helpful librarian;
- the Internet.

Secondary data are usually readily available and sufficient to assess quickly, at least in a preliminary sense, the macro-level domains – overall market and industry attractiveness. The questions your secondary data need to answer are those detailed in Chapters 3 and 4. Secondary data can also usually tell you about competitors and substitutes, so you'll gain some idea about whether someone else is already doing what you propose to do.

If the secondary data don't kill your idea, the next step is to collect primary data that can answer the remaining questions to fill any gaps in your macro-level assessment and assess your market and industry at the micro-level, as we examined in Chapters 2 and 5.

For readers who have not done research like this before, Chapters 11 and 15 outline a hands-on approach to the marketing research process from beginning to end. Doing much of the research yourself is a great way to build or extend your network. Doing so also adds considerably to your credibility and can help you answer the tough questions that financiers will throw at you later. The most important outcome, though, is that customer problems that your venture might solve – or the lack thereof – should become clear to you. The technique demonstrated in Chapter 11 may prove quite helpful in this regard. Without this kind of input, you can't shape your opportunity to maximize its potential, you cannot prepare an evidence-based sales forecast and you certainly cannot write a compelling business plan. Your primary research should also enable you to identify your industry's CSFs, information you'll need to flesh out your entrepreneurial team.

> **❝ doing much of the research yourself is a great way to build or extend your network ❞**

So, don't hide behind your Internet connection. Read the trade magazines. Get into the library. Get out in the field. Attend some trade shows. Crank up your confidence. There simply is no other way.

An evidence-based sales forecast: OK, but how?

A SWAG – a silly wild @*~# guess or an evidence-based forecast? Which will you use in your business plan? Without a top-line revenue number, you simply cannot prepare the financial statements your plan will require. Without evidence to support that top-line number, your plan will be worth little more than the paper it is written on. But how can you prepare an evidence-based forecast for something that doesn't even exist? Good question, and an important one. It's also a good test to see whether you have what it takes to reduce the overwhelming uncertainty inherent in your new venture into something more tangible that you and others can make sense of.

There are two kinds of forecast you'll probably want to do. The first is a forecast of market potential. Just how large is the market you'll serve, measured in different ways – number of units sold, revenue, numbers of customers? Secondary data and a little mathematics should get you here without great difficulty.

The second forecast – and the more difficult one – predicts how much you'll sell for the three to five years your business plan will cover. There's no point in even thinking about writing a business plan until you have these numbers. Most often – but not always – forecasting a new venture's sales involves collecting primary data. How? Chapter 16 reviews the various approaches to creating evidence-based sales forecasts. As you'll see, doing so is by no means a perfect exercise, but it's far more credible than a SWAG, and it should bolster your confidence in the merit – or lack thereof – of the opportunity you will pursue.

The customer-driven feasibility study

So, with opportunity in hand, your research gathered (the research never stops, actually, but at some point you'll have done enough of it to either abandon your opportunity or move forward with it) and an evidence-based sales forecast prepared, what else should an entrepreneur like you do before you write a business plan? If your conclusions about your opportunity are positive, then you should prepare a customer-driven feasibility study that covers the seven domains (see Box 10.1). The discipline of making yourself actually write what you have learned is a good one, for it forces you to confront the clarity of the logic that underlies the attractiveness of the opportunity you have assessed. It's a concise memo to yourself or your team – no more than a page or so for each of the seven domains. Including an executive summary up front and a final summary and conclusion at the end, it need not exceed ten pages.

---

box 10.1

What's entailed in a customer-driven feasibility study?

1 Executive summary that briefly sets what follows (tells the reader(s) – you and your team – what you are going to tell them).

2 Micro-level market assessment:

▦ target market and its pain identified; compelling benefits of your solution identified, with evidence that those in this segment are willing to pay a price that works;

▦ target market segment, size and growth rate;

▦ options to grow into other segments.

3 Macro-level market assessment:

▦ overall market size and growth rate;

▦ macro-trends analysis to assess future market growth and attractiveness.

4 Macro-level industry assessment:

▦ five forces analysis: whether or not the industry is attractive;

▦ likely changes therein going forward.

5 Micro-level industry assessment:

▦ any proprietary elements;

▦ any superior organizational processes, capabilities or resources identified that are not easily duplicated or imitated;

▦ economic viability of business model established:

– revenue forecast;
– customer acquisition and retention costs, and time required to obtain a customer;
– gross margins;
– capital investment required;
– break-even analysis;
– operating cash cycle characteristics.

6 Team assessment:

▦ team's mission, aspirations and propensity for risk;

▦ team's ability to execute on the CSFs in this industry;

▦ team's connectedness up, down and across the value chain.

7 Summary and conclusions (tell the reader(s) the key highlights of what you've told them):

▦ why this opportunity is – or isn't – attractive and on what one (or, at most, two) domain(s) you rest your case.

Such a feasibility study is *customer-driven* because, unlike most organization charts that put the entrepreneur or CEO at the top and the people serving the customer at the bottom (the me-first approach), the feasibility study begins with the target customer, without whom there will be no business. It begins in the lower left corner of the seven domains model, by identifying the target market and the customer pain you intend to resolve, and it examines the benefits you plan to deliver to your target market along with evidence that your market is willing to pay. It then proceeds clockwise through macro-level market and industry analyses; it assesses the sustainable advantage of the proposed venture; and it closes with an assessment of the entrepreneurial team and its dream: its mission, aspirations and propensity for risk; its ability to deliver results for the particular opportunity at hand; and its connections up, down and across the value chain.

> **❝ once the feasibility study is complete, you will find yourself halfway towards crafting a business plan ❞**

Once the feasibility study is complete, you – provided you and your team are satisfied that the opportunity meets your mission and aspirations and is sufficiently feasible – will find yourself halfway towards crafting a business plan. You'll also find your understanding of the opportunity to have been sharpened by the analytical scrutiny to which it has been subjected.

On the other hand, if the feasibility study has identified obstacles or flaws that render your opportunity unattractive, then the work of developing a strategy and preparing detailed financial statements necessary for a business plan can be delayed or even shelved altogether. You can then turn your attention to reshaping the opportunity or pursuing another potentially more promising one.

The feasibility study and the business plan: how are they different?

In this entrepreneurial age, there's plenty of good advice available to entrepreneurs for how to write a business plan, including books, articles and software. (In my view, the best short article on this topic is Sahlman.[4]) Surprisingly, however, there has until now been no widely accepted model for how entrepreneurs should assess opportunities for which they write business plans, in pursuit of the investment capital they need to fulfil their entrepreneurial dreams. Such a model is the subject of this book. But how do the seven domains model and the customer-driven feasibility study differ from what's in a good business plan?

To be sure, there is considerable overlap in the content of a customer-driven feasibility study and a business plan. In fact, all of the analyses we advocate are essential, though not sufficient, for crafting a thoughtful business plan. So, what's new here? What's different from a business plan?

■ *Customer focus:* The feasibility study is focused on the customer. As Peter Drucker wrote many years ago, the purpose of any business is to win a customer. The feasibility study homes in on that purpose, one quite different from that of most business plans – to win an investor. If there is no likelihood of there being customers, there will be no investors.

■ *Fundamental economics:* The feasibility study addresses succinctly the fundamental economics of the business, by identifying the key drivers of cash flow: revenue, customer acquisition and retention costs and timelines, gross margins, required capital investment, and the working capital characteristics of the operating cash cycle. If these drivers are satisfactory, then detailed strategies – for marketing, operations and financing – can probably be developed to make the venture economically viable, provided the market, industry and team elements are sufficiently attractive. If they are not, there's little point in wasting time developing such strategies nor the spreadsheets that reflect them.

■ *Mindset:* The customer-driven feasibility study asks the critical questions necessary to satisfy the entrepreneurial team's curiosity about the attractiveness of the opportunity itself, and makes it possible to answer these questions before developing the detailed strategy necessary for the completion of a business plan. Thus, its mindset is to ask (and answer) questions, not to sell the venture's merit. In contrast, the business plan organizes the answers delivered by the feasibility study and goes on to develop marketing, operating and financing strategies in an effort to sell the opportunity, in a sharply focused way, to investors and other stakeholders.

Why bother?

'Are these differences worth the effort?' you might ask. Why shouldn't you, as a would-be entrepreneur, simply skip the feasibility study and proceed directly to preparing a business plan?

■ First, researching and preparing a customer-driven feasibility study gives you a chance to opt out early in the process, before investing the time and energy in preparing a complete business plan. Thus, it can save weeks or months of time that might be wasted on a fundamentally flawed opportunity.

- Second, for opportunities that do look promising, the feasibility study jump-starts the business planning process and provides a clear, customer-focused vision about why your proposed venture makes sense – from market, industry and team perspectives, viewed independently and collectively. It identifies the customer pain and how you'll resolve it, and the one or two domains that make the opportunity stand out. These factors become the drivers of your business plan.

- Third, by ensuring that all aspects of the opportunity are examined, your analysis reduces your risk of entering a fatally flawed venture.

Asking the feasibility questions with an open mind – deliberately, objectively and comprehensively – is an important first step that entrepreneurs ignore all too often. If you'd like to do the feasibility work in the company of others, Chapter 17 suggests a few ways you can find some support and perhaps some like-minded individuals as well.

No car-buyer would buy a new car without a road test, and that's a far less risky decision than the one you are about to make. A customer-driven feasibility study is the entrepreneur's new business road test. Entrepreneurs who proceed without doing one do so at their own risk.

Business planning books

So, your road test looks good and it's time to write your business plan. How should you proceed? Writing a business plan is beyond the scope of this book but, if you've found this book's advice useful, then you may be ready for some additional thoughts on business planning. There are dozens of books on the subject, from all kinds of authors. How should you separate the wheat from the chaff?

If I were to write another business plan today, here's what I would do. First, I would re-read Bill Sahlman's superb article.[5] It's every bit as valid today as when it was written. Then, if I wanted more depth, I'd look for a book that's customer-focused, not me-focused or idea-focused. I'd look for a book that – unlike a cookbook – makes you think, instead of giving you simple recipes and checklists. Look carefully and you may find one.

What about software?

Virtually all business plans today are written with some kind of software. There's an abundance of commercially available software designed explicitly for the business-planning task. These packages usually combine both word-processing and spreadsheet elements in a single package. Should you use one of these? My recommendation is absolutely not! As consultant Joel Marks remarked in the *Wall Street Journal*, 'I can spot [a business plan prepared using such software] a mile away – there is no depth, no real analysis, no tests done to back up projections.'[6] In short, no credibility for you, the writer. And without credibility, you're dead.

What's wrong with such software? My research identified at least four common shortcomings, in addition to the concerns Joel Marks noted.

■ There's usually far too little flexibility. Some programs ask you to analyze three key competitors, for example. What if there are four or five important ones? What about substitutes, players from other industries who also serve your market?

■ The financial models are too rigid. The chart of accounts, i.e. the list of all relevant categories of revenue, expense and investment, differs for each industry. It looks different for service businesses than for manufacturers, for distributors or for retailers. Different from country to country, where accounting and tax conventions vary. What you will need to do is develop your own chart of accounts based on the categories of expense and reporting structure that are relevant for your industry and locale. That's best done using one of the major general-purpose spreadsheet packages. There's no greater credibility killer than filling a business plan with financial projections that simply don't conform to the standards of your particular industry. For many businesses, this simply isn't possible with most business-planning software. Part of the research you'll conduct for your business plan should identify the chart of accounts and reporting formats you'll need to use.

■ Many packages don't distinguish between market analysis – something you've already done in your feasibility study – and marketing strategy or planning. Understanding your market at the micro- and macro-levels is one thing; developing a strategy to go after it is quite another. This straitjacket simply does not fit.

■ Many packages make it difficult to display the very real insights you've gained from doing your seven domains homework. You want your unique insights to shine through, not have them trapped in a cookie-cutter structure.

So, read Sahlman, and read a book or two if you like. But if you hope to raise capital, don't use a business-planning software package!

What investors will be looking for in your business plan

To wrap things up, let's summarize some of the key things professional investors – the ones looking to make boatloads of money from *their* capital and *your* entrepreneurial efforts – are looking for. Some of what follows you have read in earlier chapters, but it warrants repeating in the context of the business plan you may soon be ready to write.

- Professional investors are not very interested in your idea or technology. Instead, they want to know that your business will offer differentiated solutions to real customer problems or pain, solutions that offer real competitive advantage. Better, faster or cheaper. A customer-focused business plan, following from your customer-focused feasibility study, will help you make this point.

- Investors generally look to invest in large and growing markets. Why? They want to know your venture can reach a sizeable scale, and they want to know your market is large enough to accommodate more than one successful new entrant.

- Investors seek industries that are not competitively brutal; they like entry barriers to be high enough to make it difficult for others to enter.

- Investors look for evidence that your initial advantage can be sustained. Why won't someone else steal your thunder?

- Investors look for committed lead entrepreneurs and entrepreneurial teams who can deliver on the promises contained in their business plans and whose mission, aspirations and propensity for risk are aligned with those of the investors. Life leading an entrepreneurial, venture-capital-backed company is simple really. Perform or move on. Having executed previously on the industry's CSFs, and being well connected enough to see the need to move to plan B – or, as we saw for Palm Computing, plan Z – when conditions so dictate, are important indicators of this capability.

- Finally, professional investors will measure your financial performance by cash flow, not profits. Cash is king when it comes to results so that's where your financials and your discussion thereof should focus.

When it comes to business plans, there are also a few red flags worthy of mention.

■ *The reluctance of the entrepreneur to put their own money at risk:* 'The amount isn't as material as the importance of having senior management vest a financial stake in the company,' according to Paul Mannion Jr, President of HPC Capital Management Corporation.[7] A $40,000 commitment from an owner who has $50,000 can be more persuasive than a $1 million pledge from an entrepreneur with a $15 million nest egg. Entrepreneurs are likely to be more careful with money when it's their own at stake.

■ *A poorly cited business plan:* If you've done the research, cite your sources, both secondary and primary. Data and hard evidence are credible. Your opinions ('We feel that . . .') are not. Worse, they are an indication of a lack of research that might support your point better. Credibility can be lost – or built, by citing your research – in this way, too.

■ *Overly aggressive or unsupported financial forecasts:* It's all too easy to change the assumptions in your spreadsheets to make the numbers look attractive. But changing the reality that will ultimately unfold is much harder. Investors want to see financials for which each and every number is well supported. Blind assumptions and SWAGs won't do.

In the final analysis, a good business plan should close its sale with the people – people who will attract customers and deliver cash flow – who will turn your entrepreneurial dream into reality. As we've seen in the case histories in this book, the entrepreneurs who have made these stories happen have been insightful, motivated and very capable people. Once your venture gets started, people will make all the difference. As Margaret Mead said so wisely, 'Never doubt that a small group of thoughtful, committed citizens can change the world. Indeed it is the only thing that ever has.'[8] You can, too!

Part 2

Toolkits for your road test

11

How to learn what you don't know you don't know[1]

Despite your confidence in your nascent opportunity, there are – if you'll admit it – a few things you *know* you don't know about your idea and the customers who, if you are successful, will buy it.

What you *know* you don't know

What do you *know* you don't know about your idea and about customers' likely response? You probably know you don't *really* know at least a few important things:

- whether customers, or enough customers, will buy what you propose to offer;

- whether they will pay the price you think they will pay;

- whether you've designed your goods or services in the best way to maximize their appeal, whether you had got the offering just right;

- which target market is the most promising one – you probably lack the resources to go after everyone, so where should you start?

There's also lots of other information you know you don't know, above and beyond the customer issues, issues that are dealt with in other parts of this book. The focus in this chapter, though, is on customers and their needs. More specifically, this chapter will show you how to interview prospective users of whatever it is you plan to offer, whether a good or a service, to help you answer some of the key questions that you know you don't know, like those bulleted above. More importantly, though, you'll learn how to get customers to tell you *what you don't know to ask them*!

What you *don't know* you don't know

Why is learning what you don't know you don't know – or what your customers don't know *they* don't know – important? If customers already know they need what you plan to offer, they've probably already told someone about it, including your competitors. Many of the most exciting breakthroughs that entrepreneurs bring to market are innovations that customers haven't known they needed. 'Why didn't I think of that?' we hear, after such breakthroughs come to market.

Did anyone tell Steve Jobs that they needed a personal computer? Did anyone tell Dan Bricklin and Bob Frankston, the developers of VisiCalc, the first spreadsheet application for PCs, that such an application for the Apple II was needed?[2] Ditto for the first word processor, for email, for the Web and so on. Did anyone tell British Airways, the operator of the London Eye, the huge observation wheel – sort of a high-tech Ferris wheel – that's a magnet for tourists and London locals alike, that such an attraction would pack them in on the South Bank of the River Thames?

What most of these innovations have in common is that they resolved some sort of customer pain. That is, they made it much easier – or better or faster or more efficient – for customers either to do something they already did, perhaps quite differently (PCs, spreadsheets, word processors, email) or to do something they had not done before (bring information quickly and conveniently to one's desktop; or see London, a low-rise city for the most part, from a panoramic bird's eye vantage point).

Where was the customer pain that these innovations resolved? PCs, once relevant applications software came along – word processors, spreadsheets and so on – made certain kinds of office work dramatically easier and faster and less frustrating to do and to revise. As Dan Bricklin later noted, 'VisiCalc took 20 hours of work per week for some people and turned it out in 15 minutes and let them become much more creative.' Email resolved, among other things, the customer pain of always getting people's voicemail and wasting time trying fruitlessly to connect with them. These sorts of innovations are painkillers in that their main reason for being is to resolve customer pain. Of course, email has now engendered its own customer pain, as it consumes increasing numbers of hours in people's workdays!

The World Wide Web and the London Eye, on the other hand, are enablers – innovations that enable people to do things they had not really been able to do previously.

One way to think about entrepreneurs' roles is as the developers of new painkillers and enablers. In doing so, however, it helps if the entrepreneur really understands (for painkillers) the customer's pain. For enablers, the trick is to discern whether what's enabled is something that customers would actually embrace. Either way, interviews are good tools for gaining such understanding. To the extent that you can find, in the arena where your business seeks to play, some sort of customer pain that others have not recognized and found a way to address, you'll have an opportunity that's miles ahead of the mundane ones that everybody else is pursuing.

> **❝ interviews are good tools for gaining such understanding ❞**

Fortunately, there's a technique that can be borrowed from the social sciences[3] that turns out to be a great way to do all this. It's especially useful for entrepreneurs trying to find ways to solve customers' needs, including the kinds of needs that customers don't yet know they have, or cannot easily articulate. It's called the long interview, and this chapter will tell you how to do it.

The long interview

You've probably already talked with lots of people about your idea for a new venture. If so, you're off to a great start. If you are like most entrepreneurs, though, chances are you've made one or more of the following mistakes that will have limited what you've learned from these conversations.

- You've let your enthusiasm show through. Doing so is great for selling, but it can limit the amount of honest feedback you'll get when your purpose is to learn rather than to sell. Most people don't like to disagree in the face of enthusiasm like yours.

- Rather than asking first about the customer's needs, any shortcomings or unmet or poorly met needs in the way they do things now, you've jumped right into 'me' or 'my idea'. Doing so too quickly can inhibit your learning about alternative solutions to the customer's problem, some of which might be slight tweaks of your idea or even something completely different, and perhaps even better than your initial idea.

- You've asked leading questions: 'Do you think this is faster?' The implication that it's faster will prompt some people simply to agree, whether they've really thought about it or not.

> ■ You've asked questions that can be answered with a 'yes' or a 'no'. Such questions tend to close off the conversation, rather than keeping it open to see where it might lead.

The long interview technique we propose here addresses each of these problems. It serves two key purposes:

- ■ it lets you seek answers about the things you *know* you don't know;
- ■ but first, and more importantly, it encourages the customer to tell you things you do not know to ask and that they would not otherwise think to tell you, helping you learn what you *don't know* you don't know.

Let's use an example to bring the technique to life. Suppose you are an aspiring entrepreneur. You love yogurt and find it a healthy and delicious snack, good throughout the day whenever you need a pick-me-up. You've been mixing yogurt with fruit juices and other nutritious ingredients and drinking it as a beverage, rather than eating it with a spoon. There might be a business here, you think.

Planning the long interview

To conduct a fruitful long interview to better understand your prospective customers and their pain, you need first to construct an interview guide, which is easily done on a single sheet of paper. Doing so involves two steps:

- ■ reviewing what you think you *know* about your idea and its use;
- ■ reviewing what you know you *don't know*.

What do you think you *know* about your drinking yogurt? Your drinking yogurt is:

- ■ delicious;
- ■ nutritious;
- ■ thick like a smoothie;
- ■ convenient and easy to consume;
- ■ easily combined with fruit or other flavours;
- ■ good between meals;
- ■ good for breakfast;
- ■ good for dessert;
- ■ loved by women;

▦ in need of refrigeration;

▦ and more.

What might you think you *don't know* about drinking yogurt?

▦ to whom it should be targeted;

▦ how thick or thin it should be;

▦ what flavours people will want;

▦ how it should be packaged;

▦ how you should price it;

▦ where it should be sold;

▦ how it should be pitched: thirst-quenching, as an energy source, as a party drink, like beer, as a between-meal snack;

▦ and more.

Preparing these lists serves two purposes. The lists will provide some structure for your interview, hence your learning. Further, by acknowledging what you think you know and don't know, they will help you remain distant enough from your own assumptions so you can learn. The lists will also help you identify aspects or relationships between yogurt and life that have perhaps not previously been addressed by the current marketers of yogurt in your market: drinking yogurt with herbal additives, for example.

❝ lists will provide some structure for your interview ❞

With these lists now in hand, you're ready to develop your interview guide. In fact, you are almost done, though you've barely started. Your interview guide will consist of five elements.

1 A brief introduction and some opening biographical questions to put the customer at ease.

2 A few (probably just two) 'grand tour' questions: broad, open-ended questions to encourage the respondent to tell you, from their own perspective, two things:

   ▦ everything that's relevant *to them* about the occasions in which they might consume drinking yogurt – note, though, that this question is not about your product at all, it's about them, their attitudes, motivations and behaviour;

   ▦ everything that comes to their mind – not yours – about your drinking yogurt concept.

3   The third element consists of three 'floating' prompts for each of the interview drivers. There are three kinds of these floating prompts, which you can use at any point in the interview to get the respondent to say more about something they've just mentioned:

   ■ raising your eyebrows following something the respondent has just said (maybe they've suggested that it would be good to be able to drink herbal supplements), a topic which you'd like them to go deeper into and tell you more about;

   ■ repeating a word the respondent has just said – 'Herbal supplements?' – with a questioning tone.

   ■ saying, 'What do you mean, herbal supplements?'

   The purpose of these floating prompts is to get the respondent to tell you more about what they've just mentioned. It might be a topic that's already on your lists of what you think you know or don't know, but go ahead and listen to what they have to say, so they can either confirm or refute your current knowledge. Or it might be something not on your lists (e.g. herbal supplements). These are the nuggets of gold: things *you don't know you don't know*. You are hoping to glean from your interviews the one or two of these nuggets that might turn into revolutionary ideas that will reinvent your thinking, and perhaps the yogurt category (or the herbal category!)

4   The fourth element of your interview guide comprises your lists of what you think you know and don't know, determined earlier, preceded by the phrase 'What about . . .' or occasionally 'What if . . .'. These are your 'planned' prompts. Here, the purpose is to get the respondent to talk about each of the topics about which you already think you know or don't know the answers. But here, at least, you know the questions to ask! You will use these planned prompts to cover any of these issues that the respondent does not touch upon as a result of your one or two grand tour questions, though many if not most of them will undoubtedly be addressed there.

5   Finally, to complete your interview guide, there are two other kinds of useful prompt, each beginning with 'What about . . .' or 'What if . . .'.

   ■ *Contrast prompts.* Use these to ensure that all the alternatives are fully examined. The key word in contrast prompts is usually 'not'. For example, 'What if it's *not* for between meals?'

   ■ *Exceptional incident prompts.* Use these to explore non-obvious uses or situations where your idea may have utility. For example, 'What about not drinking it at all?'

Here the purpose is to get your respondent to stretch their thinking in ways neither you – nor they! – had previously thought of. You may find some more nuggets of gold this way, too, more things you don't know you don't know.

Let's now take a look at what a complete interview guide for the drinking yogurt entrepreneur might look like (see Box 11.1).

---

box 11.1

Interview guide for drinking yogurt

Thanks for agreeing to speak with me today. As I mentioned on the phone, I'm studying what people do for drinks and snacks between meals these days, and I'd welcome your views. First, can we touch on a few biographical questions for my records?

What's the correct spelling of your name? _____

In what city or town do you live? _____

Do you sometimes eat between meals? _____

Enter gender and approximate age (observe, don't ask): Approximate age _____ Sex _____

Let's begin this way. Would you please tell me what your typical day is like between mealtimes?

Floating prompts

▨ Eyebrow flash

▨ _____?

▨ What do you mean, _____?

Planned prompts

▨ What about in meetings?

▨ What about in your office?

▨ What about at home?

▨ What about nutrition?

▨ What about health?

▨ What about convenience?

▨ What about thirst?

▨ What about hunger?

▨ What about energy?

Other prompts

▨ What about drinks and snacks at other times of day?

▨ What about meals, rather than between meals?

▨ What about weekends?

▶

OK, thanks. Now I have a second broad question to ask you. It involves a concept for a new kind of yogurt you can drink. Here's a description of the concept. Would you take a look? (Let them read the concept statement. When they are finished, ask:) What's your reaction?

Floating prompts

▪ Eyebrow flash

▪ _____?

▪ What do you mean, _____?

Planned prompts

▪ What about taste?

▪ What about nutrition?

▪ What about texture?

▪ What about convenience?

▪ What about flavours?

▪ What about between meals?

▪ What about breakfast?

▪ What about dessert?

▪ What about refrigeration?

▪ What about packaging?

▪ What about pricing?

▪ Where should it be sold?

▪ What about thirst?

▪ What about hunger?

▪ What about energy?

▪ What about parties?

▪ To whom should it be targeted?

Other prompts

▪ What about other uses?

▪ What about other occasions?

As noted above, the guide begins with a few biographical questions, simply to put the user at ease. You're really not trying to learn much here, though you should record the answers, in case a pattern develops among different kinds of respondents – older versus younger persons, or men versus women, for example.

Next comes the first grand tour question. I've phrased it very carefully to avoid the four mistakes interviewers often make. Note that:

■ there's no enthusiasm for the drinking yogurt idea here – just an enquiry about the respondent's between-meal snacking;

■ in fact, there's no mention of the idea at all – that will come later, as the second grand tour question;

■ it's not a leading question, and lets the respondent begin wherever they wish and wander as far afield as they like;

■ the question cannot be answered with 'yes' or 'no'.

Then come the three kinds of floating prompts. These are here to remind you to use one of them when you hear something in the respondent's remarks that you'd like to explore further.

After that come some of your planned prompts, taken from your first two lists. Some items on your list will be about the customer, so they fall under the first grand tour question. The others, about your product itself, will fall under the second grand tour.

You won't end up using all of your planned prompts, as the respondent will mention some – perhaps most – of them spontaneously. You may find it useful to tick them off as the respondent covers them, so you know which ones are left that you must ask.

> **❝ you won't end up using all of your planned prompts ❞**

Then come the contrast and exceptional incident prompts, to make sure you cover any non-obvious territory that the respondent has not yet mentioned.

Finally the process repeats itself, with the focus of attention now turned to your drinking yogurt idea itself. Note how open-ended the second grand tour question is: 'What's your reaction?' There's no overt enthusiasm or bias, no implied direction at all. In order to hear the respondent's reaction, however, you need to state your concept quite clearly and succinctly, yet comprehensively. One good way to do so is to write a succinct concept statement, perhaps including some nice graphics, if they help connote what you intend to offer. See Box 11.2 for what a concept statement might look like for drinking yogurt.

> **box 11.2**
>
> ### Concept statement for drinking yogurt
>
> *Refresh is a new concept in yogurt. Unlike yogurt you eat with a spoon, you can drink Refresh straight out of the bottle. It comes in a variety of flavours and sizes ranging from individual portions to containers to serve the whole family.*
>
> Note to the reader:
>
> Note how succinct and factual the concept statement is. Since a key purpose of your interviews is to refine your concept, you do not want to hype it or describe it in excessive detail. You want your interviews to *give* you the detail. The version below is how *not* to do it.
>
> *Refresh is a delicious new concept in yogurt. Unlike yogurt you eat with a spoon, you can drink Refresh straight out of the bottle. It comes in a variety of scrumptious fruit flavours, plus coffee and chocolate flavours, and in sizes ranging from individual portions to containers to serve the whole family. It's tasty, nutritious and convenient for between-meal snacks or for when you have to eat on the run.*
>
> Don't forget that what you are doing is researching, not selling. The difference is crucial!

Conducting the long interview

With an interview guide now in hand, you are ready to pick up the phone and line up some appointments. But there are a few more questions you'll have to address in order to do so and to conduct the interviews.

- Whom should I interview?
- Face-to-face or on the telephone?
- How many interviews should I conduct?
- How should I present myself in the interviews?
- Should I record the interview, or simply write very fast?
- Can I update my interview guide after I've done the first interviews and learned a few things?

Choosing respondents

'Should I interview my friends, or strangers?', you may ask. One problem with friends is that they are likely to tell you what they think you want to hear. Perfect strangers are better, and you want a very diverse pool, sampling as widely as possible, so you are more likely to hear diverging views. Should you interview experts or novices? In general, experts are *too* knowledgeable and too wedded to the way things are now. It's good to include a few experts in your sample, but they should not dominate it, unless your area of enquiry is so specialized that experts are the only realistic people to talk to.

Face-to-face or by telephone?

If you can get people to meet with you, that's far better. They'll talk longer than they will on the phone and you'll get their full attention. In my experience, an hour to an hour and a half is a common length, even from a short interview guide like the example shown here, which means you'll learn more than you would in a shorter phone call. But if the phone is the best you can get, take it. The technique – OK, not the raised eyebrows – will still work just fine.

How many interviews should I conduct?

Experienced researchers who use this technique find that the answers begin to get repetitive once the number of interviews gets into the teens. By about interview number 20, in my experience, you'll have heard virtually everything there is to hear. It's time to stop, draw your conclusions and get on with the rest of your seven domains analysis.

What about my interview persona?

Here's the hard part. You don't want to appear too clever, like you know all the answers – in fact, quite the opposite. Your interview persona should be benign and agreeable, not aggressive; accepting of whatever they say, but curious enough to ask your endless floating and planned prompts; a bit dim or naïve, to encourage them to enlighten you with all they know. With this sort of persona, you will present no danger that they will lose face in any way.

What about recording the interviews?

My experience is that people are happy to have you record what they say, as long as you tell them their remarks will remain confidential. The small micro-cassette recorders available at office supply stores are great for this purpose. I've found that buying a plug-in microphone makes the sound quality better, thus making the tapes much easier to transcribe when you go back to review what was said. Another way to go is to do your interviewing with a partner, where one person does the asking and careful listening and the other one writes.

What about updating my interview guide?

It's almost certain that, in your very first interview or two or three, your respondents will address some issues that you simply had not thought of. This is good news! You'll want to add some or all of these issues to your list of planned prompts for the rest of your interviews, to allow you to get additional perspectives on them.

Consolidating your learning

Having completed your interviews, there are a few possible outcomes for each of your two grand tour questions. From your first grand tour and its subsequent prompts, you'll have learned much about how your idea might or might not fit into your intended users' current attitudinal, motivational and behavioural patterns. You might find your idea fits quite nicely. You might find some opportunities to adjust your concept, though you are generally on track. You might find there's a mismatch. You might also find there's something else the customers need more than what you were thinking about, which may prompt you to redirect your entrepreneurial efforts entirely.

From your second grand tour and its subsequent prompts, there are several likely outcomes. One is that the respondents will have widely turned 'thumbs down' on your idea. While this result does not necessarily mean you should abandon your idea entirely, it certainly does raise your risk! If this is what you hear, however, you may decide to pursue something else that looks more promising.

Another possible outcome is that you get concrete suggestions about how to improve your offering to give it more utility or appeal. You might, if you are lucky or especially insightful, get rave reviews that indicate you have a potential winner on your hands. While this is good news, it does not mean you are ready to go to market yet, for there are other questions raised in the seven domains for which you'll also want answers before you invest months or years of your life and lots of your and other people's money.

> **❝ you might, if you are lucky or especially insightful, get rave reviews ❞**

If in your interviews you find enough promising regard for your concept, one good way to wrap up your learning is to edit your concept description to embrace the useful input you have obtained. Revise your offering to respond to what you've learned. Rarely does an entrepreneur fail to get useful feedback from an exercise like this, feedback that can help further develop the offering.

Other uses for this long interview technique

Chapter 5 examined the likelihood that your proposed venture can develop sources of sustainable competitive advantage. As you saw, one element in doing so is ascertaining whether the business model you propose is viable. Long interviews can be useful for this purpose.

Chapter 7 addressed whether you and your entrepreneurial team can execute on the handful of critical success factors that prevail in your industry. Long interviews can be useful for identifying what these factors are for the industry in which you plan to compete.

12

Market analysis worksheet

This worksheet is intended to stimulate your thinking about market size and growth rates and the various kinds of trends that are likely to influence demand for what you propose to offer. The points of this exercise are twofold:

- to identify the extent to which the proposed venture can reach a sizeable scale or whether it's more likely to be a lifestyle business;

- to identify the extent to which future demand is likely to grow or decline, based on trends that are likely to influence your customers' buying habits.

These trends may be in any of six broad categories.

- *Demographic trends:* trends towards greater or lesser numbers of people (or businesses, for business-to-business offerings) in various demographic groups, based on age, income, gender, education, ethnicity, etc. Census data are useful in quantifying these trends. *Example: the trend towards an increasing number of people in older age groups in most developed countries.*

- *Sociocultural trends:* trends towards greater or lesser numbers of people (or businesses) engaged in various lifestyle or other activities based on social or cultural trends. *Example: trends towards organic and vegetarian diets in some countries are creating increased demand for foods in these categories.*

- *Economic trends:* changes in income levels, economic growth, interest rates and other economic indicators can have profound effects on demand for many kinds of goods and services. *Example: the rapidly growing purchasing power of families in many developing countries is creating increased demand for many kinds of consumer goods in Asia and elsewhere.*

■ *Technological trends:* developments in mobile telephony, biotechnology and a vast array of other technologies portend powerful effects on demand for many other kinds of goods and services. *Example: the development of global positioning satellites has spurred new demand for products and services for backpackers, mobile phone users and drivers caught in rush-hour traffic.*

■ *Regulatory trends:* changes in laws and government policies affect demand in many ways. *Example: changes in legislation for how older people are housed and cared for in developed countries has spurred demand for new kinds of housing alternatives and other services for the elderly.*

■ *Natural trends:* global warming, the depletion of natural resources and other natural trends can influence some kinds of demand. *Example: demand for winter resort accommodation in the Alps is likely to decline if global warming makes alpine snow sufficiently unreliable.*

The challenge for the entrepreneur is to identify trends in any of these categories that are likely to have a significant effect – whether favourable or unfavourable – on demand for what is proposed to be offered. The effects of such trends can be far more powerful than one might imagine.

ff the challenge for the entrepreneur is to identify trends in any of these categories that are likely to have a significant effect on demand for what is proposed to be offered JJ

The best places to look for such trends are in trade magazines and trade associations for your industry, government reports, consumer data sources like Key Note and Mintel in the UK and similar sources elsewhere, and in the general and business press. Finding objective sources of specific trends – and citing them – provides valuable indications to either support or detract from the viability of the entrepreneur's vision of how eager customers are likely to be to accept what is to be offered. Later, at business planning time, these data provide a powerful boost to the entrepreneur's credibility and can give important support for the veracity of estimates of market potential.

So, here are the data that are needed to complete a comprehensive macro-level market analysis:

■ market size, ideally measured in any or all of the following ways:

– number of customers for the category of goods or services (athletic shoes or whatever) you will offer;

– total spending in the category;

– total units bought in the category;

▣ recent market growth rate, measured in any or all of:

  - population changes;
  - total spending in the category;
  - total units bought in the category;

▣ forecasted market growth rate from credible sources, measured in any or all of:

  - population changes;
  - total spending in the category;
  - total units bought in the category;

▣ favourable trends, with sources cited, in any or all of the six macro-trend categories:

  - demographic;
  - sociocultural;
  - economic;
  - technological;
  - regulatory;
  - natural;

▣ unfavourable trends, with sources cited, in any or all of the six macro-trend categories:

  - demographic;
  - sociocultural;
  - economic;
  - technological;
  - regulatory;
  - natural.

Overall conclusions result from answers to the following questions.

▣ Is this an opportunity for a lifestyle business or one that can reach sizeable scale?

▣ What few specific and crucial macro-trends are important to the future of the venture? What are their implications for market attractiveness?

▣ Overall, based on the data you have gathered and cited, how attractive is the market you intend to serve?

13

Industry analysis checklist[1]

" keep in mind that it is your *industry* that you are assessing, not your proposed *venture* " This checklist is useful for asking the questions necessary to assess the attractiveness of the industry you propose to enter, based on Michael Porter's five forces framework.[2] Reading Porter's original article will broaden your understanding of this tool. The task here is to assess each of the five forces to determine whether their implications for industry attractiveness are favourable or unfavourable, and then to draw an overall conclusion based on all five forces taken together. Keep in mind that it is your *industry* (food retailing, software, restaurants or whatever) that you are assessing, not your proposed *venture*, without regard to whether you actually enter the industry.

In the discussion that follows, there's a chart showing the various drivers of each of the five forces. For example, in the first chart – threat of entry – you'll see that threat of entry is most severe when *all* of the drivers are at low levels. For an industry you are considering entering, you can rate each of the drivers as low or high, depending on the conditions that prevail given your examination of your industry.

If you find all the threat of entry drivers to be low (e.g. low economies of scale, little product differentiation and so on), that's generally bad news for you, as it indicates that your industry is marked by severe threat of entry. If you find all of the drivers to be high in your industry (e.g. lots of economies of scale, much product differentiation and so on), that's much better news, suggesting that, with regard to threat of entry, your industry is favourable.

Following each of the charts, you'll find an example of a particular industry that dramatizes that force (i.e. one of the five) and its impact on industry attractiveness.

Threat of entry

In general, industries are more attractive when the threat of entry is low, meaning that competitors cannot enter easily to copy your initial success. This also means that it may be difficult for your venture to get started, but that's the price you pay for the ability to compete where others cannot easily follow.

Threat of new entrants into an industry is most severe when within the industry:	High	Low	Conditions for your industry (high or low)	Implications for industry attractiveness*
economies of scale are		XX		
product differentiation is		XX		
capital requirements are		XX		
companies' control of distribution channels is		XX		
companies' level of proprietary knowledge is		XX		
companies' control over access to raw materials is		XX		
government and legal barriers are		XX		
expected retaliation by established producers is		XX		

Summary evaluation

* Indicate whether favourable (implying little threat of entry) or unfavourable (severe threat of entry).

Example: Threat of entry is extremely severe in the restaurant industry, since almost anyone can open a restaurant, perhaps in a fully furnished location vacated by a recently failed restaurant. For the restaurant industry, all factors in the chart above are low, except perhaps for product differentiation and expected retaliation, indicating severe threat of entry.

Now, consider the industry you propose to enter. Gather the information needed to complete the chart, and draw a conclusion about the threat of new entrants. Overall, is the threat of new entrants into your industry:

- highly favourable;
- moderately favourable;
- moderately unfavourable;
- highly unfavourable?

All conditions are not equal. Which, if any, of these conditions, singly or taken together, might make severe threat of entry a fatal flaw for your opportunity?

What specific obstacles, if any, will your venture have to overcome to enter this industry?

Supplier power

In general, industries are more attractive when their suppliers (of raw materials, labour, facilities and other necessary inputs) have little power to set the prices, terms and conditions under which you will buy. Here we are examining *your* suppliers, not you as a supplier to your customers.

Power of suppliers is strong when:	High	Low	Conditions for your industry (high or low)	Implications for industry attractiveness*
size and concentration of focal industry companies relative to supplier companies are		XX		
total volume or percentage of suppliers' products purchased by the focal industry companies is		XX		
product differentiation of suppliers is	XX			
switching costs for focal industry companies are	XX			
threat of forward integration by suppliers is	XX			
suppliers' knowledge about focal industry companies' cost structure is	XX			
extent of suppliers' profits is	XX			
cost savings for the focal industry companies from the suppliers' products are	XX			

▶

Power of suppliers is strong when:	High	Low	Conditions for your industry (high or low)	Implications for industry attractiveness*
importance of the suppliers' input to quality of the focal industry's final product is	XX			
cost of suppliers' products relative to the focal industry companies' total cost is	XX			

Summary evaluation

* Indicate whether favourable (implying weak supplier power) or unfavourable (strong supplier power).

Example: Intel and Microsoft, both key suppliers to the personal computer industry, enjoy very strong power as suppliers to that industry, an unfavourable factor for personal computer makers.

Now, consider *your* industry. Based on your analysis of the drivers above, is supplier power in your industry:

- highly favourable;

- moderately favourable;

- moderately unfavourable;

- highly unfavourable?

All conditions are not equal. Which, if any, of these conditions, singly or taken together, might make strong supplier power (power of *your* suppliers, not you *as* a supplier) a fatal flaw for your opportunity?

If the power of suppliers in your industry is unfavourable, what activities (e.g. product differentiation, switching costs) could you or other potential entrants undertake to reduce their power?

Buyer power

In general, industries are more attractive when buyers (your customers) have little power to set the terms and conditions under which they will buy.

Power of buyers is strong when:	High	Low	Conditions for your industry (high or low)	Implications for industry attractiveness*
size and concentration of buyers relative to focal industry companies are	XX			
total volume or percentage of focal industry companies' products purchased by the buyers is	XX			
product differentiation by focal industry companies is		XX		
switching costs for buyers are		XX		
threat of backward integration by buyers is	XX			
buyers' knowledge about focal industry companies' cost structure is	XX			
extent of buyers' profits is		XX		
cost savings for the buyers from the focal industry companies' product are		XX		
importance of the focal industry companies' input to quality of the buyers' final product is		XX		
cost of focal industry companies' product relative to the buyers' total cost is		XX		

Summary evaluation

* Indicate whether favourable (implying weak buyer power) or unfavourable (strong buyer power).

Example: As customers of the tyre manufacturing industry, car manufacturers like Toyota and Ford have considerable buyer power.

Consider *your* industry. Overall, is buyer power of the customers served by your industry:

- highly favourable;
- moderately favourable;
- moderately unfavourable;
- highly unfavourable?

All conditions are not equal. Which, if any, of these conditions, singly or taken together, might make severe buyer power (power of *your* customers, not you *as* a customer) a fatal flaw for your opportunity?

If the power of buyers is unfavourable in your industry, what activities (e.g. product differentiation, switching costs, cost savings for buyers) could you or other potential entrants undertake to reduce their power?

Threat of substitutes

In general, industries are more attractive when the threat of substitutes is low, meaning that goods or services from other industries cannot easily serve as substitutes for your industry's products.

Threat of substitutes is most severe when:	High	Low	Conditions for your industry (high or low)	Implications for industry attractiveness*
buyer propensity to substitute is	XX			
relative price–performance relationship of substitutes compared with industry product is	XX			

Summary evaluation

* Indicate whether favourable (implying little threat of substitutes from other industries) or unfavourable (severe threat of substitutes).

Example: Threat of substitutes is severe in the glass packaging industry, as numerous other industries produce packaging (aluminium can industry, paper and plastic packaging industries and so on) that can substitute for glass.

Overall, for your industry, is the threat of substitutes:

- highly favourable;
- moderately favourable;
- moderately unfavourable;
- highly unfavourable?

All conditions are not equal. Which, if any, of these conditions, singly or taken together, might make the severe threat of substitutes a fatal flaw for your opportunity?

If the threat of substitutes is unfavourable, what activities could a potential entrant undertake to reduce the threat's likelihood?

Competitive rivalry

In general, industries are more attractive when competitive rivalry is more genteel and less intense, meaning that competing companies do not undercut one another to win customers' business.

Intensity of competitive rivalry within the industry is most severe when:	High	Low	Conditions for your industry (high or low)	Implications for industry attractiveness*
number of companies or number of equally balanced companies is	XX			
industry growth rate is		XX		
fixed or storage costs are	XX			
product differentiation is		XX		
switching costs for buyers are		XX		
diversity of competitors is		XX		
exit barriers are	XX			
strategic stakes are	XX			
Summary evaluation				

* Indicate whether favourable (implying little competitive rivalry) or unfavourable (severe competitive rivalry).

Example: Rivalry in the aluminium can industry is severe, as can-makers compete for the business of the major beverage manufacturers. All the factors in the chart above are unfavourable, except perhaps for switching costs for buyers, since cans are typically manufactured on the beverage company's premises.

Overall, is competitive rivalry in your industry:

■ highly favourable;

■ moderately favourable;

■ moderately unfavourable;

■ highly unfavourable?

All conditions are not equal. Which, if any, of these conditions, singly or taken together, might make severe competitive rivalry a fatal flaw for your opportunity?

If competitive rivalry is unfavourable, what activities could a potential entrant undertake to reduce the level of rivalry?

Overall evaluation of industry attractiveness

Now, consider your industry on all five of the forces. If three or four of the five forces are unfavourable, then your industry is brutally unattractive. If only one or two are unfavourable, then industry conditions may be moderate, though if those one or two are severe enough they could be sufficient to render the industry as unattractive in spite of the other more favourable forces.

Of the five forces, how many did you place in each category:

- highly favourable;
- moderately favourable;
- moderately unfavourable;
- highly unfavourable?

Based on the above analysis, what is your overall assessment of the attractiveness of your industry:

- highly attractive industry;
- moderately attractive industry;
- moderately unattractive industry;
- highly unattractive industry?

Which of the five forces impact most significantly on the overall structure of the industry, positively and negatively?

Does one of the forces single-handedly make the industry especially attractive? Which one? Why?

If severe threat of entry is a problem in your industry, is it reasonable to expect that you can enter and exit (by selling your business) successfully before subsequent entrants can catch up with you? Why? If not, or if such a strategy is not consistent with your entrepreneurial dreams, how will you resolve the threat of entry problem?

Based on your analysis, what changes do you anticipate in this industry – i.e. what trends will affect the five forces and make industry conditions better or worse? What can your venture do to take advantage of or influence these changes?

Finally, how might you shape or reshape your opportunity to cope with its industry setting? Is there another industry that's more attractive from which to pursue the market you seek to serve?

14

Determining the viability of your business model[1]

Chapter 5, in considering whether or not your business is likely to enjoy sustainable competitive advantage, raised a number of questions you can ask to determine whether or not your proposed business model is likely to be viable (see Box 5.1 on page 106). The thorniest of these questions are those around revenue, margins, your operating cash cycle and so on. Why? It's because most of these questions cannot be answered without real-world feedback from the market itself. Boldly stated – but unfounded – assumptions simply aren't going to suffice. Is there a systematic way, a process perhaps, to gain some clarity around these issues? Indeed there is. Let's consider a few well-known companies that have managed to address them and, in the process, create business models that have rewritten the rules in their industries.

Consider this. If the founders of Google, Starbucks or PayPal had stuck to their original business plans, we'd likely never have heard of them. Instead, they made radical changes to their initial models, became household names and delivered huge returns for their founders and investors. How did they get from their plan A to a business model that worked? Why did they succeed when most new ventures crash and burn?

Every aspiring entrepreneur, whether they desire to start a new company or create something new within an existing company, has a plan A. Virtually all of these individuals believe that *their* plan A will work. Unfortunately, they are usually wrong. But what separates the ultimate successes from the rest is what they do when their first plan fails to catch on. Do they lick their wounds, get back on their feet and morph their newly found insights into great businesses, or do they doggedly stick to their original plan?

Let's face an uncomfortable fact: the typical start-up process, largely driven by poorly conceived business plans based on untested assumptions, is seriously flawed. That's why this book and its new business road test exist.

❝ the typical start-up process is seriously flawed ❞ Most new ventures, even those with venture capital backing, share one common characteristic. They fail. But there is a better way to launch new ideas – without wasting years of your time and loads of investors' money. This better way is about assessing your opportunity *before* you write your business plan and by working systematically to *discover* a business model that really works: a plan B, like those of Google and Starbucks, which grows out of the original idea, builds on it and, once it's in place, enables the business to grow rapidly and prosper.

Most of the time, breaking through to a better business model takes time. And it takes experimentation and error, too, error from which you learn. For Max Levchin, who wanted to build a business based on his cryptography expertise, plans A to F didn't work, but plan G turned out to be the ubiquitous PayPal we know today.

Getting to plan B at Apple

Were Sergey Brin and Larry Page of Google, or Howard Schultz of Starbucks, or PayPal's Max Levchin simply lucky? Or is there something systematic about their successes that any entrepreneur can learn? Indeed, there is. Let's let the story of Apple's transition from a creative but struggling maker of personal computers to a consumer electronics and music phenomenon show us the way.

First, let's ask whether Apple's combination of the iPod and its iTunes music store was really all that new. Well, not exactly. Consider the Sony Walkman for a moment ... it made music personal and portable back in 1979! By 2000, over 300 million Walkmans had been sold. The Walkman analogue suggested that demand for personal listening devices was real.

Then there was Napster, another analogue, whose 26 million users were downloading music one tune at a time, illegally, as the courts soon decided. But analogues – predecessor companies that are worth mimicking in some way – are only part of the story. For Apple there were *antilogues*, too: predecessor companies compared to which you explicitly choose to do things *differently*, perhaps because some of what they did has been unsuccessful. For the iPod and the iTunes store there were several important antilogues. There were MP3 players like the Rio, whose clunky user interfaces were far from user-friendly. There were online music stores like MusicNet and Pressplay, whose very limited music selection and limited rights made them not very appealing to music lovers.

For Apple, there was one more analogue that put all the pieces together, courtesy of Gillette's razors and razor blades. Gillette sold razors at low, break-even prices and made its money selling the blades. Apple's Steve Jobs, ingeniously, flipped the model upside down. That he could do so profitably was, however, an unproven leap of faith. Jobs' hypothesis was that people would pay for easy to use, licensed, downloadable music and that a business model of high gross margins on the iPod with razor-thin margins in the iTunes store would be profitable while keeping the music industry off his back.

Apple's revenue on iPod sales in the first year alone was $143 million. And when the iTunes store was launched in 2003, over 1 million songs (at 99 cents each) were downloaded the very first day. Paying for downloaded music had suddenly become cool.

Getting to plan B in *your* business

So how can you break through to a business model that will work for your business? First, you'll need an idea to pursue. If you're this far along in reading this book, we hope your idea is now in place. The best ideas, as we've seen earlier, resolve somebody's pain, some customer problem you've identified for which you have a solution that might work. Alternatively, some good ideas take something in customers' lives that's pretty boring and create something so superior it provides true customer delight, as was the case for the Walkman and the iPod.

Next, you'll need to identify some analogues, portions of which you can borrow or adapt to help you understand the economics of your proposed business and its business model. And you'll need antilogues, too. As we have seen from the Apple story, analogues and antilogues don't only have to be from your own industry, though. Sometimes the most valuable insights come from rather unusual sources.

Having identified both analogues and antilogues, you can quickly reach conclusions about some things that are, with at least a modicum of certainty, known about the economics of your venture. But it is not what you know that will likely scupper your plan A, of course. It's what you *don't know*. The questions you cannot answer from historical precedent lead to your *leaps of faith* – beliefs you hold about the answers to your questions despite having no real evidence that these beliefs are actually true.

To address your leaps of faith, you'll have to leap! Identify your key leaps of faith and then test your hypothesis in some kind of experiment. That may mean opening a smaller, perhaps temporary, shop than you aspire to operate, just to see how customers respond. It may mean trying different prices for your newly developed gadget to see which price makes sales pop. By identifying your leaps of faith early and devising ways to test hypotheses that will prove or refute them, you are in a position to learn whether or not your plan A will work before you waste too much time, and money.

> **❝ to address your leaps of faith, you'll have to leap ❞**

But what do you actually need to consider as you proceed in the process of developing your business model? Every business model needs *quantitatively* to address five key elements.

1 *Your revenue model:* Who will buy? How often? How soon? At what cost? How much money will you receive each time a customer buys? How often will they send you another cheque?

2 *Your gross margin model:* How much of your revenue will be left after you have paid the direct costs of what you have sold?

3 *Your operating model:* Other than the cost of the goods or services you have sold, what else must you spend money on to keep the lights on?

4 *Your working capital model:* How early can you encourage your customers to pay? Do you have to tie up money in lots of inventory waiting for customers to buy? Can you pay your suppliers later, after the customer has paid?

5 *Your investment model:* How much cash must you spend up front before enough customers give you enough business to cover your costs?

So how do you put these building blocks to work? Box 14.1 is your organizing framework. A series of dashboards that change as you learn (see Box 14.2) are your guide for your discovery journey. Your task to begin putting flesh on the bones of your business model, without writing a business plan just yet, is to fill in at least one or more of the cells in each row of the grid.

---

box 14.1

The business model grid

Your current idea and the customer pain that it resolves or the consumer delight it offers: _____

_____

_____

Business model element	Column A: Relevant analogues and the numbers they give you	Column B: Relevant antilogues	Column C: Leaps of faith around which you will build your current dashboard	Column D: Hypotheses that will prove or refute your leaps of faith
Row 1: Revenue model				
Row 2: Gross margin model				
Row 3: Operating model				
Row 4: Working capital model				
Row 5: Investment model				

For your revenue model, for example, you might have an analogue or two that can tell you with some confidence just how, from whom and at what cost your revenue will be generated. If so, that's the detail – a short paragraph to yourself, including numbers, please – that you need for cell A1. Perhaps your analogues and some antilogues lead to a leap of faith that you'll need to examine experimentally about how your revenue model will play out. If so, that is another paragraph to yourself for cell C1, with your hypothesized answer – again, most of the time with numbers, please – to that leap of faith in cell D1.

A draft of the dashboard you will use to guide your experimental path and signal any necessary midcourse corrections in developing your revenue model is next (see Box 14.2). With these steps completed, you'll have jump-started your critical thinking about your revenue model.

A prototype dashboard for discovering your better business model

Hypotheses	Metrics	Actual period 1	Actual period 2	Actual period 3	Insights obtained, course corrections needed
Leap of faith 1:					
Hypothesis H1:					
Hypothesis H2:					
Leap of faith 2:					
Hypothesis H3:					
Hypothesis H4:					

Uncovering the right analogues and antilogues, identifying your most important leaps of faith and testing a series of hypotheses to inform all five elements of your business model doesn't happen in a single 'eureka' moment. Getting to a viable plan B, as PayPal's Max Levchin discovered, is a journey that can take months, even years. A dashboard – a systematic record you keep to guide and track this process – is a flexible tool for addressing your leaps of faith and guiding your journey. It focuses your attention on the critical issues and more efficiently deploys your precious time and resources to removing the critical risks. It provides a way to respond to the real-life data you generate.

❝ getting to a viable plan B is a journey that can take months, even years ❞

One element can hold the key

While all successful business models address each of the five elements, for many great companies, just a single element holds the key. The key element for Google was its revenue model, but initially there wasn't a revenue model at all, just a free search engine. Google's plan B, to license its technology to other websites, wasn't a winner, either. In order to bring money in, Google's plan C provided paid search listings alongside the 'objective' ones. Google's even more successful plan D built on its proprietary search algorithms to deliver targeted ads to other websites, which has generated more than half of Google's revenue since 2004.

For Ryanair, the low-cost European airline, the key was its operating model. The Ryanair operating model utilized only one type of aircraft, no free in-flight meals, direct-to-consumer online ticket booking to cut out ticket agent commissions and even getting rid of window shades and seat back pockets to significantly decrease the time on the ground between flights. This incredibly efficient operating model has allowed them to surpass all other European airlines in passenger traffic.

There are many more examples of businesses around the world – all told in *Getting to Plan B: Breaking Through to a Better Business Model*, from which this chapter has been adapted[2] – that have revolutionized their industries by hanging their hat on one key element of their business model. Some of these companies include:

■ China's Shanda Interactive: revenue model;

■ Japan's Toyota and the USA's eBay: gross margin models;

■ India's Oberoi Hotels: operating model;

■ the USA's Costco and Dow Jones: working capital models;

■ the UK's Skype: investment model.

For others, such as Spain's Zara, combining two or more elements has made their business models particularly difficult to imitate, creating sustainable competitive advantage and an ability to grow rapidly even in brutal industries like retailing.

The cold, hard facts

Most business plans assume that almost everything is already known up front – not the case, as our examples have now shown. As the famed American general in the second World War, Douglas MacArthur, is reputed to have once said, 'No plan ever survives its first encounter with the enemy.'

The process articulated *The New Business Road Test* – first assessing your opportunity, including some experiments to examine your most crucial leaps of faith – is a healthy alternative to the straitjacket of today's business-planning practices. It will enable you to anticipate and move beyond a failing plan A. It is a process designed for learning and discovering, rather than for pitching and selling. It's a process that recognizes the cold, hard facts – most often, what ultimately works, is not the plan A that was so persuasively articulated in the original plan. Instead, it's plan B.

15

Do-it-yourself marketing research for your new business road test[1]

You can do it. And you don't have to break the bank. Most early-stage entrepreneurs simply don't have the resources to hire professional research firms to conduct the research that's necessary to assess their ideas. Even if they had the resources, they might not choose to spend them this way, since the research may well show the idea to be a non-starter. So, if you've never done this before, how should you proceed?

What does marketing research – aka due diligence – do?

Marketing research – or due diligence, in financiers' terms – is the design, collection, analysis and reporting of research intended to gather data pertinent to a *particular* marketing challenge or situation. The word 'particular' is very important. Marketing research is intended to address carefully defined marketing problems or opportunities. Research carried out without carefully thought out objectives usually means time and money down the drain. Other portions of your research may address different objectives – identifying the CSFs in your industry, for example. Whether the research you need is marketing research or some other kind, however, the guiding principles are the same.

> **the research process is fraught with numerous opportunities for error**

Let's begin with a model of the research process that sets forth the many decisions that must be made to conduct effective and actionable research. The steps in the research process are shown in Box 15.1.

Steps in the marketing research process: what can go wrong?

Steps	What frequently goes wrong?
1 Identify managerial problem and establish research objectives	Management identifies no clear objective, no decision to be made based on the proposed research
2 Determine data sources (primary or secondary) and types of data and research approaches (qualitative and quantitative) required	Primary data are collected when cheaper and faster secondary data will do Quantitative data are collected without first collecting qualitative data
3 Design research: type of study, data collection approach, sample, etc.	These are technical issues best managed by skilled practitioners Doing these steps poorly can generate misleading or incorrect results
4 Collect data	Collector bias: hearing what you want to hear
5 Analyze data	Tabulation errors or incorrect use or interpretation of statistical procedures may mislead the user
6 Report results to decision-maker	Some users do not really want objective information – they want to prove what they already believe to be true

As this shows, the research process is fraught with numerous opportunities for error. That's why it's so important for entrepreneurs to be well-informed and critical users of the information that results from marketing and other research studies. To this end, we will now address each of the steps in the research process, in terms of the decisions that you, the researcher, will need to make.

Step 1: identify the managerial problem and establish research objectives

As for any other form of human endeavour, if you don't have clear objectives, any road will get you there. The same is true for conducting research. A good place to start is to ask what the managerial problem or question is that a proposed programme of research might address. For most entrepreneurs, in their initial enquiries about assessing an opportunity, there are numerous managerial questions to be answered. How large is the market? How fast is it likely to grow? What segments are most attractive? Is the industry attractive? Who are the key competitors, and what competitive advantages might they have and not have if we enter? What customer wants and needs are not currently well satisfied, for what groups of customers or consumers? How likely are consumers to buy the solution we propose to offer? How much might they be willing to pay?

Taking each of these managerial questions one at a time, and applying appropriate analytical frameworks to each of them – such as macro-trend analysis (see Chapter 3), Porter's five forces (see Chapter 4) and so on – provides clear guidance for the kind of information the researcher needs to obtain. The result is a set of research objectives (e.g. to determine market size and growth rate, to assess supplier power in this industry, to determine your target customers' likelihood to buy and so on) that will drive the research.

Step 2: determine data sources and types of data required

This step is critical in determining the cost-effectiveness and timeliness of the research effort. There are two key questions that the researcher must answer at this stage: should I gather data from primary or secondary sources? Whichever of these types of data source are called for, do I need qualitative or quantitative research to satisfy my research objectives, or both?

Primary data are data collected from individual research subjects – using observation, a survey, interviews or whatever – that are then gathered and interpreted for the particular research objective at hand. Secondary data already exist – on the Internet, in government documents, in the business press, in company files or wherever. Someone has already done the primary data collection and placed the data where others can access them, whether easily or with difficulty, whether free or at some cost.

Which are better – primary or secondary data? *If* (and it's an important *if*) a research objective can be met using secondary data, that's usually the best course to follow. Why? Three reasons:

■ first, it's usually *quicker* to find the data somewhere than to collect them from scratch – imagine having to collect demographic data without the census;

■ second, it's usually *less costly* simply to find existing secondary data than to collect them as primary data all over again;

■ third, secondary data are typically based on what people actually do, or how they behave – surveys, a common form of primary data, are based on what people *say* and the two are not the same, as we shall see in Chapter 16, on forecasting.

For entrepreneurs, secondary data, if they are available, should answer several important research questions, such as those on market and industry attractiveness at the macro-level. To identify sources for the particular secondary data you will need, consult a business librarian. A resourceful one who knows where to look for what you need to satisfy the research objectives you specify can save you enormous amounts of time. To explore consumers' willingness to buy the solution you propose to develop, primary data are not often necessary.

Qualitative or quantitative data and research approaches?

Where secondary data are to be collected, the entrepreneur needs to decide whether qualitative data or quantitative data are required. Most secondary research studies require both qualitative (e.g. macro-trends) and quantitative (e.g. market size) data. Fortunately, both are usually easy to find.

If primary data are necessary, a decision must be made about whether to collect the data using qualitative or quantitative research approaches.

❝ the benefit of qualitative data is that they may yield deeper insights into consumer behaviour than are available from quantitative research ❞

Qualitative research usually involves small samples of subjects and produces information that is not easily quantifiable. The benefit of qualitative data is that they may yield deeper insights into consumer behaviour than are available from quantitative research. For this reason, qualitative research is often conducted first and then used to guide subsequent quantitative research. An important drawback of qualitative research, however, is that its generally small samples may not represent fairly the larger population. Most experienced marketing researchers would say, 'Never *generalize* from qualitative research. Always follow up with a quantitative study to test the hunches developed in the qualitative study.' Such statements presume, however, that adequate research resources are available to conduct additional studies. Often, and particularly in entrepreneurial settings, such is not the case, and decision-makers are forced to rely, albeit tenuously, on small-scale qualitative studies.

Quantitative research collects data that are amenable to statistical analysis, usually from large enough samples so that inferences may be drawn with some confidence from the sample to the population from which the subjects in the sample are drawn. The principal benefit of quantitative research lies in its measurement of a population's attitudes towards or likely response to products or marketing programmes. Because of their larger sample sizes and quantitative metrics, greater confidence can be placed in quantitative studies, when conducted properly, using appropriate sampling procedures and statistical techniques. These issues are addressed in more detail below.

Qualitative research techniques

There are seemingly as many qualitative research techniques as there are stars in the sky.[2] The most commonly used ones, however, are focus groups and interviews of various kinds.[3] A focus group typically consists of 8 to 12 consumers from the marketer's target market brought together at a research facility to discuss a particular marketing problem, such as attitudes towards a proposed new product and various possible features thereof. A skilled moderator conducts the focus group, records the conversation on audio and/or video tape and writes a report of the findings. Typically, two or more groups are conducted for a single research project. Focus groups have significant limitations: they are subject to data distortion caused by a dominant person in the group, their results are difficult to interpret and they are neither representative of nor generalizable to a larger population, due to their small sample size and convenience samples. They are a good way, however, to begin a research enquiry, or to gather at least some information when research budgets are tight.

❝ focus groups have significant limitations ❞

Quantitative research techniques

In most quantitative research, questionnaires are used that enable the researcher to measure the subjects' responses on quantitative scales.[4] These scales allow the researcher to compare different product attributes, the responses of demographically different consumers, and other differences in order to better understand some crucial questions.

- What products or product attributes do your prospective customers prefer?
- Which product attributes are most important?
- How satisfied are the prospective customers with one product compared with others?
- How likely are the prospective customers to buy at different price points?

Where statistically significant differences are found, you can be relatively certain that the differences uncovered in the research reflect those actually found in the population as a whole. Examples of several kinds of quantitative scale commonly used in such research are shown in Box 15.2. Novice researchers, or those whose budgets are limited, can sometimes obtain useful market knowledge from small-scale research that begins with some qualitative research – perhaps several interviews – and concludes with a quantitative study using measures like those shown in Box 15.2.

---

box 15.2

Some commonly used types of scale for quantitative marketing research

Type of scale	Description	Example
Semantic differential scale	A scale connecting two bipolar words or phrases	How satisfied are you with your provider of cable TV? Not at all satisfied 1 2 3 4 5 6 7 Extremely satisfied
Likert scale	A statement with which the respondent shows the amount of agreement/ disagreement	I am extremely satisfied with my provider of cable TV Strongly agree 1 2 3 4 5 6 7 Strongly disagree
Quality rating scale	Rates some attribute on a scale from 'excellent' to 'poor'	My cable TV service, overall, is: Poor Fair Good Very Good Excellent
Importance scale, using semantic differential format	Rates the importance of some attribute	How important are the following criteria to your satisfaction with your cable TV provider?

		Not at all					Extremely
Answers the phone quickly	1	2	3	4	5	6	7
Prompt repair service	1	2	3	4	5	6	7
Cleans up after installation	1	2	3	4	5	6	7
Service never goes dark	1	2	3	4	5	6	7

Type of scale	Description	Example
Intention to buy scale	Measures how likely the respondent is to buy at some price	How likely are you to sign up for the new InterGalactic Channel for an extra $4.95 per month?

Definitely   ☐
Probably   ☐
Might or might not   ☐
Probably not   ☐
Definitely not   ☐

Step 3: design the research

Designing secondary research is a simple matter of finding sources of information sufficient to satisfy the research objectives, and to ensure that the sources are credible ones. For primary qualitative research, such as focus groups or interviews, detailed guides must be prepared for conducting the research to specify what questions are to be asked. For primary quantitative research, research design is the most technical and most difficult step in conducting the research. It's a good place to get professional help if you can afford it. The key decisions to be made in primary research design are to determine the data collection method and prepare the research instrument, to determine how to contact the participants in the research and to design the sampling plan.

Determine the data collection method and prepare the research instrument

There are several methods of collecting qualitative primary data, of which the most common are observation, survey and experiment. Observation is just that: observing subjects doing something relevant to the objectives of the research. Typically, a form is prepared on which the observer records what is being observed. Many Japanese companies favour the use of observation to better understand not only consumers but also salespeople and distribution channel members.[5]

Surveys involve writing a questionnaire, which will include questions and either scaled answers (like those shown in Box 15.2) or spaces for open-ended answers, all of which are intended to capture whatever the researcher wants to learn. Demographic information about the respondent is also usually requested to aid in market segmentation and market targeting decisions. Constructing survey questions and formats for the answers is more difficult than one might expect, and is beyond the scope of this chapter, but several sources cited herein can help bring you up to speed on these tasks. Any business school marketing research text will have a chapter on questionnaire design.[6]

❝ one common use of experiments is to examine the consumer's likelihood to buy a new product at different price points ❞

Experiments are studies in which the researcher manipulates one or more variables, such as price or product features, either within the context of a survey or in a laboratory or field setting, in order to measure the effect of the manipulated variable on the consumer's response. One common use of experiments is to examine the consumer's likelihood to buy a new product at different price points. Different respondents are given different prices for the product, and the researcher tests differences in consumers' likelihood to buy as the price changes. This procedure entails less bias than asking consumers what they would be willing to pay for a product, the real answer to which is 'As little as possible'.

Determine the contact method

Once a data collection method is chosen, the researcher must decide how to contact those who will participate in the research. Common choices include face-to-face (perhaps in a shopping mall or a public place), mail, telephone, fax, email and the Internet. Box 15.3 shows some of the trade-offs that influence the choices you must make among these methods. A significant problem with survey research is that those who choose not

❝ for a mail survey five to six times the number of surveys as you hope to receive must be mailed ❞

to participate when asked ('We're eating dinner now, and please don't call back!') may differ from those who do participate. This non-response bias may distort the results of the research. Response rate can also be a problem, since many who are asked to participate will not do so. Response rates for mail surveys sent to consumers generally run around 15–20 per cent. Far lower response rates can be expected in business-to-business settings, which is one reason why qualitative research methods, which use smaller samples, are often used. The other types are better or worse, as shown in Box 15.3. Thus, for a mail survey, for example, at least five to six times the number of surveys as you hope to receive must be mailed.

---

box 15.3

Pros and cons of different contact methods for survey research

Method	Response rate	Cost	Timeliness	Non-response bias
Face-to-face	High	High	Slow	Low
Mail	Low	Low	Slow	High
Telephone	Moderate	Moderate	Fast	Moderate
Fax	Moderate	Low	Fast	High
Email	Low	Low	Fast	High
Internet	Low	Low	Fast	High

Design the sampling plan

Selecting a sample of participants for observational, survey or experimental research requires three questions to be answered.

1   Who is the population (or universe) from which the sample of respondents will be drawn?

2   What sample size is required to provide a level of confidence in the results that is acceptable to the decision-maker who will use the results of the research?

3   By what method – probability sampling (also called random sampling) or non-probability sampling (such as convenience sampling) – will the sample be selected?

Let's discuss each of these issues briefly. (For more on sampling, see the relevant chapter in any business school marketing research text.[7]) First, the population from which the sample is to be drawn must be specified clearly. Typically, this consists of the target market, defined in demographic or behavioural terms, although excluding current non-users might not be a good idea for an entrepreneur who hopes to expand the market.

Second, the sample must be large enough to provide confidence, in a statistical sense, that statistical data, such as mean responses to survey questions, are truly within some narrow enough range, sometimes called the margin of error. In general, the larger the sample size, the smaller the margin of error. Box 15.4 provides rough approximations of the margin of sampling error associated with different sample sizes.

Third, the idea behind probability or random sampling is that every person in the population has an equal chance of being selected. If non-probability samples, such as convenience samples, are used, then the sample may be biased. As a practical matter, convenience samples are used quite often for marketing research, because true random samples are more difficult and costly to obtain. Arguably, the non-response problem makes almost all samples potentially biased in the same way. An astute user should always ask what the sample selection method was. If the method is not random, then the user should enquire in detail about how the sample was selected to look for any obvious source of bias that might distort the research results.

---

box 15.4

Margin of error associated with different sample sizes

Assume a poll of eligible voters is taken to determine which candidate is in the lead. Suppose the results are that Jones has 45 per cent of the voters in her corner, Smith has 41 per cent and 14 per cent are undecided. Can we conclude that Jones leads Smith? It depends, in part, on the sample size of the poll.

Sample size	Approximate margin of error for 95 per cent confidence level	Implications for the Jones and Smith race
100	10 percentage points	Jones has 45% plus or minus 10%, or 35% to 55%. Smith has 41% plus or minus 10%, or 31% to 51%. Smith could be leading by as much as 51% to 35%.
500	4.5 percentage points	Jones has 45% plus or minus 4.5%, or 40.5% to 49.5%. Smith has 41% plus or minus 4.5%, or 36.5% to 45.5%. Smith could be leading by as much as 45.5% to 40.5%.
1000	3 percentage points	Jones has 45% plus or minus 3%, or 42% to 48%. Smith has 41% plus or minus 3%, or 38% to 44%. Smith could be leading by as much as 44% to 42%.

What will the headlines say? Probably that Jones leads Smith, 45 per cent to 41 per cent. If the sample size is 1000, typical in national or statewide political polls, is this a fair conclusion?

Source: Based on *What is a Margin of Error?'*, American Statistical Association Section on Survey Research Methods at http://www.webpages.uidaho.edu/~redgeman/Sampling%20PDF%20Files/margin.pdf

---

Step 4: collect the data

By now, the hardest parts of the research process are complete, but the most time-consuming parts have just begun. Unfortunately, the data-collection process contributes more to overall error than any other step in the process. In some cases, especially where entrepreneurs conduct marketing research themselves instead of contracting with a third party, these errors are magnified. There are several common kinds of error in face-to-face or telephone surveys that entrepreneurs should guard against:

- selection errors by the interviewer (i.e. selecting respondents who are not members of the specified population);

- collector bias: this occurs when the person collecting the data – inadvertently perhaps, in their enthusiasm for the opportunity – biases the respondents, so they tell the researcher what they think he or she wants to hear;

- interpretation and recording of answers: in their zeal to obtain research results that support the feasibility of their opportunity, entrepreneurs sometimes have difficulty in interpreting their data objectively; in the end, the only people they fool are themselves;

- in surveys conducted by fax, email or over the Internet, an additional problem is that the researcher does not really know who actually replied to the survey.

The data collection effort for surveys like these can be substantial. To complete 100 surveys with randomly selected homes using random-digit dialling, several hundred phone numbers and more than 1000 calls will likely be required.

Step 5: analyze the data

When the data have been collected, the completed data forms must be processed to yield the information that the project was designed to collect. The forms must be checked to see that instructions were followed, that the data are complete and that the data are logical and consistent within each respondent's form. Typically, the data are then entered into computer files, percentages and averages are computed and comparisons are made between different classes, categories and groups of respondents. Often, sophisticated statistical analyses are required. If you lack the skills to do these things, you may wish either to obtain professional help or to find some marketing research students at a nearby university to help you with this phase – or any of the phases, for that matter – of your research.

Step 6: report the results

This is where the rubber meets the road. If the research study began with clearly defined research objectives, then reporting the results simply returns to those objectives and reports what was found. Where research is carried out without clear objectives – as is sometimes the case, unfortunately – reporting can be difficult, as no clear conclusions may be available. Including a report

❝ including a report of the results of a well-designed marketing research study can be a source of credibility for the writer and a powerful differentiator against other business plans ❞

of the results of a well-designed marketing research study in a business plan can be a source of credibility for the writer and a powerful differentiator against other business plans. Perhaps the most common shortcoming of business plans that are rejected summarily by funding sources is that they lack any marketing research to provide support for the conclusions they draw. Wishful thinking and optimistic hand-waving are not enough.

What users of marketing research should ask

The research process described in this chapter makes clear where many of the potential stumbling blocks lie in designing and carrying out marketing research. Whether you conduct the research yourself or whether you hire someone to do it for you, an informed and critical user of marketing research should ask the following questions to ensure themselves that the research is unbiased and the results may be relied upon. These questions should be posed before the implementation of the research and again before its completion.

1   What are the objectives of the research? Will the data to be collected meet those objectives?

2   Are the data sources appropriate? Are cheaper, faster, secondary data used where possible? Is qualitative research planned first to ensure that quantitative research, if any, is on target?

3   Are the planned qualitative and/or quantitative research approaches well suited to the objectives of the research? Qualitative research is better for deep insights into consumer behaviour, while quantitative research is better for measurement of a population's attitudes and likely responses to products or marketing programmes. For most entrepreneurs, the first of these purposes is the more important.

4   Is the research designed well? Will questionnaire scales permit the measurement necessary to meet the research objectives? Are the questions on a survey or in an interview or focus group unbiased? ('Isn't this a great new product? Do you like it?') Do the contact method and sampling plan entail any known bias? Is the sample size large enough to meet the research objectives?

5   Are the planned analyses appropriate? They should be specified *before* the research is conducted.

Rudimentary competence: are we there yet?

A key objective of this chapter is to provide you, the entrepreneur, with at least a rudimentary level of competence in designing and carrying out marketing research studies. Entire courses dealing with marketing research are offered in nearly every business school curriculum, and this brief chapter does little justice to the detail and technical expertise involved in this important craft. Nonetheless, by reading this material and a few of the cited reference sources on particular research techniques, you should be able to conduct at least some useful research for an entrepreneurial venture. Such research, despite its limitations, will yield greater insights into the opportunity's attractiveness than will hunches alone.

16

Evidence-based forecasting[1]

I know of no manager or entrepreneur who has ever seen a forecast that came in exactly on the money. Some forecasts turn out too high, others too low. Forecasting is an inherently difficult task because no one has a perfect crystal ball. The future is inherently uncertain, especially in today's rapidly changing markets. Consumer wants and needs change, buffeted by the winds of ever-changing macro-trends. Competitors come and go. New technologies sweep away old ones.

Some forecasts are based on extensive and expensive research, others on small-scale enquiries, still others on uninformed hunches. Forecasting plays a central role in all kinds of planning and budgeting in all kinds of businesses and organizations. For entrepreneurs, forecasting is crucial because it's the foundation on which every business plan is based. The forecast drives the level of expenses that will be required to operate the business. It drives the level of investment needed to produce the sales. And it tells the entrepreneur whether there's enough revenue to be had from the opportunity to make it worthy of pursuit.

> **for entrepreneurs, forecasting is crucial because it's the foundation on which every business plan is based**

Given these stakes, and given the risks entailed in being very wrong with a forecast, some effort to prepare an evidence-based forecast, instead of a wild guess, is almost always called for, even if time and money are scarce. So forecast you must – but how?

A forecaster's toolkit: a tool for every forecasting setting

Before choosing a method to prepare a forecast, the entrepreneur must know first what is to be estimated or forecasted. First, there's market potential, i.e. the likely demand from all actual and potential buyers of a product or product class. An estimate of market potential often serves as a starting point for preparing a sales forecast, about which we'll talk more later.

For your venture, prospective investors will want to know how large the potential market for your goods or services will be in the coming years, measured perhaps in several ways: in numbers of potential users, numbers of units to be purchased and in pounds sterling, dollars or even Tanzanian shillings, if you are in Tanzania. There's also the size of the currently penetrated market – those who are actually using goods or services like those you propose to offer. Investors will also want to know these figures – the size of the potential and penetrated markets – for the market segments you intend to serve, i.e. your target market. Clearly, though, you will not win a 100 per cent share of this market. For the pro formas in your business plan, you will also need to forecast your sales revenues, probably for three to five years going forward – a sales forecast. How might you do all these things?

In established organizations, there are two broad approaches for preparing a sales forecast: top down and bottom-up. Under the top-down approach, a central person or people take the responsibility for forecasting and prepare an overall forecast, perhaps using aggregate economic data, current sales trends or other of the methods described shortly.[2] Under the bottom-up approach – a common approach in decentralized firms – each part of the company prepares its own sales forecast, and the parts are aggregated to create the forecast for the firm as a whole. Either of these logics may be useful in preparing a sales forecast for your new venture.

❝ there are two broad approaches for preparing a sales forecast: top-down and bottom-up ❞

For example, using the bottom-up logic, you can break your anticipated demand into pieces – either market segments or product lines – and add up the components to create the summary forecast. There are numerous advantages to using this approach. First, it will force you to think clearly about the drivers of demand for each market segment or product line and thus understand better the real potential of your opportunity and the parts thereof.[3] Second, you will be forced to make explicit assumptions about the drivers of demand in each category, assumptions you can debate – and support with evidence gathered from your research – with prospective investors and that you and they can verify later as the business unfolds. Third, such an approach facilitates 'What if . . .?' planning. Various combinations of market segments and/or product lines can be combined to build a business plan that looks viable.

So, what forecasting methods or tools can you choose from? There are six major evidence-based methods for estimating market potential and forecasting sales: statistical methods, observation, surveys, analogy, judgement and market tests.[4] A seventh method, not evidenced-based – the SWAG – is not condoned here, though there is little else to support the forecasts in many business plans.

Statistical and other quantitative methods

Statistical methods use past history and various statistical techniques, such as multiple regression and time series analysis, to forecast the future based on an extrapolation of the past.[5] Is this method useful for entrepreneurs or new product managers charged with forecasting sales for a new product or new business? Often not, for there is no history in their venture on which to base a statistical forecast. Your business may not even exist yet.

In established firms, for established products, statistical methods are extremely useful. When Michelin, the tyre maker, wants to forecast demand for the replacement car tyre market in Europe for the next year, it can build a statistical model using factors such as the number and age of vehicles currently on the road in Europe, predictions of GDP for the region, the last few years' demand and other relevant factors to forecast market potential, as well as Michelin's own replacement tyre sales for the coming year. Such a procedure is likely to result in a considerably more accurate forecast than other methods, especially if Michelin has years of experience with which to calibrate its statistical model.

❝ in established firms, for established products, statistical methods are extremely useful ❞

As with all forecasting methods, there are important limitations of statistical methods. The most important of these is that statistical methods generally assume that the future will look very much like the past. Sometimes this is not the case. US WEST, the regional Bell telephone company serving the Rocky Mountain and northwest regions of the USA, ran into trouble in the 1990s when its statistical models used to predict needs for telephone capacity failed to allow for the rapidly increasing use of computer modems, faxes and second lines for teenagers in American homes. Suddenly, the average number of lines per home skyrocketed, and there was not enough physical plant – cable in the ground, switches and so on – to accommodate the growing demand. Consumers had to wait, sometimes for months, to get additional lines, and they were not happy about it.[6] Similarly, if product or market characteristics change, then statistical models used without adequate judgement may not keep pace. When tyre makers produce car tyres that last 80,000 miles instead of 30,000 – 50,000 miles, the annual demand for replacement tyres is reduced. If car manufacturers were to change the number of wheels on the typical car from four, then the old statistical models would also be in trouble.

A variety of other quantitative forecasting methods, especially for new product forecasting, have also been developed. These include methods to model mathematically the diffusion of innovation process for consumer durables,[7] and conjoint analysis,[8] a method to forecast the impact upon consumer demand of different combinations of attributes that might be included in a new product. For entrepreneurs who are so inclined, these methods are worth a look.

Observation

Another method for preparing an evidence-based forecast is to observe or gather existing data directly about what real consumers really do in the product-market of interest. Like statistical methods, observation-based forecasting is attractive because it is based on what people actually do. To the extent that behavioural or usage data can be found from existing secondary sources – in company files, at the library or on the Internet – data collection is both faster and cheaper than if a new study has to be designed and carried out. For new-to-the-world products, however, observation is typically not possible and secondary data are not available, since the product often does not exist yet, except in concept form. Market tests, discussed later, are one way to get real purchase data about new-to-the-world products.

> **like statistical methods, observation-based forecasting is attractive because it is based on what people actually do**

Surveys

Another common way to forecast sales or estimate market potential is to conduct surveys. These surveys can be done with different groups of respondents. Consumers, after being shown a statement of the product concept[9] or a prototype or sample of the product, can be asked how likely they are to buy it. Buyers can also be asked about their current buying behaviour: what they currently buy, how often or how much they use. The salesforce can be asked

> **there are important limitations of surveys, however**

how much they are likely to sell. Experts of various kinds – members of the distribution channel, suppliers, consultants, trade association executives and so on – can also be surveyed.

There are important limitations of surveys, however.

■ What people *say* is not always what people *do*. Consumer surveys of buyer intention are always discounted heavily to allow for this fact. For one common approach to doing so, see Box 16.1.

---

box 16.1

A survey of buyers' intentions: what people *say* is not what they *do*

When Nestlé's refrigerated foods division in the USA was considering whether to acquire Lambert's Pasta and Cheese, a fresh pasta maker, it wanted to forecast the likely first-year sales volume if the acquisition were completed. To do so, Nestlé used a concept test in which consumers were asked, among other things, how likely they were to try the fresh pasta product. The results were as shown in the first two columns in the table below.

Purchase intent	Percentage response	Rule of thumb reduction for forecasting purposes	Percentage of market deemed likely to actually buy
Definitely would buy	27%	Multiply by .8	27% x .8 = 21.6%
Probably would buy	43%	Multiply by .3	43% x .3 = 12.9%
Might or might not buy	22%	Count as zero	
Probably or definitely would not buy	8%	Count as zero	
Totals	100%		21.6% + 12.9% = 34.5%

Even though 70 per cent of consumers surveyed indicated they were likely to buy, Nestlé's experience indicated that these 'top two box' percentages should be cut sharply: 'Definitely' responses were reduced by 20 per cent, while 'Probably' responses were reduced by 70 per cent. 'Maybe' responses were considered as 'No'. These adjustments, shown in columns three and four, reduced the 70 per cent figure by more than half, to 34.5 per cent. Most consumer product manufacturers who employ concept tests use similar rules of thumb when interpreting purchase intent data for forecasting purposes, because they have learned that what people *say* they will buy exceeds what they will *actually* buy. Similar logic is useful in a variety of forecasting situations.

Source: Based on Marie Bell and V. Kasturi Rangan, 1995, *Nestlé Refrigerated Foods: Contadina Pasta and Pizza*, Harvard Business School Publishing, Boston, MA.

■ The people who are surveyed may not be knowledgeable, but if asked for their opinion they will probably provide it.

■ What people imagine about a product concept in a survey may not be what is actually delivered once the product is launched. If consumers are asked whether they will buy an 'old-world spaghetti sauce with home-made flavour', they will surely provide a response. Whether they will actually *like* the taste and texture of the sauce that the lab develops is another story.

In general, statistical and observational methods, where adequate data or settings are available in which to apply them, are superior to survey methods of forecasting, because such methods are based, at least in part, on what people have actually done or bought (e.g. the number of old cars actually on the road), while survey methods ('Are you likely to buy replacement tyres this year?') are based on what people say, a less reliable indicator of their future behaviour.

Analogy

An approach often used for new product forecasting where neither statistical methods nor observations are possible is to forecast the sales or market potential for a new product or new venture by analogy. Under this method, the product is compared with similar products that were introduced earlier, for which historical data are available. When Danone, the French marketer of yogurt, plans to introduce a new flavour of packaged yogurt, its managers will likely look at the sales history of earlier introductions to forecast the sales for the newest flavour. This method is also used for new-to-the-world high-technology products, for which product prototypes are often either not available or are extremely expensive to produce.

ff an approach often used for new product forecasting where neither statistical methods nor observations are possible is to forecast the sales or market potential for a new product or new venture by analogy 🗩

Rather than conduct surveys to ask consumers about their likelihood of buying a product they can hardly imagine (what would someone have said in 1978 about their likelihood of buying a personal computer?), forecasters consider related new product introductions with which the new product may be compared. Early forecasts for high-definition television (HDTV) were done this way, comparing HDTV with historical penetration patterns for colour TV, video recorders, camcorders and other consumer electronic products.[10]

As always, there are limitations. First, the new product is never exactly like that with which the analogy is drawn. Early video recorders penetrated their markets at a much faster rate than did colour TV. Which analogy should be used for HDTV? Why? Second, market and competitive conditions may differ considerably from when the analogous product was launched. Such conditions need to be taken into account.

Judgement

While we hesitate to call this a forecasting method of its own, since capable and informed judgement is required for *all* methods, forecasts are sometimes made solely on the basis of experienced judgement or intuition. Some decision-makers are intuitive in their decision processes and cannot always articulate the basis for their intuitive judgements.

Said a footwear buyer at Nine West Group, 'Trend forecasting is a visceral thing that cannot be trained. I rely on my sense of colour and texture, but at times I cannot explain why I feel a certain way . . . I just know.'[11] Those with sufficient forecasting experience in a market they know well may be quite accurate in their intuitive forecasts. Unfortunately, it is often difficult for them to defend their forecasts against forecasts prepared by evidence-based methods when these forecasts differ. Nonetheless, the importance of experienced judgement in forecasting, whether it is used solely and intuitively or in concert with evidence-based methods, cannot be discounted.

Market tests

Market tests of various kinds are the last of the commonly used forecasting methods. Used largely for new products, market tests may be carried out under controlled experimental conditions in research laboratories, on the Internet or in live test markets with real advertising and promotion and real distribution in real stores. Use of test markets has declined over the past few decades for three reasons:

- they are expensive to carry out, since usually significant quantities of the new product must be produced and marketing activities of various kinds must be paid for;

- in today's data-intensive environment, especially for consumer products sold through supermarkets and mass merchants, competitors can buy the data collected through scanners at the checkout and learn the results of the test market without bearing the expense to conduct it;

■ competitors can engage in marketing tactics to mislead the company conducting the test, by increasing sampling programmes, offering large discounts or buy-one-get-one-free promotions, or otherwise distorting normal purchasing patterns in the category.

The coming of the Internet has made possible a new kind of market test: an offer directly to consumers on the Web. Offers to chat rooms, interest groups or email lists of current customers are some of the approaches that have been tried. Entrepreneurs' use of such techniques will likely increase, due to their ability to carry out such tests quickly and at low cost.

---

box 16.2

Chain ratio forecast: trial of fresh pasta

Once Nestlé's research on fresh pasta had been completed (see Box 16.1), it used the chain ratio method to calculate the total number of households that would try their fresh pasta. The chain ratio calculation went like this.

Research results for:	Data from research	Chain ratio calculation	Result
number of households in target market	77.4 million		
concept purchase intent: adjusted figure from Box 16.1	34.5% will try the product	77.4 million x 34.5%	26.7 million households will try if aware
awareness adjustment: based on planned advertising level	48% will be aware of the product	26.7 million x 48%	12.8 million households will try if they find product at their store
distribution adjustment: based on likely extent of distribution in supermarkets, given the introductory trade promotion plan	the product will obtain distribution reaching 70% of US households	12.8 million x 70%	9.0 million will try the product

Similar chain ratio logic is useful in a variety of forecasting settings.

Source: Based on Marie Bell and V. Kasturi Rangan, 1995, *Nestlé Refrigerated Foods: Contadina Pasta and Pizza*, Harvard Business School Publishing, Boston, MA.

Mathematics entailed in forecasting

Regardless of the method used, the ultimate purpose of forecasting is to generate numbers that reflect what the entrepreneur believes is the most likely outcome – or sometimes a range of outcomes, under different assumptions – in terms of future market potential or for the sales of a product, a product line or a new venture. The combination of judgement and other methods often leads to the use of either of two mathematical approaches to determine the ultimate numbers: the chain ratio calculation or the use of indices. Boxes 16.2 and 16.3 offer examples of how to apply these mathematical approaches to arrive at sales forecasts.

---

box 16.3

Estimating market potential using indices

In most developed countries there are several published indices of buying behaviour, including the 'Annual Survey of Buying Power' published by *Sales and Marketing Management*, for the US. The buying power index (BPI) is a weighted sum of a geographical area's percentage of national buying power for the area, based on census income data (weight .5), plus the percentage of national retail sales for the area (weight .3), plus the percentage of national population located in the area (weight .2). If this calculation comes to 3.50 for a given state or region, one might expect 3.5 per cent of sales in a given category (toys, power tools or whatever) to come from that geographical area.

Category development indices (CDIs) are similar indices that report the ratio of consumption in a certain *category* (say, restaurant sales) to population in a defined geographical area. Trade associations or trade magazines relevant to the category typically publish such indices. Ratios greater than 1.0 for a particular geographic area, say metropolitan Manchester, indicate that the area does more business than average (compared to the country as a whole) in that category.

Brand development indices (BDIs) compare sales for a given *brand* (say, PizzaExpress restaurants) to population. Companies that use BDIs typically calculate them for their own use. The ratio of the BDI to the CDI for a given area is an indicator of how well a brand is doing, compared to its category overall, in that area.

These various indices are useful for estimating market potential in defined geographic areas. They are, however, crude numbers, in that they do not consider differences in consumer behaviour from region to region. The CDI or BDI for snowmobiles in Austria is far higher than in Spain, for example. Attempting to rectify this imbalance by increasing the snowmobile advertising budget in Spain would be difficult!

Note that both mathematical approaches begin with some kind of an estimate of market potential (the number of households in the target market in Box 16.2; the national market potential for a product category in Box 16.3). The market potential is then multiplied by various fractional factors that, taken together, predict the portion of the overall market potential that one firm or product can expect to obtain. In Box 16.2, which shows the more detailed of the two approaches, the factors reflect the appeal of the product to consumers, as measured by marketing research data, and the company's planned marketing programme.

Cautions and caveats in forecasting

Keys to good forecasting

There are two important keys to improving the credibility and accuracy of forecasts of sales and market potential. The first of these is to make explicit the assumptions on which the forecast is based. This way, if there is debate or doubt about the forecast, then the assumptions can be debated and data to support the assumptions can be obtained. The resulting conversation is far more useful than stating opinions about whether the forecast is too high or too low.

The second key to effective forecasting is to use multiple methods. Where forecasts obtained by different methods converge near a common figure,

❝ entrepreneurs should remember that any forecast is almost certainly wrong ❞

greater confidence can be placed in that figure. Where forecasts obtained by multiple methods diverge, the assumptions inherent in each can be examined to determine which set of assumptions can best be trusted. Ultimately, however, entrepreneurs should remember that any forecast is almost certainly wrong. Contingency plans should be developed to cope with the reality that ultimately unfolds. A key challenge for manufacturers is to be able to quickly adjust production schedules to adapt to demand that differs from the forecast.[12]

Biases in forecasting

Entrepreneurs should recognize several sources of potential bias in the forecasts they make. First, forecasts are subject to anchoring bias, where forecasts are perhaps anchored inappropriately to recent comparable or historical figures, even though market conditions have changed markedly for better or worse.[13]

Second, capacity constraints are sometimes misinterpreted as forecasts. Someone planning to open a car wash that can process one car every seven minutes would probably be amiss in assuming sufficient demand to actually run at that rate all the time. A restaurant chain that is able to turn its tables twice each night, on average, must still do local market research in order to ascertain how much volume a new restaurant will really produce. Obviously, putting similar 30-table restaurants in two different trade areas with different population make-up and density with different levels of competition will result in different sales levels.

> **❝ entrepreneurs should not assume 100 per cent awareness and distribution coverage ❞**

Finally, unstated but implicit assumptions can overstate a well-intentioned forecast. While 34.5 per cent of those surveyed (after adjustments, as shown in Box 16.1) may indicate their willingness to buy a new grocery product, such as fresh pasta, for such a forecast to pan out requires that consumers are actually made aware of the new product when it is introduced, and that the product can actually be found on supermarket shelves. In forecasting the likely sales of consumer goods and others to be marketed through distribution channels, entrepreneurs should not assume 100 per cent awareness and distribution coverage. Actual awareness and distribution levels should be estimated based on the planned marketing programme for the product and factored into the forecast via the chain ratio method (see Box 16.2).

17

Getting help with your road test

There you have it. Ten chapters of what you need to know to road test your idea, and six chapters of hands-on tools to help you get the job done. The good news is that you are not alone, not with 2 million others in the UK, or similarly large numbers wherever else you may be, doing likewise. Or maybe you're fortunate to be working on a new venture within an established company, where there are colleagues to work with. Whichever is the case for you, if you haven't yet built your entrepreneurial team, road testing your idea can seem like a lonely task. Fortunately, there are lots of places to network with others on similar paths – people in the throes of testing an idea for a new business, getting a business started or working to get their growth curve pointing skywards.

A good place to start is on the Internet, where communities of entrepreneurs and aspiring entrepreneurs are building their networks. Every country has websites for entrepreneurs, and any of the search engines are good places to find them. In the UK, though, there are a few that stand out. One is www.startups.co.uk, a site targeted at building better businesses. Their online forum receives, at the time I write, more than 100,000 site visits per month, with lots of active discussion threads running at any one time. Another useful site is www.growthbusiness.co.uk, where the focus is on growing the business after the start-up and making sure the wheels don't fall off. Lots of *New Business Road Test* readers are in this stage of their business evolution. If that's you, this site is worth a look. For those working on business plans – and that's common among our readers, some of whom have the cart before the horse! – another good resource is www.bizplans.co.uk, where various sorts of help are available to those who need a business plan to get a loan from the bank, get friends and family on board or raise capital from a business angel. Because this site operates in association with the London Business School, I know you can rely on it.

Finally, every summer the entrepreneurship faculty at the London Business School runs an Entrepreneurship Summer School, where several dozen participants from around the world come to work on their new business ideas under the guidance of a mentor from the school's extensive entrepreneurial network. There are summer programmes of various kinds at other schools, too. For those who would like to travel the road in the company of others on similar journeys, this is a good way to do it if the season fits. For details of suitable programmes for you, check the websites of the leading business schools.

In whatever manner you carry out your own road test, know that you'll have plenty of company. Tens of thousands of readers of this book's first and second editions have travelled this path before you. For many, the road test has put the brakes on a venture that was found to be fatally flawed, saving countless weeks or months of time – precious time for entrepreneurs – not to mention the money that would likely have been wasted. Time that those same entrepreneurs can now spend putting their efforts into ideas that *can* fly. Time that, with hard work and perhaps a little luck, will lead to a thriving venture that employs others, that brings business to suppliers and that delivers great solutions to customers to resolve their pain. Tomorrow's new jobs depend on people like them – and like you – because it's the community of entrepreneurs who drive the engine of economic development. You're on a noble and exciting path. May your journey be a fulfilling one!

Appendix

Research methodology

As a three-time entrepreneur with a win, a loss and a draw to my name, I've long been curious about what was for me a burning question: what is it that makes the difference between new ventures that succeed and those that fail? Eventually, I grew curious enough about this question that I moved on from my 20-year business career, went back to school to earn a PhD and began teaching and learning about entrepreneurship in a more systematic way. Not having to fight the daily fires I'd fought as an entrepreneur gave me the time to think carefully about this question, and working with bright MBA students and entrepreneurs still in the trenches challenged my thinking further.

In 2000, while on sabbatical at the London Business School, one of the world's top-ranked (among the world's top seven, according to *Business-Week*[1]) institutions in the teaching, research and practice of entrepreneurship and a remarkably entrepreneurial place in its own right, and amid the unravelling of the dot.com boom, I undertook an extensive effort to shed new light on my question. I began my research with a careful reading of the varied literature that has something to say about opportunity assessment – literature in entrepreneurship, strategic management, marketing, finance and economics. What had the world's best academic minds learned about what makes an opportunity a good one? I then formulated a series of open-ended questions that I would ask of experienced venture capital investors and serial entrepreneurs, people who, in my judgement, must be skilled at the opportunity assessment task out of necessity. In their lines of work, assessing opportunity poorly would lead quickly to failure. Their real-world perspective was essential, I knew.

I then conducted a series of qualitative interviews – typically ranging in duration between one and two hours and based on the research methodology described in Chapter 11 – with 24 serial entrepreneurs and venture capital investors in the USA and the UK – from Cambridge and London to Silicon Valley in California. My research assistants and I prepared transcripts of the interviews and analyzed the results. As a final check, I then discussed and debated the results with my London Business School colleagues and others. Finally, I provided a draft of my conclusions to a subset of those I had interviewed, and asked two questions: 'What's wrong, inaccurate or incomplete here?' and 'What, if anything, do my findings add to what people who start or fund new ventures already know?'

The key result of this research was the seven domains model that comprises the intellectual and pragmatic core of this book. To make the seven domains come alive, I worked with a talented former student – now a promising businesswoman in her own right – to identify examples of companies whose stories would show how the seven domains play out in practice. Researching these companies completed the analysis. These case histories bring the seven domains to life far better than my own words ever could.

My colleagues and I – and a growing number of entrepreneurship faculties around the world – have since used the seven domains model in our business school classrooms, most notably in the Entrepreneurship Summer School at the London Business School. There we help an average of 50 aspiring entrepreneurs each summer put their ideas through the seven domains tests, under the guidance of mentors from the school's global entrepreneurial community (see www.london.edu/summer_school for more information). We've also used the model in executive programmes in the venture capital industry, the pharmaceutical industry and elsewhere, and found that it consistently opens eyes. Markets and industries really *are* different, and that difference matters. Both macro- and micro-levels merit careful scrutiny. Entrepreneurs can't be assessed adequately by simply reading their CVs or examining their character and entrepreneurial drive. The model is comprehensive, yet simple and parsimonious. It is straightforward to understand and apply. It captures the key elements of attractive opportunities. And it works to answer the aspiring entrepreneur's most fundamental question: why will or won't this work?

Entrepreneurs and others who've used the seven domains framework have also discovered that it serves as a useful diagnostic check-up at virtually any point in a growing company's history. It's a good way to see what's changed in the environment in which the business operates, what hasn't, and whether any of the assumptions that have guided the business need to be altered or updated.

As luck would have it, the model also works to provide new insights into investors' own portfolios and the patterns inherent in their portfolios' successes and failures. Are angel investors and venture capitalists serial mistake-makers, the victims of recurring patterns of errors that make their overall success dependent on the one or two in ten investments that hit the big time or are other patterns at work? There's much yet to learn!

Notes

Chapter 1

1   Quoted in 'Venture capital has gone from one unreality to another', *Knowledge at Wharton*, http://knowledge.wharton.upenn.edu/

2   For those interested in reading more about what makes for a successful entrepreneur, see Chapter 2 in David A. Kirby, 2003, *Entrepreneurship*, McGraw-Hill, Maidenhead.

3   We distinguish between *market* opportunities – those brought about by the confluence of market and competitive factors – and *financial* opportunities, such as those where arbitrage or underpriced assets provide the primary basis for economic gain.

4   The short blocks of italicized text in this and subsequent chapters are quotations from the interviews that comprise the research on which this book is based.

5   Such environmental assessments are explained in further detail in the environmental analysis chapter of any textbook on marketing management, such as Chapter 3 in H. Boyd, O. Walker, J. Mullins and J.-C. Larréché, 2005, *Marketing Management: A Strategic Decision Making Approach*, McGraw-Hill/Irwin, Burr Ridge, IL.

6   Two useful tools for making micro-level market assessments – the buyer utility map and the price corridor of the mass – are provided in W. Chan Kim and Renée Mauborgne, 2002, 'Knowing a winning business idea when you see one', *Harvard Business Review*, September–October.

7   For more on real options, see Avinash K. Dixit and Robert S. Pindyck, 1995, 'The options approach to capital investment', *Harvard Business Review*, May–June; and Rita Gunther McGrath, 1999, 'Falling forward: real options reasoning and entrepreneurial failure', *Academy of Management Review*, January.

8   For details on how to conduct a five forces analysis, see Michael Porter, 1979, 'How competitive forces shape strategy', *Harvard Business Review*, March–April.

9   For more detail on these ideas, see the chapter on resources and capabilities in any strategic management textbook, such as Chapter 5 in R.M. Grant, 2004, *Contemporary Strategy Analysis*, Blackwell, Oxford.

10 For more on operating cash cycle characteristics and their impact on a firm's ability to grow, see Neil C. Churchill and John W. Mullins, 2001, 'How fast can your company afford to grow?', *Harvard Business Review*, May.

Chapter 2

1   Peter Drucker, 1967, *The Effective Executive*, Harper & Row, New York, p. 53.

2   Danny Bradbury, 2001, 'WAP could get a shot in the arm from iMode', *Computer Weekly*, 1 February, p. 46.

3   Figures from Census of Japan, http://jin.jcic.or.jp/stat/index.html

4   Yaeko Mitsumori, 2000, 'NTT's iMode paves the way for wireless data services', *Radio Communications Report*, 28 February, p. 108.

5   Preliminary FY1999 Statistics on Telecommunications Market in Japan, Telecommunications Carrier Association, 31 August, 2000, p. 5.

6 From www.nua.ie/surveys/?f=VS&art_id=905357352&rel=true

7 Bien Perez, 2000, 'DoCoMo boosts iMode reach; Japanese mobile operator exports version of home services while moving to create fit with partners' systems', *South China Morning Post*, 12 December.

8 See note 4.

9 Catherine Ong, 2000, 'iMode a success thanks to HTML', *Business Times (Singapore)*, 10 June.

10 From 'Why i-Mode is successful in Japan', www.nttdocomo.com/html/imode02_4.html

11 Clive Keyte, 2001, 'Learn mobile lessons from Japanese', *Computer Weekly*, 9 August, p. 18.

12 Jamie Smyth, 2000, 'I-mode set to take Europe by storm', *Irish Times*, 6 October.

13 See note 4.

14 *Communications Today*, 2000, 'Wireless industry prospers, except 3G, execs say at Wireless 2000', 29 February.

15 See note 11.

16 *ISP Business News*, 2001, 'Japan's NTT turns i-Mode toward American markets', 28 May.

17 *Japanese News Digest*, 2004, 'Japan NTT DoCoMo I-Mode Service Overseas Subscribers at 3.0 Mln End-June 2004', 12 July.

18 *PR Newswire Europe*, 2005, 'Mobile Content Market Set to Triple to More Than 7.6 Billion Euros Within a Year', 6 July.

19 *Japanese News Digest*, 2004, 'Japan NTT DoCoMo I-Mode Service Overseas Subscribers at 3.0 Mln End-June 2004', 12 July.

20 Kevin J. O'Brien, 2007, 'Forerunner of mobile Internet, i-mode is fading in Europe', *New York Times*, 17 July.

21 Greg Farrell, 1994, 'Lite weight no longer', *Brandweek*, 31 October, p. 18.

22 Fran Brock, 1985, 'Brewers need drinkers for their low-alcohol beer', *AdWeek*, 18 March.

23 Stratford Sherman, 1985, 'America's new abstinence', *Fortune*, 18 March, p. 20.

24 Figures from 'Population and housing characteristics of baby boomers 26 to 44 years old: 1990', http://www.census.gov/population/censusdata/cph-1-160h.txt

25 Bart Barnes, 1983, 'Survey indicates sports play a major role in our lives', *Washington Post*, 16 March.

26 William Oscar Johnson, 1988, 'Sports and suds: the beer business and the sports world have brewed up a potent partnership', *Sports Illustrated*, 8 August, p. 68.

27 See note 21.

28 Tony Schwartz, 1981, 'Light beer ad can be heavy work', *New York Times*, 10 December.

29 Mike Littwin, 1985, 'They're all-stars at play; the mood is light; the product is lite; results are heavy', *Los Angeles Times*, 4 February.

30 From 'Shakeout in the brewery industry', http://www.beerhistory.com/library/holdings/shakeout.shtml

31 See note 26.

32 Robert E. O'Neill, 1986, 'No stopping the light brigade (1986 supermarket sales manual – beer and wine)', *Progressive Grocer*, July, p. 49.

33 James E. Causey, 1997, 'Nation's beer drinkers see the light', *Milwaukee Journal Sentinel*, 1 June.

34 Information on Nike's case history was taken from the Nike, Inc. website at http://www.nike.com/nikebiz

35 Geraldine E. Willigan, 1992, 'High-performance marketing: an interview with Nike's Phil Knight', *Harvard Business Review*, July–August.

36   From 'Nike, Inc. – entering the new millennium', Harvard Business School Case 9-299-084, 16 March 2001, p. 1.

37   *Forbes*, 2000, 'The A-list', 5 January.

38   Fara Warner, 2002, 'Nike's women's movement', *Fast Company*, August, Issue 61.

39   See note 38.

40   2005, 'Nike analyst meeting – final', *Fair Disclosure Wire*, 28 June.

41   Mark Parker, 2009, 'Letter to the Shareholders', *Nike Annual Report*, http://media. corporate-ir.net/media_files/irol/10/100529/AnnualReport/nike-sh09-rev2/index. html#mark_parker_letter

42   From http://www.usna.com/news_pubs/publications/shipmate/2000/2000_04/brides.htm

43   *Business Wire*, 1999, 'OurBeginning.com revolutionizes wedding invitation industry with launch of first complete online sales and services site', 12 April.

44   Kathleen Kelleher, 2001, 'Birds and bees; so there are more single people, but it's still a couple's world', *Los Angeles Times*, 12 February.

45   From 'Communications and information technology', statistical abstract for the USA, http://www.census.gov/prod/2001pubs/statab/sec18.pdf

46   Nancy Pfister, 1999, 'Marketing the frou-frou to growlin' football fans', *Industry Wrapups*, 3 December.

47   Ellen Zavian, 2000, 'Women score first down as Super Bowl ads debut', *Brandmarketing*, February.

48   *Business Wire*, 2000, 'OurBeginning.com reports record quarter following Super Bowl XXXIV debut', 25 May.

49   Traffic figures in this paragraph are from Neilsen/NetRatings survey, as reported in Greg Farrell, 'Bailing out from the Super Bowl ad binge', 2000, *USA Today*, 7 June.

50   Barnet D. Wolf, 2000, 'Money can't buy name recognition on the internet', *Columbus Dispatch*, 11 June, p. 1H.

51   See note 48.

52   See note 43.

53   See note 48.

54   Kim Girard, 2002, 'Crash and learn', *Business 2.0*, June.

55   Jeffrey D. Zbar, 2001, 'Marketing agencies have learned how to handle Dot-Com phenomenon', *Sun-Sentinel*, 19 January.

56   See note 46.

57   Sandeep Junnarker, 2000, '"Dot Coms" look to score from Super Bowl ads', CNET News.com, 21 January, http://www.news.com.com/2100–1017–235943.html

Chapter 3

1   From William Shakespeare, *Julius Caesar*, Act IV, Scene iii.

2   From a Hero Honda ad campaign, http://www.herohonda.com/a/about_hist_main.htm

3   Rohit Saran, 2001, 'Hero Honda: hero no. 1', *India Today*, 10 September.

4   From http://www.eia.doe.gov/emeu/cabs/india/indiach1.htm

5   SAPRA India, 1998, 'Development in the twenty-first century: challenges ahead for India', http://www.subcontinent.com/sapra

6   See note 5.

7   From http://www.wwmr.org/indiademo.html

8   India Infoline, 2001, http://www.indiainfoline.com/fmcg/demo/po08.html

9   From http://www.wwmr.org/indiademo.html

10   See note 5.

11   From http://in.indiainfoline.lycosasia.com/lyas/econ/andb/infr/infr13.shtml

12   John Tagliabue, 1996, *New York Times*, 17 August, p. 34.

13   Cybersteering, 1999–2002, 'How did the international giants get their names?', http://www.cybersteering.com/trimain/history/names.html

14   R. Sridharan, 1998, 'The Hero Group: can the Munjals survive?', *Business Today*, 7 January.

15–16 See note 3.

17   HowStuffWorks, 2002, http://www.howstuffworks.com/two-stroke3.htm

18   See note 3.

19   Brian Carvalho and Swati Prasad, 2001, 'Bike wars', *Business Today*, 2 September.

20   See note 19.

21   See note 3.

22   From http://www.herohonda.com/a/press_main.htm

23–24 See note 3.

25   Hero Honda, 2004, 'Hero Honda Creates New Performance Records', 12 April, at http://www.herohonda.com/site/press

26   Raghuvir Srinivasan, 2003, 'Hero and Honda – Fill it, shut it, forget it?', *The Hindu Business Line*, 16 March.

27   Neha Kaushik, 2004, 'The scooter surge', *The Hindu Business Line*, 5 August.

28   Bhupesh Bhandari and S. Kalyana Ramanathan, 2005, 'A 50% market share is not easy to sustain', *Business Standard*, 3 June.

29   Swarai Baggonkar, 2009, 'For scooters, it's yesterday once more – almost', http://business.rediff.com/report/2009/jun/20/for-scooters-its-yesterday-once-more-almost.htm

30   *The Hindu Business Line,* 2009, 'Hero Honda powers ahead', 2 September.

31   Shobhana Subramian, 2009, 'It's a Long Road Ahead', *Business Standard*, 4 May.

32   Barry Janoff, 1999, 'Supermarkets go au naturel', *Progressive Grocer*, vol. 78, issue 3, p. 75.

33   Dennis Roth, 2000, 'America's fascination with nutrition', *Food Review*, January–April, p. 32.

34   S.C. Gwynne, 1998, 'Thriving on health food' *Time*, http://www.time.com/time/archive/preview/0,10987,987856,00.html

35   From http://www.wholefoodsmarket.com/products/list_preparedfoods.html

36   Steve Dwyer, 1997, 'The right prescription for maturing', *Prepared Foods*, February, p. 12.

37   Buck Jones, 'Deli update 1997', *Progressive Grocer*, vol. 76, issue 4, p. 131.

38   See note 32.

39   German Munoz, 2001, 'What's feeding organic growth?', *Natural Foods Merchandiser*, June.

40   From http://www.wholefoodsmarket.com/investor/AR00_letter.html

41   Erin Kelly, 2000, 'Health-food chains spar for baby boomers', *Fortune*, 3 April, p. 56.

42   Whole Foods Market, 2005, '2004 was the best year in our 24-year history', Annual Report 2005.

43   From Chairman's Letter, 2008 Annual Report, http://www.wholefoodsmarket.com/company/pdfs/ar08_letter.pdf; and Rachel Wharton, 2008, 'Whole Food tries to shake "whole paycheck" image with free value tours', *NY Daily News*, 8 August.

44   Paul Hemp, 2001, 'Managing for the Next Big Thing: an interview with EMC's Michael Ruettgers', *Harvard Business Review*, January, p. 132.

45   Daniel Roth, 2002, 'Can EMC restore its glory?', *Fortune*, 22 July, pp. 107–110.

46   EMC, 2002a, 'A brief history of EMC through 1998', http://www.emc.com/about/emc_story/brief_history.jsp

47–48 See note 46.

49   From http://www.emc.com

50   See note 46.

51   See note 44.

52   EMC, 2002b, 'EMC profile', http://www.emc.com/about/corp_profile/index.jsp?openfolder=all

53–54 See note 46.

55   See note 44.

56   See note 52.

57   EMC, 2001, 'EMC Symmetrix named "Product of the Year" by *Network Magazine*', http://www.emc.com/about/news/press/us/2001/20010418-876.htm

58   Nelson D. Schwarz, 1999, 'The tech boom will keep on rocking', *Fortune*, 15 February, p. 72.

59   David Kirkpatrick, 1999, 'Storage! Storage! Storage!', *Fortune*, 15 February, p. 72.

60   See note 44.

61   Daniel Lyons, 2001, 'What's eating EMC?', *Forbes*, 26 November, pp. 62–65.

62   Steve Hamm, 2005, 'From the Brink to the Big Leagues', *BusinessWeek* European Edition, 15 August, pp. 60–61.

63   See note 62.

64   Andy Reinhardt, 2004, 'Can EMC find growth beyond hardware?' *BusinessWeek* European Edition, 1 November, pp. 62–63.

65   Tim Beyers, 2005, 'EMC revs earnings engine', *The Motley Fool*, 19 April, www.fool.com/News/mft/2005/mft05041920.htm

66   EMC Corporation, *BusinessWeek*, http://investing.businessweek.com/research/stocks/earnings/earnings.asp?ric=EMC

67   Gary Taubes, 1995, 'The rise and fall of Thinking Machines', *Inc. Technology*, issue 3, p. 61.

68   Joshua Hyatt, 1985, 'Breakthrough: start-up fever may return to computer industry', *Inc.*, August, p. 15.

69   *Omni*, 1992, 'Danny Hillis: interview', October.

70–71 See note 67.

72   *The Economist*, 2001, 'Rethinking machines', 24 March.

73–75 See note 67.

76   Michael E. Knell, 1994, 'Cuts for computer maker Thinking Machines goes Ch.11', *Boston Herald*, 16 August, p. 27.

77   John Markoff, 1992, 'Company news: super-duper computer; it may be faster than anyone wants', *New York Times*, 10 June, p. D3.

78   Geoff Baum, Lee C. Patterson and Evantheia Forbes-Schibsted, 1996, 'Why they fail', *Forbes*, 7 October.

79   See note 19.

80   See note 44.

Chapter 4

1 Quoted in Herb Greenberg, 2002, 'How to avoid the value trap', *Fortune*, 10 June, p. 194.

2 Michael Porter, 1979, 'How competitive forces shape strategy', *Harvard Business Review*, March–April.

3 *Public Citizen*, 2001, 'Drug industry most profitable again', http://www.citizen.org/congress/reform/drug_industry/corporate/articles.cfm?ID=838

4 *San Jose Mercury News*, 1993, 'Study: drug profits excessive', 26 February, http://www.ibiblio.org/pub/academic/medicine/public-health/drugs3.Feb93

5 David Noonan, Joan Raymond and Anne Belli Gesalman, 2000, 'Why drugs cost so much', *Newsweek*, 25 September, p. 22.

6 *US Business Reporter*, 2001, 'Pharmaceuticals industry', 15 December, http://www.activemedia-guide.com/pharmaceutical_industry.htm

7 Anita M. McGahan, 1994, 'Industry structure and competitive advantage', *Harvard Business Review*, November–December.

8 Perry L. Fagan, 1998, 'The pharma giants: ready for the 21st century?', Harvard University Note 9-698-070, 6 May.

9 See note 7.

10 See note 5.

11 *Chemical Week*, 1984, 'A prudent boost in spending', 11 January, p. 3.

12 Alfred A. Sagarese, 1989, 'Fine chemicals: ripe for takeover', *Chemical Week*, 3 May, p. 24.

13 See note 7.

14 Elisa Williams and Robert Langreth, 2001, 'A biotech wonder grows up', *Forbes*, 3 September, p. 118.

15 American Health Line, 2005, 'Industry Profits Unlikely Until Decade's End, Report Says', 1 June.

16 Sam Cage, 2009, 'Roche's $46.8 billion Genentech deal outshines others', 12 March, http://www.reuters.com/article/topNews/idUSTRE52B1DN20090312

17 See note 14.

18 Geoffrey Carr, 1998, 'Survey of the pharmaceutical industry', *The Economist*, 21 February, p. 16.

19 Amgen, Inc., *BusinessWeek*, http://investing.businessweek.com/research/stocks/earnings/earnings.asp?ric=AMGN.O

20 See note 18.

21 See note 8.

22 Henry Dummett, 2003, 'New FDA Generics Regulations Take Effect', *WMRC Daily Analysis*, 19 August.

23 See note 18.

24–25 See note 8.

26 William C. Castagnoli, 1995, 'Is disease management good therapy for an ailing industry?', *Medical Marketing & Media*, January.

27 See note 5.

28 Ken Lacey, 2000, 'Under transformation: the pharmaceutical industry reinvents itself', *Pharmaceutical Technology Europe*, December.

29–30 See note 18.

31 See note 8.

32 See note 28.

33   See note 8.

34   See note 18.

35   Kerry Capell, Michael Arndt and John Carey, 'Drugs Get Smart', *BusinessWeek* European Edition, 5 September, pp. 76–85.

36   Congressional Budget Office, 1998, 'How increased competition from generic drugs has affected prices and returns in the pharmaceutical industry', http://www.cbo.gov/showdoc.cfm?index=655&sequence=1

37   *Fortune*, 2001, 'Most profitable industries: return on assets', http://www.fortune.com/indexw.jhtml?list_frag=list_f5_ind_mostprofit_asset.jhtml&channel=list.jhtml

38   'How the industries stack up', *Fortune*, 17 April, 2006, p. F–26.

39   *Fortune*, 2009, 'Top industries: Most profitable', http://money.cnn.com/magazines/fortune/global500/2009/performers/industries/profits/assets.html

40   See note 38.

41   *Newsweek*, 2000, 2 October, p. 74L.

42   Allison Haines, 2000, 'Gartner says consumers will spend 20 times more on e-commerce with broadband access', http://www.gartner.com/5_about/press_room/pr20001017b.html

43   M.J. Zuckermann, 2000, '"Race is fierce" to broadband sales; hints of high-quality video, sound tantalize PC users', *USA Today*, 27 June, p. 15E.

44   David A. Chidi, 2001, 'DSL options starting to trim down', *InfoWorld*, 30 April, p. 61.

45   Steven Rosenbush, 2001, 'Broadband: what happened?', *BusinessWeek*, 11 June, p. 38.

46   Tim Kenned, 2000, 'Bringing DSL home', *Telephony*, 18 September.

47   Darrell Dunn, 2001, 'DSL may finally be ready for expected breakthrough', *Electronic Buyers' News*, 12 February.

48   Roger O. Crockett, 2001, 'Broadband and Main: use of digital subscriber lines and other broadband applications in everyday life', *BusinessWeek*, 8 October, p. 86.

49   Simon Romero, 2001, 'Internet services put credibility to test', *New York Times*, 19 March, section C, p. 4.

50   Charles Waltner, 2001, 'Meet your connection: if you can avoid the pitfalls, these are great days to be shopping for communications services', *Fortune*, 1 June, p. 59.

51   *Newsweek*, 2001, 'Telecom's big tumble: after badly misjudging the market, the industry faces huge losses and a chain reaction of failures', 18 June, p. 33.

52   Todd Wallack, 2000, 'Pacific Bell rules DSL; but FCC will make it easier for rivals to compete', *San Francisco Chronicle*, 22 May, p. E11.

53   See note 44.

54   Joan Raymond, 2001, 'URL, interrupted', *BusinessWeek*, 18 June, p. SB7.

55   Tarifica Alert, 2005, 'FCC Details U.S. Broadband Growth: Will ADSL Catch Cable?', 26 July, www.tarifica.com

56   High Speed Internet, 2009, 'Tracking the Growth of Broadband Internet Usage', 11 March, http://www.high-speed-internet-access-guide.com/articles/broadband-statistics-for-2008.html

57   Bob Zider, 1998, 'How venture capital works', *Harvard Business Review*, November–December, p. 133.

58   The British Venture Captial Association, the European Venture Capital Association and the National Venture Capital Association in the USA all publish directories that identify the investing preferences of their member firms. *Pratt's Guide to Venture Capital*, available in many business libraries, provides similar information.

59   See note 45.

Chapter 5

1   Philip Van Munchen, 1998, 'The devil's adman', *Brandweek*, 15 June, p. 30.

2   Joan Holleran, 1997, 'Craft brews, a beer rabbit?', *Beverage Industry*, January, p. 8.

3   Jim Collins, 2000, 'Best beats first', *Inc.*, August, pp. 48–51.

4   Institute for Brewing Studies, 1997–1998, *North American Brewers Resource Directory 1997–1998*, Institute for Brewing Studies, Boulder, CO; National Restaurant Association, 2001, *Restaurant Industry Operations Report*, National Restaurant Association, Washington DC.

5   Constantinos C. Markides and Paul A. Geroski, 2005, *Fast Second: How Smart Companies Bypass Radical Innovation to Enter and Dominate New Markets*, Jossey-Bass, San Francisco, CA.

6   See note 3.

7   Joel Dreyfus, 1983, 'SmithKline's ulcer medicine "holy war"', *Fortune*, 19 September, p. 129.

8   See note 7.

9   Leon Jaroff, 1995, 'Fire in the belly, money in the bank', *Time*, 6 November, p. 56.

10   William E. Sheeline, 1989, 'Glaxo's goal: new wonder cures', *Fortune*, 6 November, p. 101.

11   See note 9.

12   Andrew Tausz, 2001, 'Still the one to beat; Nokia strives to maintain its lead in the wireless handset market', *Telephony*, 13 August.

13   See note 12.

14   Christopher Brown-Humes and Robert Budden, 2004, 'Nokia begins to get the message', *Financial Times*, 6 May.

15   Techtree News Staff, 2009, 'Nokia Targets Low Cost Segment in India', 20 August, http://www.techtree.com/India/News/Nokia_Targets_Low_Cost_Segment_in_India/551-105688-547.html

16   Abhinav Ramnarayan, 2009, 'Nokia Fights back for share of smartphone market', *Guardian*, 2 September.

17   See note 12.

18   Yves Doz, Jose Santos and Peter Williamson, 2001, *From Global to Metanational: How Companies Win in the Knowledge Economy*, Harvard Business School Press, Boston, MA.

19   Dan Steinbock, 2001, *The Nokia Revolution: The Story of an Extraordinary Company that Transformed an Industry*, American Management Association, New York.

20   See note 19.

21   Jonathon, D. May, Paul Y. Mang, Ansgar Richter and John Roberts, 2001, 'The innovative organization', *McKinsey Quarterly*, Spring, p. 21.

22   Katherine Doornik and John Roberts, 2001, 'Nokia corporation innovation and efficiency in a high-growth global firm', Graduate School of Business, Stanford University, Case Number S-IB-23, p. 9.

23   Tracy Sutherland, 2000, 'The Finn formula', *The Australian*, 28 November, p. 32.

24   Nokia, 2001, 'Nokia expands ventures organization with new tool for corporate innovation', http://www.press.nokia.com/PR/200112/842293_5.html

25   Daniel Eisenberg, 2001, 'Why are these CEOs smiling?', *Time*, 5 November.

26   eBay, 2002, 'Fee changes', 16 January, http://www2.ebay.com/aw/marketing.shtml#011602232649

27   From '2004 Annual Report', eBay, http://investor.ebay.com/annual.cfm

28   See note 25.
29   Whit Andrews, 1998, 'Investors betting on eBay to maintain its auction lead', *Internet World*, 5 October, p. 72.
30   Rick Spence, 2000, 'The eBay economy', *Profit*, February–March, p. 6.
31   Robert D. Hof, 2001a, 'The people's company', *BusinessWeek*, 3 December, p. EB14.
32   Michael Rappa, 2002, 'Business models on the Web', http://www.digitalenterprise.org/models/models.html
33   Tom Gardner, 1999, 'The eBay model: powerful networks', http://www.fool.com/portfolios/RuleMaker/1999/RuleMaker990128.htm
34   *Business Wire*, 2005, 'eBay Inc. Announces Second Quarter 2005 Financial Results', 20 July.
35   See note 34.
36   Gene G. Marcial, 2001, 'eBay – for hard times', *BusinessWeek*, 3 December, p. 63.
37   Laurie J. Flynn, 2009, 'EBay's income declines 31% as economy reduces traffic', *New York Times*, 22 January.
38   Doug Tsuroka, 2009, 'EBay's latest results edge analyst views, but margin tumbles', *Investor's Business Daily*, 21 October.
39   Christopher A. Bartlett, 1985a, *EMI and the CT scanner (A)*, Harvard University Press, Boston, MA.
40   David J. Teece, 2000, *Managing Intellectual Capital*, Oxford University Press, Oxford, p. 93.
41   Christopher A. Bartlett, 1985b, *EMI and the CT scanner (B)*, Harvard University Press, Boston, MA.
42   Pier A. Abetti, 1989, 'Technology: a key strategic resource', *Management Review*, February, p. 37.
43–44 See note 41.
45   *BusinessWeek*, 1976, 'Can Britain's EMI stay ahead in the US?', 19 April, p. 122.
46   *BusinessWeek*, 1980, 'GE gobbles a rival in CT scanners', 19 May, p. 40.
47   Saul Hansell, 2001, 'Online grocery goes to the checkout lane', *Milwaukee Journal Sentinel*, 10 July, p. 1A.
48   John Case, 2001, 'Food for thought: the on-line grocery business just keeps growing. So why can't anybody make any money at it?', *Inc.*, September, pp. 44–46.
49   Carol Emert, 2000, 'Webvan sees sales surge 136%', *San Francisco Chronicle*, 28 July, p. B1.
50   Dana Canedy, 1999, 'Need asparagus? Just click it; on-line grocers take aim at established supermarkets', *New York Times*, 10 September, p. C1.
51   Carolyn Said, 2000, 'Webvan sees revenue losses grow', *San Francisco Chronicle*, 14 April, p. B1.
52   *Los Angeles Times*, 2001, 'Online grocers hurt by delivery costs, apathy', 22 May, Business Section, p. 7.
53   Monica Soto, 2001, 'When a company fails to deliver', *Seattle Times*, 7 May, p. A1.
54   See note 50.
55   Vanessa Hua, 2001, 'Running out of gas; Webvan's efforts to keep on truckin' not likely to succeed, analysts say', *San Francisco Chronicle*, 27 April, p. B1.
56   See note 48.
57   Andy Reinhardt, 2001, 'Tesco bets small – and wins big', *BusinessWeek*, 1 October.
58   Nomensa: Humanising Technology, 2009, 'Tesco's online sales hit £1 billion', 6 October, http://www.nomensa.com/news/industry-news/2009/10/tescos-online-sales-hit-1billion.html
59   See note 9.

Chapter 6

1 Indira Gandhi, 1982, *Indira Gandhi: My Truth*, Grove Press, New York.

2 Quoted from Edmond Rostand, 'La Princesse Lointaine', 1980, *The Oxford Dictionary of Quotations*, 3rd edn., Oxford University Press, Oxford, p. 410.

3 Howard Schultz and Dori Jones Yang, 1997, *Pour Your Heart into it: How Starbucks Built a Company One Cup at a Time*, Hyperion, New York.

4 Howard H. Stevenson, H. Irving Grousbeck, Michael J. Roberts and Amarnath Bhide, 1999, *New Business Ventures and the Entrepreneur*, McGraw-Hill/Irwin, Burr Ridge, IL.

5 Most of what follows is based on Schultz and Yang (1997), see note 3.

6–8 See note 3.

9 Alex Witchel, 1994, 'Coffee talk with: Howard Schultz; by way of Canarsie, one large cup of business strategy', *New York Times*, 14 December, p. C1.

10 See note 3.

11 Matt Rothman, 1993, 'Into the black', *Inc.*, January, p. 59.

12–17 See note 3.

18 Dori Jones Yang, 1994, 'The Starbucks enterprise shifts into warp speed', *BusinessWeek*, 24 October, p. 76.

19–20 See note 3.

21 Stanley Holmes, 2002, 'Planet Starbucks', *BusinessWeek*, 9 September, pp. 100–110.

22 From 'Starbucks Corporation Fiscal 2004 Annual Report', http://www.starbucks.com/aboutus/investor.asp

23 *Fortune*, 2005, '100 Best Companies to Work For', 24 January.

24 See note 21.

25 Andy Serwer, 2009, 'Starbucks fix: Howard Schultz spills the beans on his plans to save the company he founded', *Fortune*, 18 January.

26 Starbucks Newsroom, 2009, 'Starbucks Posts Strong Third Quarter Fiscal 2009 Results', 24 July, http://news.starbucks.com/article_display.cfm?article_id=249

27 See note 25.

28 See note 3.

29 From a speech given at Stanford University, 23 October 2002.

30 See note 3.

31 Scott S. Smith, 1998, 'Grounds for success (interview with Starbucks CEO Howard Schultz)', *Entrepreneur*, May, p. 120.

32–33 See note 3.

Chapter 7

1 From William Wordsworth, *The Prelude*, book xi, 1.11.

2 Howard Schultz and Dori Jones Yang, 1997, *Pour Your Heart into it: How Starbucks Built a Company One Cup at a Time*, Hyperion, New York.

3 Andrea Butter and David Pogue, 2002, *Piloting Palm: The Inside Story of Palm, Handspring and the Birth of the Billion Dollar Handheld Industry*, John Wiley & Sons, New York.

4–8 See note 3.

9 Paul E. Teague, 2000, 'Father of an industry', *Design News*, 6 March, p. 108.

10 See note 3.

11 See note 9.

12   Rae Dupree, 2001 'Words to live by from an apostle of simplicity', *U.S. News and World Reports*, 15 January, p. 35.

13   Katie Hafner, 1999, 'One more ultimate gadget', *New York Times*, 16 September, p. G1.

14–16 See note 3.

17   David A. Kaplan, 1997, 'The cult of the Pilot', *Newsweek*, 21 July, p. 35.

18   See note 3.

19   Joanna Pettitt, 1998, 'Palm Computing hangs on to control of handheld market', *Computer Weekly*, 16 April, p. 21.

20   See note 3.

21   Kim Clark, 2004, 'Round two at Palm', *U.S. News and World Reports*, 1 November.

22   'Palm Reports Q4 and FY 2009 Results,' http://files.shareholder.com/downloads/ PALM/755201276x0x302996/fc5f86a8-8a30-4c60-93ca-347e9d3797b9/ PalmReportsQ4AndFY09Results.pdf

23   Tricia Duryee, 2009, 'Former Apple Exec Jon Rubinstein Replaces Ed Colligan as Palm's CEO', *moconews.net*, 10 June, http://www.washingtonpost.com/wp-dyn/ content/article/2009/06/10/AR2009061003344.html

24   See note 23.

25–26 See note 3.

27   Michael Treacy and Fred Wiersema, 1993, 'Customer intimacy and other value disciplines', *Harvard Business Review*, January–February, pp. 84–85.

28   See note 27.

29   The details in the case history that follows were reported in Judith Crown, Glenn Coleman and Drew Wilson, 1993, 'The fall of Schwinn', *Crain's Chicago Business*, 11 October.

30   See note 29.

31   Based on 'Bicycle makers: kids' stuff', *The Economist*, 3 June 1989, p. 101.

32   Jennifer Foote, 1987, 'Two-wheel terrors', *Newsweek*, 28 September, p. 72.

33–38 See note 29.

39–40 See note 3.

41   See note 29.

Chapter 8

1   This case history is taken from Lloyd *et al.* (2001a, 2001b). See notes 2 and 7.

2   Julian Lloyd, Eileen Rutschmann and John Bates, 2001a, 'Virata (A)', London Business School.

3–6   See note 2.

7   Julian Lloyd, Eileen Rutschmann and John Bates, 2001b, 'Virata (B)', London Business School.

8   3i, 2005, '3i backs Virata vision', at www.3i.com/ourportfolio/successstories/ ss_virata.html

9   Quoted from an interview with Hermann Hauser on 7 April 2000.

10   This case history is taken from David Allison, 1988, 'Ken Olsen interview', http:// www.americanhistory.si.edu/collections/comphist/olsen.html

11   John C. Whitney Jr and Bruce C. Greenwald, 1987, *Invisible barriers to successful marketing in new environments*, Working Draft, University of Wisconsin.

12   Allison (1988), see note 10.

13–14 See note 10.

15   Jones Telecommunications and Multimedia Encyclopedia, 'Digital Equipment Corporation (DEC)', http://www.digitalcentury.com/encyclo/update/dec.html

16   See note 10.

17   Interview with Jean Micol on 12 September 2002.

18   Saras Sarasvathy, 2001, 'What makes entrepreneurs entrepreneurial', working paper, University of Washington.

19   Andy Grove, 1996, *Only the Paranoid Survive*, Currency/Doubleday, New York.

Chapter 9

1   Quoted from Oliver Wendell Holmes, 'The Professor at the Breakfast Table', 1980, *The Oxford Dictionary of Quotations*, 3rd edn., Oxford University Press, Oxford, p. 253.

2   Herb Greenberg, 2002, 'How to avoid the value trap', *Fortune*, 10 June, p. 194.

3   Heesun Wee, 2002, 'The challenge in store for Gap', *Business Week Online*, 9 October, http://www.businessweek.com

4   V. Kasturi Rangan and Marie Bell, 1997, *Nestlé Refrigerated Foods: Contadina Pasta and Pizza (A)*, Harvard Business School Press, Boston, MA.

5   See www.navigationzone.com for details.

6   Harper W. Boyd Jr, Orville C. Walker Jr, John Mullins and Jean-Claude Larréché, 2002, *Marketing Management: A Strategic Decision Making Approach*, McGraw-Hill/Irwin, Burr Ridge, IL.

7   Bob Zider, 1998, 'How venture capital works', *Harvard Business Review*, November–December.

8   Kopin Tan, 2002, 'USA: venture capitalists still detect red flags in lots of proposals', *Wall Street Journal*, 7 August.

9   See note 8.

Chapter 10

1   Quoted from Institute for Intercultural Studies, 2001, 'Margaret Mead 1901–1978', http://www. mead2001.org

2   Peter F. Drucker, 1985, *Innovation and Entrepreneurship,* Harper & Row, New York.

3   Amar V. Bhidé, 2000, *The Origin and Evolution of New Businesses*, Oxford University Press, Oxford.

4   William H. Sahlman, 1997, 'How to write a great business plan', *Harvard Business Review*, July–August.

5   See note 4.

6   Kopin Tan, 2002, 'USA: venture capitalists still detect red flags in lots of proposals', *Wall Street Journal*, 7 August.

7   See note 6.

8   See note 1.

Chapter 11

1   Adapted from a working paper of the same title, John W. Mullins, London Business School, 2005.

2   Mary Bellis, 'Inventors of the Modern Computer, The First Spreadsheet – VisiCalc – Dan Bricklin and Bob Frankston', http://inventors.about.com/library/weekly/aa010199.htm

3   See Grant McCracken, 1988, *The Long Interview*, Sage Publications, Newbury Park, CA. Much of this chapter is based on McCracken's interviewing methodology.

Chapter 13

1   Adapted with permission from the work of Robert McGowan and Paul Olk of the University of Denver.

2   Michael Porter, 1979, 'How competitive forces shape strategy', *Harvard Business Review*, March–April.

Chapter 14

1   Chapter 14 has been adapted, with permission, from John Mullins and Randy Komisar, 2009, *Getting to Plan B: Breaking Through to a Better Business Model*, Harvard Business School Press, Boston, MA.

2   See note 1.

Chapter 15

1   Adapted with permission of The McGraw-Hill Companies, from Chapter 7 of Boyd *et al.* (2001), *Marketing Management: A Strategic Decision Making Approach*, 4th edn.

2   For additional qualitative research techniques, see Abbie Griffin, 1996, 'Obtaining Customer Needs for Product Development', in M. D. Rosenau, ed., *The PDMA Handbook of New Product Development*, John Wiley & Sons, New York; and Gerald Zaltman, 'Rethinking marketing research: putting the people back in', *Journal of Marketing Research*, November 1997, pp. 424–437.

3   The definitive guide to conducting in-depth interviews is Grant McCracken, 1988, *The Long Interview*, Sage Publications, Newbury Park, CA. Chapter 11, the first of the toolkit chapters in this book, is based on McCracken's approach.

4   For a useful guide to conducting surveys, see www.whatisasurvey.info

5   Malcolm Gladwell, 1996, 'The Science of Shopping', *New Yorker*, 4 November, pp. 66–67; and Gary Hamel and C. K. Prahalad, 1991, 'Corporate Imagination and Expeditionary Marketing', *Harvard Business Review*, July–August.

6   Joseph F. Hair, Robert P. Bush and David J. Ortinau, 2000, *Marketing Research: A Practical Approach for the New Millennium*, McGraw-Hill, Maidenhead.

7   See note 6.

Chapter 16

1 Adapted with permission of The McGraw-Hill Companies, from Chapter 7 of Boyd *et al.* (2001), *Marketing Management: A Strategic Decision Making Approach*, 4th edn.

2 Peter L. Bernstein and Theodore H. Silbert, 1982, 'Are economic forecasters worth listening to?', *Harvard Business Review*, July–August.

3 F. William Barnett, 1988, 'Four steps to forecast total market demand', *Harvard Business Review*, July–August.

4 David M. Georgeoff and Robert G. Murdick, 1986, 'Manager's guide to forecasting', *Harvard Business Review*, January–February.

5 Arthur Schleifer Jr, 1996, *Forecasting with Regression Analysis*, Harvard Business School Publishing, Boston, MA.

6 Deborah Solomon, 2000, 'Local phone companies put customer service on hold, critics charge', *Wall Street Journal*, 6 July, p. B1.

7 Frank M. Bass, 1969, 'A new product growth model for consumer durables', *Management Science*, January, pp. 215–227; Trichy V. Krishnan, Frank M. Bass and V. Kumar, 2000, 'Impact of a later entrant on the diffusion of a new product/service', *Journal of Marketing Research*, May, pp. 269–278.

8 Robert J. Dolan, 1990a, *Conjoint Analysis: A Manager's Guide*, Harvard Business School Publishing, Boston, MA.

9 Robert J. Dolan, 1990b, *Concept Testing*, Harvard Business School Publishing, Boston, MA.

10 Fareena Sultan, 1991, *Marketing Research for High Definition Television*, Harvard Business School Publishing, Boston, MA.

11 Colin Welch and Ananth Raman, 1998, *Merchandising at Nine West Retail Stores*, Harvard Business School Publishing, Boston, MA.

12 Marshall L. Fisher, Janice H. Hammond, Walter R. Obermeyer and Ananth Raman, 1994, 'Making supply meet demand in an uncertain world', *Harvard Business Review*, May–June.

13 Amos Tversky and Daniel Kahneman, 1974, 'Judgment under uncertainty', *Science*, vol. 185, pp. 1124–1131.

Appendix

1 *BusinessWeek* Online, www.businessweek.com

Index

Comprehensive. Authoritative. Trusted

FT Guides will tell you everything you need to know about your chosen subject area

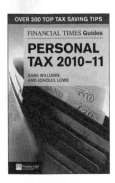

OVER 200 TOP TAX SAVING TIPS

FINANCIAL TIMES Guides

PERSONAL TAX 2010–11

SARA WILLIAMS AND JONQUIL LOWE

9780273735694

FINANCIAL TIMES Guides SECOND EDITION

VALUE INVESTING

HOW TO BECOME A DISCIPLINED INVESTOR

GLEN ARNOLD

9780273724520

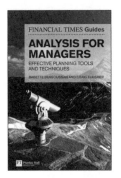

FINANCIAL TIMES Guides

ANALYSIS FOR MANAGERS

EFFECTIVE PLANNING TOOLS AND TECHNIQUES

BABETTE BENSOUSSAM AND CRAIG FLEISHER

9780273722014

FINANCIAL TIMES Guides

MAKING THE RIGHT INVESTMENT DECISIONS SECOND EDITION

HOW TO ANALYSE COMPANIES AND VALUE SHARES

MICHAEL CAHILL

978027372984

FINANCIAL TIMES Guides

SELECTING SHARES THAT PERFORM FOURTH EDITION

10 WAYS TO BEAT THE STOCK MARKET

RICHARD KOCH AND LEO GOUGH

9780273712671

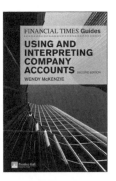

FINANCIAL TIMES Guides

USING AND INTERPRETING COMPANY ACCOUNTS SECOND EDITION

WENDY McKENZIE

9780273723967

FINANCIAL TIMES Guides

EXCHANGE TRADED FUNDS AND INDEX FUNDS

HOW TO USE TRACKER FUNDS IN YOUR INVESTMENT PORTFOLIO

DAVID STEVENSON

9780273727835

FINANCIAL TIMES Guides

BUSINESS START UP 2010

THE ONLY ANNUALLY UPDATED GUIDE FOR ENTREPRENEURS

SARA WILLIAMS

978027373029

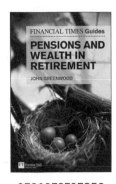

FINANCIAL TIMES Guides

PENSIONS AND WEALTH IN RETIREMENT

JOHN GREENWOOD

9780273727859

FINANCIAL TIMES Guides

INVESTING

THE DEFINITIVE COMPANION TO INVESTMENT AND THE FINANCIAL MARKETS SECOND EDITION

GLEN ARNOLD

9780273723745

FINANCIAL TIMES Guides

USING THE FINANCIAL PAGES SIXTH EDITION

ROMESH VAITILINGAM

9780273727873

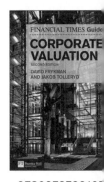

FINANCIAL TIMES Guides

CORPORATE VALUATION SECOND EDITION

DAVID FRYKMAN AND JAKOB TOLLERYD

9780273729105

Change your business life today

FT Prentice Hall
FINANCIAL TIMES